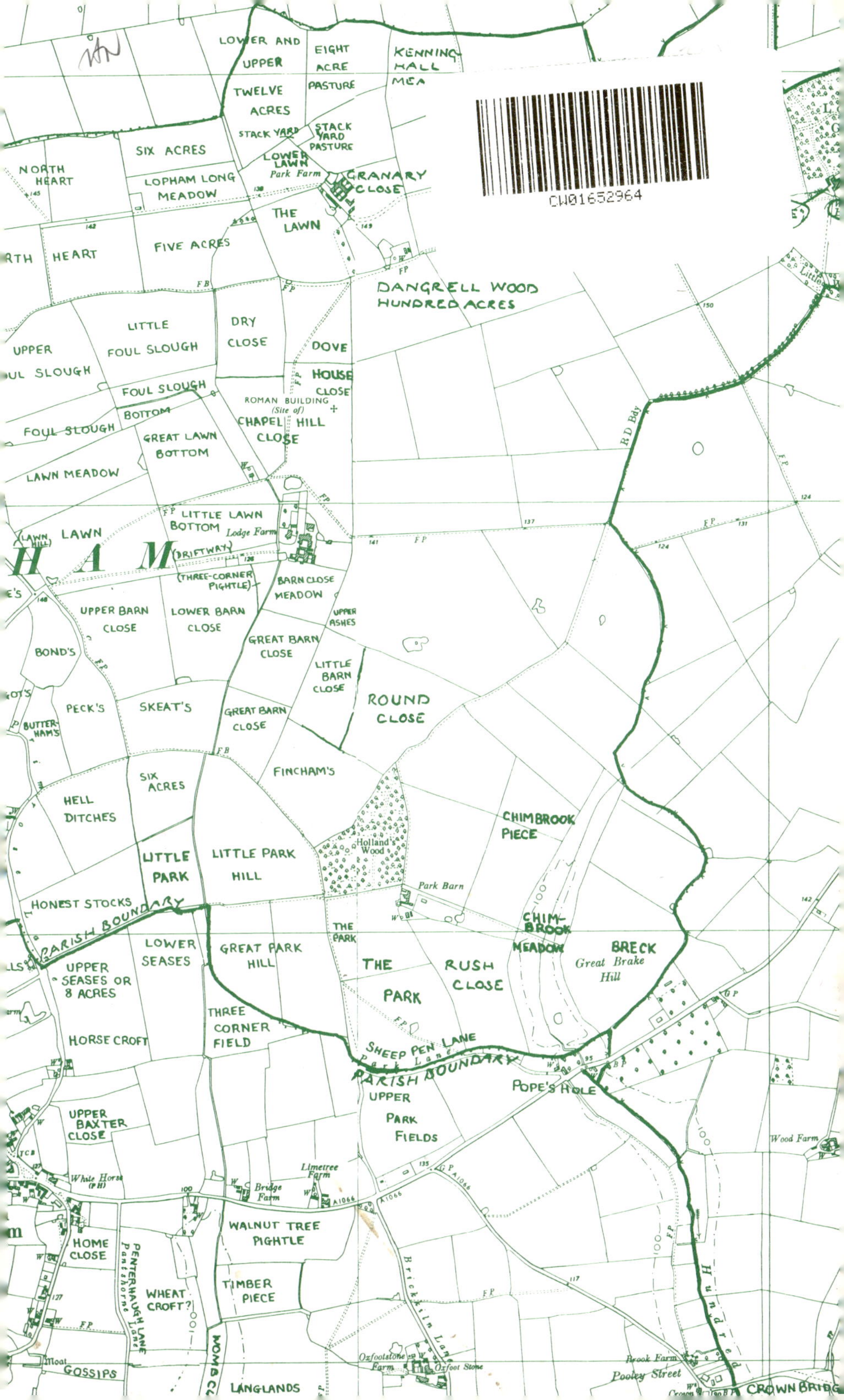
LOWER AND UPPER TWELVE ACRES
EIGHT ACRE PASTURE
KENNING HALL MEA
STACK YARD
STACK YARD PASTURE
SIX ACRES
NORTH HEART
LOPHAM LONG MEADOW
LOWER LAWN
Park Farm
GRANARY CLOSE
THE LAWN
RTH HEART
FIVE ACRES
DANGRELL WOOD HUNDRED ACRES
UPPER
UL SLOUGH
LITTLE FOUL SLOUGH
DRY CLOSE
DOVE HOUSE CLOSE
FOUL SLOUGH BOTTOM
FOUL SLOUGH
ROMAN BUILDING (Site of)
CHAPEL HILL CLOSE
GREAT LAWN BOTTOM
LAWN MEADOW
R D Bdy
LITTLE LAWN BOTTOM
Lodge Farm
(LAWN HILL) LAWN
H A M
(DRIFTWAY)
(THREE-CORNER PIGHTLE)
BARN CLOSE MEADOW
UPPER BARN CLOSE
LOWER BARN CLOSE
UPPER ASHES
BOND'S
GREAT BARN CLOSE
LITTLE BARN CLOSE
ROUND CLOSE
PECK'S
SKEAT'S
BUTTER-HAM'S
GREAT BARN CLOSE
FINCHAM'S
SIX ACRES
HELL DITCHES
Holland Wood
CHIMBROOK PIECE
LITTLE PARK
LITTLE PARK HILL
Park Barn
HONEST STOCKS
PARISH BOUNDARY
LOWER SEASES
GREAT PARK HILL
THE PARK
CHIM-BROOK MEADOW
BRECK
Great Brake Hill
UPPER SEASES OR 8 ACRES
THE PARK
RUSH CLOSE
THREE CORNER FIELD
HORSE CROFT
SHEEP PEN LANE
Park Lane
PARISH BOUNDARY
POPE'S HOLE
UPPER PARK FIELDS
UPPER BAXTER CLOSE
Wood Farm
White Horse (P H)
Limetree Farm
Bridge Farm
A1066
WALNUT TREE PIGHTLE
HOME CLOSE
PENTERHAUGH LANE
Pantshorne Lane
WHEAT CROFT?
TIMBER PIECE
Brickkiln Lane
Hundred
Moat
GOSSIPS
Oxfootstone Farm
Oxfoot Stone
LANGLANDS
Brook Farm
Pooley Street
CROWN BRIDG

A HISTORY OF THE LOPHAMS

The Tower of South Lopham Church, drawn and etched by J. S. Cotman, 1819. Reproduced by courtesy of the Colman Rye Librarian, Norwich Public Library.

A HISTORY
OF
THE LOPHAMS
by
Michael Friend Serpell

The Oxfoot Stone

PHILLIMORE

1980
Published on behalf of
THE LOPHAM BOOK COMMITTEE
by
PHILLIMORE & CO. LTD.
London and Chichester
Head Office: Shopwyke Hall,
Chichester, Sussex, England

ISBN 0 85033 371 7

Printed and bound in Great Britain
by W & J Mackay Limited, Chatham

DEDICATED TO
the Memory of
the Reverend Francis BLOMEFIELD
who wrote:

"Some perhaps may censure me if they hit on a Thing that I have not seen, or perhaps been mis-informed about; Others there are, I don't doubt, who will think me too particular in many Things, and others perhaps, not particular enough; so that as it is a Thing impossible to please All, if it is but approved of by my *Subscribers*, (to whom only I am obliged) I care for nought else . . ."

Patrons

Miss G. Allen & Mr. D. Livingstone
Mr. & Mrs. J. D. Alston
Anonymous
Mrs. O. V. Aston
Mr. & Mrs. W. G. Avery

Mrs. M. Baldwin
Mr. A. Barnard
Mrs. E. Baskerville
Mrs. R. D. Bishenden
Mr. H. Bowyer
Mr. & Mrs. J. M. A. C. Brown
Mr. D. Brundell
Mr. & Mrs. J. W. Bush

Mrs. A. E. Cook
Mr. A. L. Cooney
Mr. & Mrs. A. A. Crook
Mrs. G. Crook

Mr. & Mrs. J. Deards
Mr. & Mrs. J. Divall

Mr. V. C. Frost

Mr. & Mrs. J. Goddard
Mrs. S. J. Gooderham
Mr. M. Grover

Mrs. B. Hoskins

Mr. A. A. Kerry

Mr. & Mrs. J. P. Mackay-Miller
Miss B. I. S. Malson
Captain M. A. N. Mansbridge
Mr. & Mrs. J. Morgan
Mr. & Mrs. I. Murdoch

Mr. & Mrs. S. Newstead
Mrs. J. Nunn

Mr. & Mrs. E. Pearce
Mr. & Mrs. E. Pond

Miss C. Ralph
Mrs. V. Read
Mr. & Mrs. A. Rednall
Mr. & Mrs. P. Reeder

Mr. & Mrs. W. Sayer
Mrs. E. A. Serpell
Mr. & Mrs. L. G. Shaw
Mr. A. Sheldon
Mrs. A. Solly
Mr. & Mrs. W. Speer

Mrs. Jean Turnbull-Crook
Mr. & Mrs. R. Twidle

Mr. R. H. & Mrs. J. M. Vere
Mr. & Mrs. W. Vernon

The Book Committee wish also to acknowledge the generous help they have received from residents and friends of both the Lophams in the support and administration of fund-raising occasions organised for this book. They are much obliged to the author for his work and to Mr. J. P. Mackay-Miller for his technical advice and assistance on the problems of book production.

Contents

Foreword by the Duke of Norfolk *ix*
Preface *xi*

Part One

The Lophams from prehistoric times until A.D. 1570

		Page
Chapter 1	Oldest Lopham	3
Chapter 2	The First Settlement	7
Chapter 3	The First Address	10
Chapter 4	The First Christening	13
Chapter 5	The First Valuation	19
Chapter 6	The Lost Lopham	22
Chapter 7	Lopham Churches	25
Chapter 8	Lopham Lands and Lords	33
Chapter 9	Mediaeval Lopham Life	39
Chapter 10	Lopham Developments 1350–1570	48

Part Two

Social and economic changes in the Lophams between 1570 and 1900

Chapter 11	Tudor Lopham	69
Chapter 12	The Beginnings of Lopham Linen	78

Chapter 13	New Times, New Thoughts and Old Inclinations	88
Chapter 14	Some Lopham Names and Fames	101
Chapter 15	Eighteenth Century Lopham	108
Chapter 16	Disaffection and Dissent	113
Chapter 17	Property and Poverty	121
Chapter 18	One Green Oasis	137
Chapter 19	Ructions	150

Part Three

Twentieth Century Lopham

Chapter 20	Educations	175
Chapter 21	The Losing of the Looms	184
Chapter 22	The Good Old Days	199
Chapter 23	The First World War and Afterwards	225
Chapter 24	The Second World War and Twentieth Century Lopham	255

APPENDIX 267

INDEX OF PARTS ONE TO THREE 299

Foreword

by His Grace the Duke of Norfolk
E.M., C.B., C.B.E., M.C.

The first earls of Norfolk, the Bigods, inherited the manor of Lopham from Roger Bigot, who had received it at the hands of William the Conqueror, as a comrade-in-arms. The lordship of the manor returned to the Crown in 1302 but by the end of the fourteenth century it had passed from the royal family by marriage to the Mowbrays, who became the first dukes of Norfolk.

On the death of the last Mowbray dowager duchess in 1506/7 Lopham came into the Howard inheritance and my family have owned land there ever since. Lopham Lodge, built or rebuilt in the sixteenth century, once commanded a park of many acres, and was recommended by Thomas, the fourth Howard duke, to his children as an alternative residence to Framlingham, Thetford and Kenninghall. It will be seen in this book that the first identifiable settlement in the Lophams, a Roman villa, was discovered near the site of the present-day Lodge Farm.

I am delighted therefore to be asked to write the foreword to this interesting story of the Lophams, and would strongly recommend it to anybody who wants to know more of the history of this fascinating area.

NORFOLK

Arundel, February 1980

Acknowledgements

The section of Faden's map of Norfolk which appears on the jacket and on pages 162–163 is reproduced by courtesy of the Norfolk Record Society.

The end-papers are based on the 6 inch Ordnance Survey of 1925. The place names, drawn mostly from the Inclosure Awards, have been entered by the author and Mrs G. F. Brown, who also made the drawing on the title page.

Preface

The neighbouring parishes of North and South Lopham lie one above the other in the hundred of Guiltcross on the southern border of Norfolk, in Latitude 52.24N, Longitude 1.00E. North Lopham,* which is five miles west-north-west of Diss, has an area of 817 hectares and is bordered on the west by the parish of Garboldisham; on the north by Kenninghall; on the east by Fersfield; and on the south by its sister parish. South Lopham,† five miles west of Diss, has an area of 791 hectares and is bordered on the west by Blo'Norton and Garboldisham; on the north by its sister parish; on the east by Bressingham; and on the south by the county boundary with Suffolk. The parish churches of North and South Lopham are about a mile apart and there is a common village hall halfway between them. North Lopham's population, according to the 1961 Census, was 461, while South Lopham's was 360. The figures given in 1971 were 470 and 374 respectively.

The idea of this book was conceived by Mr. A. A. Crook of North Lopham, who made a preliminary agreement with the writer in December, 1976. In January, 1977, he arranged a meeting with supporters who established the Lopham Book Committee, with the following members:

Mrs. G. F. Brown of North Lopham,
Mr. A. A. Crook of North Lopham,

* Ordnance Survey reference 136 TM 0382.
† O.S. reference 136 TM 0481.

Mrs. A. A. Crook, honorary treasurer, of North Lopham,
Mrs. P. E. Howard, honorary secretary, of South Lopham,
Captain M. A. N. Mansbridge, honorary chairman, of South Lopham,
Mr. E. A. Pearce of South Lopham.

The project has been welcomed by the parish councils and other institutions of North and South Lopham, and a list of patrons is annexed to this preface.

The writer must first of all express his thanks for much help and kindness shewn to him by the committee both collectively and separately. In congratulating the Lophams on the lively interest they have shewn in their history he would like to express his admiration for the enterprise and hard work of their Book Committee, especially in the raising of funds and the collection of information. At the same time he would like to thank all Lopham residents, past and present, who have helped him with information, advice, admission to their houses, and the loan of documents and photographs. Mrs. Jennie Arnold of North Lopham has typed his drafts with skill and patience.

By the courtesy of the Duke of Norfolk and his archivist, the late Dr. F. W. Steer, the writer was given access to manuscripts at Arundel Castle and permission to quote from them. The lord of the manor of Lopham, Miss B. I. S. Malson of Chesterfield, kindly allowed him the same facilities with her manuscripts. His particular thanks are also due to Lieutenant Commander Brian Willson, R.N. (retired) and Mrs. Willson for their loan to him of the manuscript of an unpublished book on the history of the linen industry, written by Mrs. Willson's mother, the late Mrs. R. O. Pickering ("Elizabeth Harland"); to Mr. C. W. Farrow of the Norfolk and Norwich Genealogical Society for certain recondite information about the "Mid-Anglian Light Railway"; to Mr. Simon Cotton of the Norfolk Churches Trust for references to certain wills; to Mr. Tony Gregory of the Archaeology Department, Norwich Castle Museum for information about archaeological finds in and near the Lophams; to Miss Alison Maddock, formerly curator of the Thetford Museum, for access to Coleby Cobb's loom and other information; and to

Mr. David Orr of Redgrave for information about *Dolomedes Plantarius* and its habitat.

The Public Record Office and the British Library's Department of Manuscripts have given the writer their customary understanding and efficient help, but his heaviest obligation is to the Norfolk Record Office, the patient and constructive assistance of whose management and staff is a model for such institutions. He must also acknowledge the quick and resourceful services of the Colman-Rye librarians in the Norwich Public Library.

Much information has been gathered from the local Press, and the writer would like to acknowledge the courtesies shewn to him by the Eastern Daily Press and allied newspapers. All printed sources of the text are cited in the references, together with the names of their authors where these are known.

The only unacknowledged authority: his partner at interviews, his remembrancer, adviser, editor, and all-patient reader or listener, is the writer's wife.

NOTE: In Part One, at the Committee's request, original English spellings have been preserved. In the rest of the book, except where they are evidently original, spellings have been modernised. Proper names and place names are in their original spelling, however, and some original spellings have been cited in case they illustrate pronunciation.

PART ONE

The Lophams from prehistoric times until A.D. 1570

CHAPTER ONE

Oldest Lopham

The Wonders of Lopham are famous but no-one agrees how many there are. Stories range from an inexhaustible well and an exuberant milch cow to the undying love between the two Lophams and their unquenchable thirst.[1] Probably there is competition with the Seven Wonders of the ancient world, but the oldest printed record of them was content with Three. When the Reverend Francis Blomefield wrote about the Lophams in 1739, he said that

"This Town is remarkable among the Country People for the three WONDERS, (as they call them) the First is, the *Selfgrown Stile*, being a Tree grown in such a Manner, that it forms a regular Stile, and serves for such in a common Foot Path . . . The Second is, thc *Ox-foot Stone*, which lies in a Meadow so-called . . . The Third is called *Lopham Ford*, at which place the *Ouse* and *Waveney*, (those disagreeing Bretheren as *Spelman* calls them) have their Rise . . ."[2]

For the purpose of this history it is remarkable that these three Wonders can all be related to the oldest days of the Lophams. The Selfgrown Stile, long vanished, was characteristic of the ancient times when, as Blomefield put it, "this Town was most Wood".[3] The Oxfoot Stone, which still exists, is older than any historical woods, and may have slid into the place where it still lay in Blomefield's time, with the help of a glacier, perhaps in the last Ice Age between 100,000 and 80,000 B.C. As for the Ford, this may have been the first reason for a human settlement in the place where the Lophams were to be.

Mrs. Norah Womack, Miss Emily Brown & the inexhaustible well of North Lopham. By courtesy of E. Counties Newspapers Ltd.

To begin then with the senior Wonder, the Oxfoot Stone, this is a flattish slab of sandstone, measuring about three feet by two and from six to nine inches thick. On one surface there is a sharp but shallow impression which resembles the hoof-print of an ox but which in all probability marks where some fossil bivalve was once embedded. The stone was moved to its present position alongside Oxfoot or Oxfootstone Farm in recent times for safety's sake.[4] It may have been moved from earlier sites more than once before. In 1815 it seems to have lain in an acre of copyhold land known as the "Oxfootpiece" in South Lopham, and to judge from a deed in the writer's possession, it was still there in 1841.[5] But a report in the *Eastern Daily Press* of September 13th, 1929, said that this "wonderful relic . . . after being removed from its original site, was used for years as a roadside mounting block by equestrians". Whatever trials the stone may have suffered, Lopham's respect for tradition seems to have saved it from becoming road-metal or building stone, and the "oxfoot-print" remains clear and unweathered.

When this erratic block first grounded East Anglia was still joined to the Continent behind a coastline which ran from Yorkshire round the Dogger Bank to the western shores of Jutland. The first men to see it in what was to become Norfolk may have been nomadic hunters from the future Europe, travelling overland in the Middle Stone Age, the Mesolithic, between 6,000 and 5,000 B.C.[6]

But the earliest known traces of man in the Lophams date from the Late Stone Age, the Neolithic, between 2500 and 1500 B.C. Britain had become an island by 5,000 B.C. but our following history may suggest that westward migrating drives continued from the continent long after the land bridge had foundered in the new North Sea.

A neolithic stone implement, a "celt", was found at Lopham Ford about 1884. It was described at the time as "a thin, highly-polished axe of green grey diorite 6½ inches long".[7] Celts were handy tools used by our remote ancestors as hoes, chisels, axes, and no doubt as weapons of war when occasion arose. For whatever purpose it was being used and however it came to be lost, the place where this particular celt was found is significant. Lopham Ford is not only on the borderline between Norfolk and Suffolk; it marks one of the oldest trackways in East Anglia.

In the Late Stone Age much of Norfolk and Suffolk was covered with thick woodland but, where the vegetation was thin, neolithic men began to make clearings and settlements, for example in Breckland and in the region of present-day Ipswich.[8] Archaeological finds indicate that there were passages through the forests from one inhabited spot to another, and that a particular track ran between the Ipswich and the Breckland settlements across the narrow watershed which now divides the Waveney from the Dune or Little Ouse.[9] The causeway at Lopham Ford is just eighty-six feet above sea-level, but for many centuries it must have been the only hard standing between miles of dangerous fens. The last Ice Age, which may have bequeathed to the Lophams their Oxfoot Stone, is believed to have left another legacy in a great sheet of water stretching over and around the present-day Fens of Roydon, Bressingham, Lopham, Redgrave, Hinderclay, Blo' Norton and Thelnetham.[10] As time went on, this lake broke down into a tract of deep marshland and meres. In neolithic days Lopham Ford may have been the only safe passage through this tract, and its possession could have had strategic importance between warring tribes for hundreds of years to come.

In case these considerations seem too remote to be real, let it be known that in the war of 1939–1945 a British land-mine was laid beneath the Redgrave Road on the Norfolk side of "Lopham Gate", as Lopham Ford is often called.[11] It was to have been detonated whenever the invading German tanks roared up from Redgrave and over the Norfolk border, thus driving them into the boggy ground on either side of the causeway. This is by no means the only occasion when British defence tactics have been dictated by ancient tradition. Perhaps we may feel justified in believing therefore that the celt found at Lopham Ford in 1884 was lost some three or four thousand years before in battle.

CHAPTER TWO

The First Settlement

Given the strategic importance of Lopham Gate, perhaps it became not only the scene of fighting but sometimes a frontier post. A mile and a half north west of the causeway a polished flint axehead of neolithic date was found in 1955 near the Blo' Norton Road.[12] In the same year, another two miles to the north west, part of a stone axe-hammer of comparable age was found off King's Head Lane in North Lopham.[13] The traces of a village or hamlet called Lopham Ford are discussed below in Chapter Six, but the existence of such a place may strengthen the possibility of a frontier post established at some long-forgotten date.

Without archaeological research such a date cannot be recovered and up to the present time no proof of settlements in the Lopham region, north or south of the county boundary, has been found of earlier age than Roman times. But the most ancient traces of settlement may lie beneath the longest-lasting places of dwelling or resort, whether cottages, inns or churches, and the fact that no tools, weapons or other evidence of humanity have been found for the two or three thousand years between the celt at Lopham Ford and the Roman villa near Lopham Lodge Farm need not mean that the area was uninhabited.

What we should like to know is when and how agriculture and civilisation began in the Lophams, but on these questions we can only speculate. To judge from the evidence found in neighbouring parts of East Anglia, the succeeding Ages of Bronze, beginning about 1500 B.C., and Iron, perhaps a thousand years later, brought not only better means and methods of livelihood but also suffering and slaughter. A few miles from where the Lophams were to be there are traces of farming with oxen, sheep and primitive wheat, together with the spinning of yarn, as early as 500 B.C.[14] It may be significant of the troubled times that this West Harling settlement has been judged by archaeologists to have lasted no more than one or two generations.

For the forests to become fields, where the Lophams were to be, there needed not so much war as an agricultural revolution. Perhaps both came together in the Late Iron Age with a confederation of warrior tribes known to the Romans as the Belgae. These Celtic-speaking invaders from the Rhineland were not only fighters but farmers, and their ploughshares were as good as their swords. Their skill in metalwork enabled them both to cut down the big timber and to cultivate the heavy loam beneath it with broader bladed coulters than the natives had ever seen.[15]

The Belgae arrived in south-east England about 100 B.C. and by the time of the second Roman invasion in A.D. 43 they seem to have fought their way north to a frontier with the Iceni along the Little Ouse.[16] Whoever there may have been living in the future Lophams at that time was therefore in the front line, and at both a crossing-point and a turning-point in local history.

Whatever went on between the Iceni and the Belgae during the next four years—conflict, infiltration, intermarriage and alliance—it was the Iceni who made their first revolt against the Romans in A.D. 47–48. Perhaps as part of their suppression the Romans gave them a tributary king, Prasutagus, who took himself a wife from among the Belgae, Boudicca, known to later history as Boadicea. The relevance of these events to the history of the Lophams is uncertain but it may be noted that after the second rebellion of the Iceni under their Belgic leader, Boudicca, in A.D. 60–61, they and their allies are said by Suetonius to have been deported in thousands to work as convict gangs on the reclamation of the Fenland.[17] Evidence of Roman-directed reclamation work in Lincolnshire is questionable;[18] it is interesting to speculate whether such labours began nearer home and whether the uppermost reaches of the

Mr. Charles Brown at Lodge Farm, North Lopham, *c.* 1885.

Waveney and the Little Ouse, which are clearly artificial channels, were first dug for the Romans by Icenian prisoners-of-war.

The first clear signs of settlement in the Lophams are Roman. It was modern agriculture, in 1954, which brought to light the remains of a group of buildings with stone foundations, mosaic floors, bath houses and heated rooms, near Lodge Farm, North Lopham.[19] These remains have been accepted as traces of a prosperous landed gentry of Roman stock established on a "villa" estate here between perhaps 150 and 350 A.D. The native working farmers and their labourers, who would have been needed to support such an establishment, were probably housed in wooden barn-like buildings and small huts of which traces would be hard to find. Some sixteen or seventeen centuries would have to go by before their descendants enjoyed the Roman luxury of central heating.

CHAPTER THREE

The First Address

It is plain then that there were people living and farming here in the second century A.D., but we do not know what they called their dwelling-place. In East Anglia the slate of Celtic and Romano-British place-names has been wiped nearly clean by the waves of immigrants and invaders who swept over the land in the latter end of the Roman occupation and afterwards. LOPHAM, like many neighbouring place-names, shews a sometime stranger's footprint, at least in its second half. "Hām" is a very old English word for "home", "homestead", or "village", and it was spread far and wide in England by immigrants from Northern Europe.[20] As for the first syllable, its meaning seems less sure.

It is notorious that a place tends to become known by the name of its possessor, and that Mr. Smith, who decorates his new habitation with a white trim and the title of "Ivory Towers", is likely at best to hear it called "Smith's place", but more likely "Brown's place" or "Jones's place" after the names of former owners. The modern school of English place-name interpreters, however, may have taken this lesson too much to heart. They seem to prefer a "former owner" explanation to almost any other descriptive solution. The *Oxford Dictionary of English Place-Names*, for example, interprets LOPHAM as "*Loppa*'s HĀM", and says that the mysterious Loppa's people had another place at Loppington in Shropshire. According to a grant made by Edward III on March 2nd, 1334, there was also a place called Lopholm in the neighbourhood of Boston, Lincolnshire.[20A] Perhaps the rules of the game do not allow the Dictionary to refer to the island of Loppa in the sea of Lopp on the far northern coasts of Norway.

The spelling LOPPHAM is indeed on record as early as the twelfth and as late as the seventeenth century, but in the eleventh century *Domesday Book*, on whose orthography the Dictionary so largely depends, LOPHAM is always spelt the way it is today. In 1225 the spelling of "Luppeham" and "Northluppeham" were recorded.[21A] If amateur guesses are allowed in place-name explanation, is it a possible alternative that the first syllable refers to no shadowy personage or tribe of "Loppa" but to a typical pioneering task in an area of primeval forest? The origins of the word "lop" in its cutting sense are obscure but its present-day meaning seems at least to hail from the same times and places as the word "hām".[21] That there may be some substance in this explanation, or at least that our ancestors believed in it, is suggested by a fifteenth century document from Lopham, preserved in the Norfolk Record Office. This names two places in South Lopham as "lopthorne" and "lopthorne furlong".[22]

Considering the importance of Lopham Gate as a crossing-point through the fens, another explanation might be found in the words "loup" or "lope", which are of Old Norse origin and can mean to leap or stride across.[23] "Lope-staves" were used to traverse East Anglian fens as late as the seventeenth century,[24] whilst in Kent a "lop-way" meant a private path.[25] Did LOPHAM once mean "the village at the crossing", or, as we now say, "the gate"?

There is one more alternative which deserves perhaps less serious consideration. The large raft spider, *Dolomedes plantarius*, the biggest spider of Britain, was officially discovered in Redgrave and Lopham Fens by Dr. Eric Duffey in 1956[26] but Dolomedes and many other kinds of spider had been there who knows how long before he was identified. Now the Anglo-Saxon word for spider was "lobbe"[27] which in English became "loppe". Geoffrey Chaucer was still writing of spiders and cobwebs as "loppes" and "loppewebbes" at the end of the fourteenth century.[28] May we indulge ourselves therefore with the picture of Anglo-Saxon invaders floundering in the fen, brushing the lopwebs and lopthreads from their

The Great Raft Spider, *Dolomedes Plantarius*—female with egg sac. An ancient & modern inhabitant of Lopham Fens. By courtesy of Mr. David Orr, producer of "*Reed Grove*, the story of a Nature Reserve".

sweating faces, failing to make Dr. Duffey's discovery by some fifteen hundred years, but naming with curses the place they were attacking "Spider Village", in the language of today?

CHAPTER FOUR

The First Christening

Whether the name of Lopham was a tribal address or a nickname, it appears to have roots in Northern Europe and to have been given to this place by people whom historians call, collectively, the Anglo-Saxons. There are various times and ways in which the first wave of such people might have arrived here. Before the end of the fourth century A.D. the Roman government of Britain was hiring foreign mercenaries to defend East Anglia from Saxon pirates. Some of these mercenary forces were themselves Saxon, and dug themselves in as the first "Anglo-Saxon" colonies in Britain. As Roman rule decayed, the mercenaries sometimes became their own masters and would move from the coast inland.[29] But wherever they went they were likely to find themselves fighting fresh invaders from the Scandinavian shores. Some of these no doubt came up the Waveney which was wider than it is today and gave perhaps a higher reach to boats of shallow draught. But it was the Anglo-Saxons who gave this river its name, and a translation, "Quaking Bog River",[30] suggests the trouble that raiders would be in if they tried to land above Roydon.

So the former Roman settlement above Lodge Farm and whatever dependencies went with it, may have been seized first by freebooters who came overland and later by invaders from overseas. The nearest datable evidence of Scandinavian strangers was found at Kenninghall Butts in 1869, a cemetery in which bodies had been buried between 500 and 600 A.D.[31] In the graves were ornaments of a type which modern archaeology has traced from southern Sweden through northern Jutland to Ipswich, where there is a larger cemetery of comparable date.[32] It may be therefore that the sixth and seventh century inhabitants of Kenninghall were of the race known as the "Ipswich people", and had made their way through the Suffolk forests over the Norfolk border. If so, they are likely to have come by Lopham Gate and to have occupied whatever settlements they found behind it.

The "Ipswich people" sported large square-headed brooches of gilded bronze. Some of these, found at Kenninghall Butts, were cruciform, in a pattern which has been incorporated in the Kenninghall village sign. But this "sign of the

North Lopham Church, *c*. 1950.

cross" was not Christian. There are faint and scattered traces of the Christian religion in East Anglia dated as early as the fourth century A.D. but nothing has been found yet to connect them with the Lopham region.

It may be supposed that there were pagan shrines in the earliest Lopham settlements and that their sites were sometimes adopted by successive cults. The oldest possible trace of such a site may survive in a place-name, Fivestone Lane, now known as Fyson's Lane. Documentary records of a place called "Five Stone" or "Five Stones" survive in various forms from at least the middle of the sixteenth century. It is conceivable that there were once five "standing stones" not far from the site of South Lopham church, and that they had a magical or ritual significance in some pagan era.

The site of North Lopham church as a "holy place" may be a great deal older than the present building, and it could be significant that the base of a Roman vase was found in 1950 some five hundred yards away.[33] A resident of South Lopham has pointed out to the writer that the churches of both villages lie in an almost straight line with Redgrave church.[34] Such an alignment of shrines has no known origin in Christian customs and might conceivably arise from some forgotten pagan practice, such as a fire festival.*

From the "Ipswich people" there rose a dynasty of kings, the Wuffings, who conquered all East Anglia and ruled over it from 550 until A.D. 740.[35] They began to receive Christian baptism before A.D. 617, and it is likely that Christianity reached the Lophams during the same seventh century. Christian policy, enjoined by Pope Gregory I upon Mellitus his missionary to Britain in A.D. 601, was to respect the pagan sanctuaries; not to destroy them but to purify them for Christian worship.[36] If churches were consecrated at North and South Lopham on top of pagan shrines in this manner, it is possible that their first dedications were decided in Rome. Gregory had recommended that the temples of the heathen should be sanctified with holy water and with the relics of Christian martyrs. It may be supposed that there was no local shortage of the latter in those barbarous times. Again,

* On the other hand it may be mere coincidence like many other alleged "ley" lines.

however, it is possible that foreign imports were preferred, since Gregory is known to have provided his missionaries not only with church equipment but to have sent to them in Britain "relics of the holy apostles and martyrs" from Rome.[37] Relics already held such a wonder-working importance in Christian teaching that there must have been an element of competition with magical objects exhibited in pagan temples.

Gregory's recognition of the need to compete with heathen rites is shewn in a letter he wrote about recent converts in Britain. He pointed out that these people had been accustomed as heathens to plentiful sacrifices of oxen to their devils. The solemnity of such celebrations ought to be maintained, but with a new meaning. For the anniversary of a church dedication, or for the birthdays of saints whose relics were preserved there, lean-to shelters of branches should be built round the walls now converted from pagan to Christian use; and religious feasts held under them. On such occasions animals should be killed, not to appease the devil but to glorify God and to give Him thanks for a well-filled stomach. Gregory said that if these physical pleasures were maintained the converts would be brought more easily to appreciate the joys of the spirit.[38]

It will be seen later in this history how the Lophams may have continued this tradition of church junketings well into the Middle Ages.

Gregorian Christianity in East Anglia had some two hundred and fifty years to spread and settle before it came under pagan attack from the Danish invaders of the ninth century. From what is known about the movements of the "Great Heathen Army" between 865 and 870 A.D.[39] it is likely that any churches the Lophams might have possessed at that time would have been desecrated or destroyed. In 878, however, King Alfred forced Christianity upon Guthrum, the Danish leader, by conquest, and although most of Norfolk and Suffolk continued under Danish rule for the next forty years, it is possible that some Christians in Lopham survived the loss of their church or churches, and even that the dedications of Gregorian days were not forgotten.

The first thing to be said about the two Lopham church dedications is that they are at present (1980) the wrong way round. There is evidence from a number of early wills, for example that of Edmund Clerk in 1375,[40] and from the *Norwich Domesday Book* of perhaps an even earlier origin,[41] that the church of North Lopham was dedicated to Saint Andrew and the church of South Lopham to Saint Nicholas. To judge from the second of the authorities quoted, there was even a time when the northern village was known as "Lopham Saint Andrew" and the southern as "Lopham Saint Nicholas". At various times in English church history, however, saints have gone out of fashion, and the Lopham Parish Registers, for example, refer only in geographical terms to the churches of North and South Lopham. Nevertheless Norfolk's principal historian, the Reverend Francis Blomefield, who was rector of a next-door parish, made no question of the mediaeval dedications when he published his account of the Lophams in 1739.[42] He was still the accepted authority when his book was republished with the same allotment of dedications in 1805. In 1829, however, Mr. John Chambers, who drew heavily on the work of Blomefield and Parkin, published an anonymous "General History of Norfolk" in which, apparently by carelessness, he recorded the saints of North and South Lopham in the wrong order.[43] This mistake seems to have been copied by the County Directories from 1836 onwards, and when saints came into vogue again in the mid-eighteen-thirties the clergy followed suit. For a hundred and fifty years therefore the dedications have been reversed,* but in the present history Saint Andrew and Saint Nicholas will return to their proper places.

Andrew is much the more ancient patron saint. It would be rash to assume that a church at North Lopham was dedicated to him as long ago as the days of Gregory the Great and his missionary Saint Augustine. Nevertheless Augustine's dedication in A.D. 604 of the church which became S. Andrew's Cathedral at Rochester had many early parallels in Britain. Both Gregory and Augustine were old boys of S. Andrew's monastery at Rome. Gregory was abbot there at the time of his election to the papacy in A.D. 590, and his devotion to this senior apostle and martyr had been recognised already by the

* But not by scholars such as John L'Estrange in his *Church Bells of Norfolk*, 1874.

Eastern Emperor Tiberius II in the gift to him of one of S. Andrew's arms.[44] Traditions of this devotion and of the relics which went with it may be apparent in the five hundred and seventy-seven pre-Reformation churches dedicated to S. Andrew in England, one hundred and six of them in Norfolk alone.[45]

In the same county there are only twenty-nine such dedications to S. Nicholas.[46] The fame of this popular saint in Western Christendom dates from 1087 when his miracle-working relics were the subject of a sensational burglary by merchants of Bari in southern Italy.[47] Their pious theft was from Myra in Asia Minor, where Nicholas was supposedly a bishop in the fourth century. The significance of this post-Conquest dedication at South Lopham will be discussed in Chapter Seven.

CHAPTER FIVE

The First Valuation

The history of the Lophams turns towards facts instead of speculation in the pages of *Domesday Book*. King William the Conqueror, however, did not command this survey of his conquests to be made for the benefit of historians. What he wanted was a record of how his English lands were held and what they were worth in money, service and kind.[48] So although we learn the first recorded names of Lopham inhabitants—unless we believe in "Loppa"—; the rough size of the population; some of the farming that went on and the livestock that were kept; a good many interesting questions about eleventh century Lopham are left unanswered.

We have to guess at the geography. *Domesday Book* records three different places by the name of Lopham, all held of King William I in 1086 by Roger Bigot, the founder of the house of the Bigod earls of Norfolk, as tenant-in-chief. The first two holdings are distinguished from each other by the names of "Lopham" and "the other Lopham"; the third is merely called "Lopham".[49] It has been deduced that the second of these must have been what is now called South Lopham since it adjoined another holding in Blo' Norton ("Nortuna" in *Domesday Book*). This circumstance, however, could have applied also to Lopham Ford if, as the next chapter suggests, there was a third Lopham settlement in that place. The first holding, which was the largest, may have been the original North Lopham, or Lopham-Magna as it was sometimes called in later days. The third holding, which was the smallest and had the least woodland, is perhaps the most likely site of the "Lost Lopham", down by the fen at Lopham Ford.

On these assumptions, and counting each numbered sub-tenant as the head of an average family of four, the population of North Lopham might be reckoned at about 150, South Lopham at about 80, and Lopham Ford perhaps at 40: altogether some 270 souls. This may be an underestimate. Despite the afflictions of fire and sword which East Anglia had suffered from the ninth to the eleventh centuries the total population shewed a marked increase between A.D. 850 and 1066. It has been estimated that in the hundred of Guiltcross, where the Lophams lie, the inhabitants in 1086 averaged 10.8 to the square mile.[50]

The only names in *Domesday Book* of Lopham inhabitants refer to the days of Edward the Confessor, the last of the Anglo-Saxon kings. In his time a freeman named Ofl had held a manor in what is believed to be North Lopham, while another freeman, Alsi, had held a manor consisting of lands in a Lopham holding and in Blo' Norton. There is argument among historians about the freedom and independence of "freemen" compared with the lot of other kinds of tenant listed in *Domesday Book*.[51] A relatively large concentration of "freemen" is recorded in East Anglia and it has been suggested that these were survivors of "a once more wide-spread class, who had managed to retain their economic independence because they dwelt on richer lands or were more efficient cultivators".[52] If there is any substance in this theory it should be noted that in the smallest of the Lopham holdings there were no less than five freemen in 1086, whereas the other two seem to have had only one freeman between them. Could this mean that the smallest holding, possibly identified as Lopham Ford, was the oldest of three Anglo-Saxon settlements?

Domesday Book tells us that all three holdings had plough-land but there is nothing said about the crops. There were some eight ploughteams in all, each of eight oxen, and the stock of "beasts", including the cows from which the oxen were bred, had risen from two to sixteen between 1066 and 1086. On the other hand, while the meadowland remained at a total of some thirty acres the number of sheep had fallen from two hundred to one hundred and twenty. The woodland, amounting to perhaps three hundred and thirty acres in all the holdings, does not seem to have dwindled since the Conquest, but *Domesday* suggests that there was room and mast enough for many more swine. There had been at least one Norfolk rebellion in the Conqueror's time and perhaps the Lophams lost both pork and mutton to the opposing forces.

In addition to the stock, the largest holding had two "rounceys" or work-horses, and the second largest had one. The second also had ten hives of bees, valuable in the Middle Ages as a source of mead, wax and sugar. Despite their loss of stock both holdings were reckoned to have grown in prosperity during the twenty years since the Conquest. The "whole of Lopham", whatever that may have meant, was taxed at two shillings and tenpence halfpenny a year, precisely the same rate as the combined taxes of East Harling and Quidenham.[53]

CHAPTER SIX

The Lost Lopham

Some grounds for belief in a third Lopham have been described in Chapters One, Two and Five. It may be useful at this juncture to sum up the remaining evidence.

> "Twixt Lophàm forde and Shimpling Thorne
> England shalbe woonn and lorne."

This mediaeval jingle is said to have been copied from a manorial court book of Shimpling Thorne, which lies between Bury S. Edmund's and Sudbury.[54] Whatever it meant as prophecy it suggests pictorially that there may have been a landmark at each of the two places. In 1375 Edmund Clerk (which is not likely to have meant "Edmund, priest" since he had a wife and sons) bequeathed a mark (thirteen shillings and fourpence) "towards the repair of the cross at Lophamford".[55] He had left the same substantial amount, in the money of those days, to the fabric of the church of St. Nicholas, South Lopham, and it looks as though Lophamford Cross had then some religious function. It may have served also as a boundary mark and even as a market cross. Blomefield blames Leland, a sixteenth century antiquary, for calling Lopham Ford *Lopham Market* "without any Authority",[56] but perhaps a cross was still standing in Leland's day.

In 1618 Robert Reyce, writing about Suffolk, said:

". . . there bee two ryvers the one called the Ouse which is the lesser by some called the Dune, the other the Waueney, both which arising almost out of one head between Lopham and Foord and running cleane contrary courses doe devide this shire from Norfolk."[57]

"Foord", which may be identified as Lophamford, seems here to refer to a village on the Suffolk side of Lopham Gate. There are contemporary maps which print the word "Ford" in the same situation but which may refer to the actual causeway between the fens.

There is no ambiguity about the location given by John Adams in his *Index Villaris* of 1690. In this gazetteer he listed three distinct Lophams, starting with "Lopham-Ford" in the county of Suffolk and the hundred of Blackborn at the "Latitude" of "52 27" and the "Longitude" of "1 02*E*". He went on to tabulate Lopham North, to which he gave the same Latitude, and Lopham South which he credited with the rectory and "One Gentleman". Unfortunately the geographical calculations of that date cannot be regarded as reliable.

Forty years later Cox and Hall in the Suffolk volume of their *Magna Britannia* mentioned

"*Lophamford*, a Village remarkable only for a marshy Ground, out of which the Rivers *Ouse the less* and *Waveney* rise, at a little Distance one from another, dividing this County from Norfolk . . ."[58]

There is evidence that Blomefield, who published his account of the Lophams nine years afterwards, had read at least the Norfolk volume of *Magna Britannia*,[59] but he does not discuss Lopham Ford as a separate village. In correcting Leland about the misnomer of "Lopham Market" he describes *Lopham Ford* as "the Place where the Goal" (sc. Gaol) "of the Duke of *Norfolk's* Liberty was kept",[60] and he goes on to give a long account of the Liberty.

The "Liberty", granted by King Edward IV in 1468 to the last Mowbray duke of Norfolk and his duchess, applied to certain of their lands in Norfolk, Suffolk, Essex, Surrey and Sussex, and it gave them and their heirs "for ever . . . all manner of Fines, Profits, Amerciaments, Penalties, &c. of all Residents in the said Liberty . . . with full Power for the Duke's Officers to seize for any of them . . ."[61] A gaol would have been useful therefore near the border of Norfolk and Suffolk, and some sign of its location appears in the name of

"Gaol House" about half a mile north of Lopham Gate. Two successive "squarsons" of Wortham Hall, the Rev. George Betts (ob. 1766) and his son of the same name (ob. 1822) owned a small freehold farm at this spot, which was described in 1773 as "near the Frith* and supposed to be near the old Goal" (sic) "house on the Common."[62] The original building therefore seems to have disappeared by that date, and what is now called "Gaol House" was described in a map of about 1790 as "Lopham Ford Farm".[63]

It is tempting to think that Gallows Hill in Redgrave, about the same distance south of the border, is the site of another convenience to the duke's "Liberty", but Hangman's Barn is a long step back into Norfolk.

The picture of a village or hamlet of "Lophamford" emerging from these quotations is not very clear, but there can be little doubt that such a place existed and that most or all of it belonged in recent times to Suffolk. The crossroads on Redgrave Common, known as "Crossway", might seem to be a good site for the fourteenth century cross, but it is difficult to distinguish this area from Redgrave. A local story given to the writer was that the lost Lopham stood at Crackthorn Bridge, midway between Redgrave and Thelnetham.

* The Frith consisted of sixty acres in two pieces, called the Little Frith and the Great Frith, bounded by the Redgrave Road, the Hopton Road and the river Dune. It was "taken off the Common", says Blomefield, "by the Lord's Consent, of whom they now hold it, it is Marsh Ground, and lett at 8 *l*. per Ann. the Income of which is given to the Poor by the Feoffees every *Christmas* and *Easter*".[64] The Appendix shews that this income is still devoted to charitable uses.

CHAPTER SEVEN

Lopham Churches

Both before and after the Norman Conquest churches had valuations like other property, based on the income they got from their glebelands, from tithes, and from the "oblations" or offerings of the faithful. But there is no word of any Lopham church in *Domesday Book*. The same silence applies to a number of places in Norfolk where it is known or believed that a church was standing in 1086.[65] Sometimes the value of the church was included in that of the manor; sometimes no doubt it was excluded from *Domesday* for reasons unknown to us; and sometimes perhaps the church was in ruins or otherwise valueless for the time being.

At South Lopham one part of the church at least must have been standing up as plainly in 1086 as it does today. The high round window set in the thick wall of the nave points moreover to a large Saxon church of some importance. Perhaps it had been one of the "minsters" which were built in East Anglia during the return of Christianity in the tenth century, and which were designed to serve whole hundreds before parishes and parish churches were established.[66] A former minster might be expected to have connections outside the parish, particularly with the bishop's see, and this may be the explanation of a number of facts in the history of South Lopham church.

Roger Bigot had won favour in the eyes of King William, apparently by his merits as a comrade-in-arms in the Conquest. *Domesday Book* shews that this favour had brought him many possessions in East Anglia. The three Lopham

South Lopham Church from N.W. shewing Anglo-Saxon round window in North wall of nave, 1949. By courtesy of the National Monuments Record.

holdings were among them with much else, including both a monastery and a church in Thetford. The monastery has not been identified but the church, says Blomefield, ". . . as I take it, was St. *Nicholas*'s which always belonged to the Abbey".[67] As Chapter Four has shewn, however, neither the Thetford nor the South Lopham church is likely to have belonged to S. Nicholas until after 1087. On the other hand, by 1089 Bigot's conquering Norman cousins in Apulia were building a great pilgrimage cathedral at Bari to receive the wonder-working bones acquired from Myra.[68] This foundation was dedicated of course to S. Nicola, and such was its fame that Bigot may well have decided to celebrate the saint in East Anglian dedications.

By "the Abby" Blomefield meant the Cluniac Priory of S. Mary which was founded by Roger Bigot at Thetford in 1103. In atonement for the sins he had committed as Steward to William Rufus and to Henry I, Bigot had planned, it is said, a pilgrimage to Jerusalem. He had been persuaded from this expensive and dangerous enterprise by his own steward, who argued that the money such a journey would cost him could be laid out just as effectively in the foundation of a monastery, where monks could pray continuously for all Bigots, past, present and to come.[69]

The monastery he already held in Thetford may have been amalgamated by Bigot with the new foundation, and S. Nicholas, Thetford, was presumably one of the first endowments. But it was Great S. Mary's, on the Suffolk side of the river, which was converted into the first Priory church, for reasons of prestige and perhaps for other advantages. Between 1075 and 1095 Great S. Mary's had been the cathedral church of the diocese and, to judge from a firm letter sent to the Prior by Bishop Herbert Losinga in 1114, the Priory exploited this fact to the detriment of the Bishopric's "ancient episcopal rights".[70] We can only guess that these "rights" were profitable. For example, if South Lopham church was once a minster Great S. Mary's may have had rights over it dating from her cathedral days; and if, as may appear, that former minster retained possessions outside its present parish, its presentation or "restitution" by Roger Bigot to the inheritors of Great S. Mary's could have meant a loss of revenue to the new see at Norwich.

It is commonly said that the "church of Lopham" was first granted to Thetford Priory by Roger's son William Bigo*d*, as he is generally called. But William's charter, given between 1107 and 1120, appears to be firstly a confirmation of his father's grants and secondly an undertaking to pay compensation for churches, Lopham among them, already promised to the Priory but not yet delivered.[71]

This state of affairs might have a bearing on the architectural history of S. Nicholas, South Lopham. Authorities agree that the earliest Norman work at this church may be dated

South Lopham Church, North door, built *c*. 1150; restored *c*. 1866.

before 1120. At Thetford the Bigods' rebuilding of the Priory, now transferred to the Norfolk side of the river, was completed in 1114.[72] Is it possible that William Bigod then sent his builders up the Little Ouse, perhaps with a surplus of imported ashlar from Thetford, to modernise the Saxon church at South Lopham?* If so, the labourers must have found the digging of the tower foundations in Lopham clay a sticky change from their task at Thetford, where, as a chronicler reports, they had to dig "mighty deep" because of sand.[73] The once splendid north door of the nave, blocked and 'restored' about 1866, marked perhaps the completion of the Bigod rebuilding some seven hundred years before.

Between 1154 and 1177 a charter of Henry II confirmed the Priory's ownership of "the church of Joppham", as someone misspelt it, "with all its appurtenances".[74] We are not told what these "appurtenances" were, but this conventional phrase still had a meaning and it was applied to few of the churches listed in the charter. We may at least assume that they were ecclesiastical properties or "spiritualties", as they were called, and in a catalogue of such properties belonging to the Priory in 1291, we find there were "portions" in the church revenues of Winfarthing, Shelfanger, Blo' Norton S. Andrew, and Garboldisham S. John.[75] These particular "portions" do not seem to be named among the previously recorded endowments of the Priory, but had they, and perhaps others, once belonged to the "appurtenances" of S. Nicholas, South Lopham? The advowson of S. Nicholas had been repossessed by the Bigods before 1291, but perhaps the appurtenances, a shadow of a long-forgotten South Lopham Minster, were retained by the Priory.

Much less is known about the early history of S. Andrew's, North Lopham. Despite what the Norfolk county directories have said for so many years, there is no Norman work in the south porch of this church, and nothing earlier than the fourteenth century now appears above ground. According to the so-called *Norwich Domesday Book* of the fourteenth or fifteenth century, the church of Lopham S. Andrew was

"... a chapel depending from the other church of S.

* The Norman fabric exhibits a variety of building material: perhaps even Roman brick on the west face of the much-repaired tower.

The Church, North Lopham, from south-east.

Nicholas, and thirty parishioners belong to it; and thereat is there baptism and burial and a manner of belfry in the churchyard, with two bells hanging in a certain tree."[76]

The thirty parishioners may be understood as the heads of thirty families, married perhaps at Lopham S. Nicholas. The description of the belfry suggests that the whole account of the parish dates from before the 1470s when the present west tower was begun. Churchyard belfries without bell-towers can still be seen, for example at East Bergholt in Suffolk, but the North Lopham bells, hanging perhaps in some ancient oak, must have been a remarkable sight. Perhaps one of them gave the old "Bell" inn nearby its name.

We should not jump to the conclusion that S. Andrew's church was built as a "chapel of ease" to S. Nicholas. If that had been its purpose why is it at the extreme southern end of North Lopham street and barely a mile by road from the parent church? As Chapter Four suggests, the present building may stand on an ancient holy place. Its dedication to S. Andrew, however, could date from the twelfth or thirteenth

The Bell Inn, North Lopham, *c*. 1935.

centuries when monks of Thetford Priory were serving the cure. At an uncertain date the Priory became known as 'S. Mary's and S. Andrew's the Great'',[77] and the representative monks might have copied the second dedication.* But there is a possibility of a much earlier derivation. In 1544 John Levold of North Lopham bequeathed his "body to be buryed in the churche or churchyarde of Saint Andrew of North lopham beforesaide . . . Allso to our mother churche in Norwiche xiid . . ."[78] By 1544 Thetford Priory had been dissolved and therefore could perform no longer the functions of a "mother church", whatever these may have been. But it is a fairly long stride to suppose that such functions were formally transferred to S. Andrew's of Norwich. Although the fabric of that church appears to be all of the fifteenth and sixteenth centuries or later, it was founded in fact before the Conquest.[79]

A Cecily de Lopham, "formerly wife of *Rob. de Bump-*

* See Chapter Ten for a possible reference to this dedication on North Lopham church tower.

stede" was buried there in 1389.[80] She may have been a member of the family descended from Ivo, a twelfth century North Lopham tenant of the second Bigod earl of Norfolk.* They took their patronymic from Lopham, and Blomefield records among them: "Henry (of *Lopham*) the Chirurgeon" (1248) "Symon de Lopham, Clerk, in 1334, and Dionise de Lopham his Son, who was a famous Notary Publick".[81] It is just possible therefore that John Levold referred to a link with Norwich that was older than any monkish connections with Thetford.

The building of North Lopham tower is discussed in a later chapter but it is worth noting here that the builders of the lowest storey in the last quarter of the fifteenth century did their best to prevent their descendants from forgetting the dedication. They wrote in stone an "A" for "Andrew" at the corner nearest the church south door.† The tower of S. Mary at Kenninghall has her monogram in the same situation.

There may be one other ecclesiastical site in the Lophams: Chapple or Chapel Hill, a field which lies north of Lodge Farm in North Lopham. A map made in 1612 of "Lopham Parke"[82] gives a rough sketch of the Lodge as it then stood, a building with four gables and a detached barn or stable, both within an enclosure, possibly hedged, with a stream running through it, and apparently under the house, from north to south. Round the enclosure lies "The Lawne", an area of 423 acres, 2½ roods. Various field-names are given but there is no "Chapel Hill" and it may be that at this date a chapel, or the remains of one, was inside the house. Apart from the Howard family's observance of the Roman Catholic religion, the house as a manor-house was far enough away from both North and South Lopham churches to make a domestic chapel necessary in the Middle Ages. But at Arundel Castle the earliest map to shew "Chapple Hills" dates from about 1812. The name is applied to a field lying east of "Dovehouse Close".

* Robert de Lopham, possibly her father, was associated while a bailiff of Norwich with Peter de Bumstede, a burger of the same city, in 1303 and 1320.[80A]

† The fourteenth (?) century wrought iron fish on the door itself is also one of S. Andrew's emblems.

CHAPTER EIGHT

Lopham Lands and Lords

In the early eighteenth century Blomefield would remark that the commons of the Lophams, including "Fenn Common",

> ". . . Contain as much Land as the whole Towns beside."[83]

(The word "town" does not seem to have been used in its modern sense until after the Norman Conquest, and it continued concurrently to apply to villages and smaller hamlets for more than seven hundred years.[84])

In *Domesday Book* there is no reference to these commons, even as pasture or waste, presumably because much of the commons-to-be were still under the forest, whilst undrained fenland would have seemed worthless. The omission may have proved an initial advantage to the peasants in so far as it left large areas to which no landlord had yet staked particular claims. There was room for the development of vested interests in common use.

Felling trees for buildings, fences, fuel and more fields must have cut steadily into the forest edges. Such names as Hewtree, Cuttings and Knaveings (i.e. Gnawings), Stubbinges, Shortstubbyng, and lopthorne may bear witness in both North and South Lopham to the labour of the woodlanders. By the beginning of the twelfth century at least one landlord, Bishop Herbert Losinga of Norwich, was trying to check the destruction of his woods by his peasants. We do not know in Lopham whether or when restrictions on felling began, nor can we say when parts of the surviving woodland were first conserved by lords of the manor within park pales. By 1301, however, the last of the Bigod lords had a manor house, a park, and three hundred and thirty five acres of demesne land here, including fifteen of meadow and twenty of pasture. ("Demesne" land originally meant all the ground cultivated for the lord's own use, but by the fourteenth century it could include holdings of the peasants who worked for him.[85]) Some of the pasture may have been land recovered from the fens, for a charter of the previous century shews that a certain John delepol of Lopham had one and a half acres in "Lopham marsh".[86]

The last Bigod lord was another Roger, the fifth Earl of Norfolk. He quarrelled about money with brother John, his heir, and, apparently in spite, surrendered to King Edward I in 1302 his Earldom, the Marshalcy of England and most of his lands,[87] including the manor of Lopham. The property did not stay long with the Crown for in 1310 King Edward II assigned it to his own brother, Thomas of Brotherton, who was made Earl of Norfolk in 1313 and Earl Marshal three years later. Not long before his death in 1338 Earl Thomas was accused of oppression and seems to have undergone some restraint in his lordship. The Lophams may have voiced complaints against him for on March 16th, 1337, King Edward III, at the request of Countess Mary (born de Brewose), the earl's second wife, released all the earl's tenants, free and bond, "in Lopham and elsewhere in England and Wales" for ever from a tallage called "le Wrongeyeld."[87A] A tallage was an arbitrary tax levied by a lord upon his feudal dependants and the name given to this one may describe what was thought of it. King Edward himself seems to have visited Lopham on June 8th–10th and 12th, 1338.[87B]

The manor of Lopham passed in due course to Margaret, the new Earl's elder daughter, and, by 1375, his sole surviving heir. In 1377 she was created Countess of Norfolk in her own right, and when she died in 1399 the Earldom and her lands went to her grandson, Thomas de Mowbray, the first Duke of Norfolk.[88] The lordship of the manor of Lopham passed eventually with that share of the Mowbray inheritance which was allotted to the Howard family, but in 1486, while Thomas Howard was still in the Tower for fighting on the wrong side at the battle of Bosworth, King Henry VII granted Lopham, with other manors, to Elizabeth, the widow of the last Mowbray duke, for life. This lady, who appears to have spent some of her widowhood at Easthall in her neighbouring manor of Kenninghall, lived until 1506/7.[89] The lordship of the manor of Lopham returned to the Howard family, but was sold in 1872 by trustees for Henry, the fifteenth Howard duke of Norfolk, to Henry Edwin Garrod, a lawyer of Diss.[90]

In 1383 Margaret Marshal, Countess of Norfolk, had at least sixty acres of wood in her park at Lopham, and whether from this manor or another, she had recently provided all the timber for the new stalls of Greyfriars Church in London, at a cost of three hundred and eighty marks.[91] She was troubled, like other lords of Lopham, by poachers, and in 1374 brought complaints against a number of people for breaking into her park at Lopham and entering her free warrens elsewhere, hunting there without license and carrying away pheasants from the warrens and deer from the park.[91A]

It is not known where the Bigod, Marshal or Mowbray manor houses stood in Lopham, but field-names may provide some clues. A privilege belonging to many lords of manors in the Middle Ages was the monopoly of dovecotes on their lands. The word "dove" or "dowe" originally applied to all sorts of pigeon, and these birds, fattened on the crops of lord and commoner alike, provided in the dovecote fresh meat for the lord's table and dung for his fields. The dovecote therefore was usually close to the manor house, and it may be significant that in South Lopham fields called "Dowhouse Acre" and "Dowes Close" were both in the neighbourhood of the present-day hall. The hall is mainly a modern building but its site, opposite the church, is a traditional position for the manor house.

In North Lopham too we have noticed the field-name of "Dovehouse Close", nowadays called "Duffy's Close",[92] near the site of the old Lodge and the much older site of the Roman villa. The building sketched in the Arundel map of 1612 was possibly put up by the Howard dukes of Norfolk at some date before 1571. But "The Lawne"* surrounding it probably took its name from the ancient word "lawn" or

* The term appears as a field-name in both North and South Lopham.

"laund", meaning a glade or open space among woods. This takes us back to the earlier days of Lopham and may mean that there was another mediaeval manor house on the site of Lopham Lodge. Both these theoretical sites of manor houses have nearby fragments of woodland, at Lopham Grove and at Holland's Wood, either of which might be a remainder of Margaret Marshal's sixty acres.

The Bigods, the Marshals and the Mowbrays all had many manors and we need not suppose that any of them were frequently in residence at Lopham. The Lopham manorial courts were ruled on most occasions by the lord's steward, or his deputy, and the farming of the demesne land would be managed by a bailiff. The bailiff would be assisted by a reeve, who was supposed to be elected by his fellow-tenants as the best husbandman of them all. One way of rewarding the reeve for his services was to allow him land additional to his regular holdings, and there seem to be traces of this practice in Lopham. In 1841 there were fields still known as "reeve-land", for example, "one rood of Land of Reeveland lying at Snellsmere"[93] in South Lopham. In the same village there was "half an acre of Meadow called Reeves Meadow".[94]

These names go back to the days of farming by the "open field system", when the arable land of a village was divided into two or three large fields, cultivated under a two or three years' rotation of crops. The great fields were again divided into long narrow strips, cultivated by the peasant holders according to their respective conditions of tenancy. A man's holdings were not grouped together but intermixed with other men's, as chance, inheritance and the manorial courts would have it, so that one tenant had often to look after his holdings piecemeal in different parts of the manor. Relics of this mediaeval chaos are abundantly illustrated in the 1815 maps of the Inclosure Awards at North and South Lopham.[95] Messrs. Brown & Taylor, the meticulous surveyors of the time, recorded not only exchanges of allotments of "Common Land" made in order to bring together scattered estates, but, lifting their hands in despair, had to qualify some of their estimates of acreage with such provisos as:

"Deduct Land belonging to Mr. John Porter lying intermixed and undivided in this Estate."[96]

One attempt at rationalisation may be traced at a much earlier date. The lord of the manor suffered like his tenants from the dispersal of fragments of his demesne over common lands. Such fragments were still known in eighteenth century Norfolk as "severals", and Blomefield records that one lord of Lopham, at an unspecified date, exchanged "Lands . . . then called the *Severals*, and now the *Allands* or *Ollands*" for "*Chimbrook-Meadow*", then belonging to the inhabitants of North and South Lopham, "to make his Fishery".[97] The fish-pond was made presumably by damming the stream called the Chim Brook, and a vestige of it remained in the name of "Poule Chimbrook" field, shewn on the 1612 map of Lopham Park. By that date, however, the "Fishery" had been replaced by the more fashionable device of a "Decoy", a trap for wild water-birds and another means of keeping the Lodge table supplied with fresh poultry.

The lord of the "Fishery" was glad no doubt to add to the amenities of his park. But in making the exchange he was careful to reserve to himself "the Trees, Furze and Bushes, growing, or which should ever hereafter grow on the lands" (the Severals) "so laid out, which privilege," says Blomefield in 1739, "the Lord still enjoys".[98] This is an interesting example of a feudal lord insisting upon common rights which dated from ancient and more democratic days. It is believed by a number of historians that the manorial system of the Middle Ages developed from earlier societies in which common rights played a much greater part than they did in feudal times.[99] The inefficiency of the agricultural system which has been described was set off to some extent by the communal behaviour which such a lack of system induced.

In the Lophams both the limitation and the preservation of common rights can be observed over hundreds of years in the proceedings of the manorial courts. The British Library has a collection of Lopham court rolls extending from 1399 to 1655.[100] The purposes of the courts, originally more than one, were to maintain the authority of the lord over his tenants, to settle disputes between these tenants, and to punish transgressors against laws within the court's jurisdiction. It was the practice in court rolls to recite from time to time the "custumal", reporting on rights and duties then in force. Perhaps it was from such a recital that Blomefield quoted a privilege of the tenants still in force in 1739:

". . . the Tenants can build, and pull down, fell Timber and plant on the Waste against their own Lands without Licence."[101]

This may seem a far cry from the days of "conservation areas" and "planning permission". It harks back to the days when the Lophams were pioneering settlements in forest clearings and it speaks of the vested interests so called in the second paragraph of this chapter. It explains some of the haphazard growth of buildings around and behind the main lines of the Lopham villages. More than that it illustrates the background of traditional rights for which Lopham people were to demonstrate on the enforcement of the Inclosure Act of 1812. These rights were not only of each man for himself; they maintained customs for the common good. An entry to the court rolls as late as March 20th, 1652, records that

"At this Court it is ordered that noe Inhabitant within the Towne of Lopham shall mowe any fodder upon the Fenne called Lopham Fenne to imploy for the fodderings of any Cattell, but onely such as is fitt for Charitie, upon paine of vi^{s} viii^{d} for every loade or loadings cutt or carried away . . ."[102]

The administration of Town Land on Lopham Fen for the common good continues to this day.

CHAPTER NINE

Mediaeval Lopham Life

Kings and queens, lords and ladies, bishops, priors, stewards, bailiffs and other institutions all have records enough from long ago, but it is hard to discover the lives of the people set under them. We should like to know the histories of mediaeval men and women who never knew which king was on the throne; who would not have recognised the lord of their manor if they met him; who saw the fields as the scenes of the seasons and the tasks they hated or loved; the churches as places of awe, sometimes in sorrow, often in boredom, sometimes in jovial meeting, but always with touches of magic; the lord's hall at harvest a place of lights, bountiful meat and drink and music perhaps, but with always a smell of the law.

There was another institution they knew well and used much but which has no history, the tavern. The importance of the Norfolk alehouse and the strength of Norfolk ale were celebrated about the time of Magna Carta in Latin verses; one set, by a monk of Peterborough, attacking Norfolk's drinking habits; another, by a Norfolk monk, defending them. Four lines from the first set might be translated:

> "After the market they haste to the inn
> Where what we call *buslusse* they keep soaking in,
> And then they're so drunk that they can't speak or pass
> Since for falling about they can't climb on their ass."[103]

The Peterborough analysis of this buslusse or booze will not bear translation;[104] even in the thirteenth century one county would revile the next county's beer.

North Lopham King's Head, *c*. 1935. The "Hill", a fragment of the old village green, in front.

The Lophams had no market of their own but no doubt there were taverns as soon as there were village greens. In the thirteenth century the weather the villagers would discuss over a cup of buslusse would not be so very different from today's, even though its onset were unforeseen, and its consequences uncontrolled. Without the hypnotic "presentations" of television news, the dictation of the radio or the propaganda of the newspapers, people were still able to use their own imaginations. Reflections of these have been preserved by the chroniclers, those collectors of mediaeval bar-room gossip. Thus we learn that the hail which in 1203 was "as bigge as hennes egges",[105] became in 1206 "as big as goose egs".[106] When the rainstorms of June and July, 1201, made an "outragious course of waters", which drowned men and cattle and carried away the corn and hay, "al men thought a new deluge had been come"[107]; and when "Great thunders and lightninges bursting out of the cloudes were seene" five years later, "men thought that the day of Doome had bin come".[108]

On the lighter side there were tall stories to enjoy. The Middle Ages left no flying objects unidentified, whether it was "one morning in the beginning of Lent" in 1209, when "the clouds seemed to fight with the Sun, from the Sun rising, till one of the clocke of that daie",[109] or the merman who came out of the sea at Orford in 1187 and stayed for six months at the castle. "Oftentimes he was brought to the Church, where he shewed no tokens of adoration. At length when hee was not wel looked to, he stale away to the sea, and never after appeared."[110] Sometimes, as still happens, tall stories had a touch of satire, as in the discovery in 1349 of "a serpent having two heads, and faces like women, one being shaped after the new tyre of that time: another after the manner of the old attire, and it had great wings, after the manner of a Flindermouse or Bat".[111]

Perhaps it was in those days that another tall tale with a sting in it was told for the first time in Lopham:

"How there was a wondrous ox came to Lopham, with horns and udders both, and gave such a plenty of milk to the folk of Saint Nicholas and Saint Andrew that they lacked not for butter nor cheese nor whey. So they sold their kine in Kenninghall market and spent the revenue on Lopham buslusse until they were all amazed. They could not tell the Bull from the Bell, the White Horse from the Black Horse, the Chequers from the Cherry Tree, nor the King's Head from the Crown. At last they grew hungry and must have cheese, so one was sent to get the milk for the curd. But he was so muddled with drink that instead of a pail he took up a sieve, and milked the ox till the sun went down and he stripped it dry. Then the ox bellowed and stamped away in the dark of the moon and never after appeared. But the mark of its wrath may be seen to this day on a stone they call the Oxfoot-stone."[112]

Then there were the wonders and grumbles of husbandry to be murmured and heard. In the late thirteenth century wheat, barley and hay seem to have been the main crops at Lopham. No doubt there were oxen, cows, sheep, pigs and poultry for subsistence. There is a record that in 1270 eight hundred eggs were sold in Lopham at fourpence the hundred, a halfpenny more than they cost at Caister.[113] We do not know

Mr. George Smith of the North Lopham Bull, 1884.

who bought the eggs or why but it must have been a subject of Lopham talk. It would be as unreliable to give an estimate of these prices in terms of modern money as it would be unrealistic to imagine "intensive poultry breeding" in thirteenth century Lopham.

In the following century it is reasonable to suppose that the Marshals at Lopham, like so many other landlords in Norfolk, bred sheep. In 1341 Norfolk was rated the richest wool-producing county in England, producing for one of King Edward III's taxes 2,206 sacks while Suffolk produced only 959.[114] The name of "Sheepmere"[115] in South Lopham, marking perhaps like "Oysmere"[116] (Goose mere?) the site of one of the vanished meres north of Lopham Fen, may date from this earlier period of sheep-breeding, whilst "Sheep-Pen Lane"[117] may belong to the time of the Howards discussed in Chapter Ten.

Among the griefs and fears of wars and weather and taxes the mediaeval peasant would have also the worries of murrain. In 1275 there was a visitation of foot-rot which is said to have lasted for twenty-eight years.[118] Characteristically, the Englishman blamed foreigners in his alehouse talk:

"A rich man of France brought into Northumberland a Spanish Ewe, as bigge as a calfe of two yeeres, which Ewe being rotten, infected so the countrey, that it spread over all the realme."[119]

In 1318:

"A great murrein of kine hapned, which were so mortally infected, that dogs and ravens eating of the carrion of the kine, were poisoned, and did swell to death, so that no man durst eate anie beefe."[120]

But worse than any of these afflictions, and enough to bring tavern fellowship to an end, was contagion among men. In 1341:

"There began amongst the East Indians and Tartarians a certaine pestilence, which at length waxed so general, infecting the middle region of the ayre so greatly, that it destroyed the Saracens, Turks, Syrians, Palestinians, and the Grecians, with a wonderfull, or rather incredible death . . . And the seventh yeere after it began, it came into England . . . and so wasted & spoyled the people, that scarce the tenth person of all sorts was left alive: when Church-yards were not sufficient and large ynough to bury their dead in, they chose certaine fields appointed for that purpose . . . There died from the first of Januarie, to the first of July, in the City of Norwich 57104 persons, besides Ecclesiasticall Mendicants and Dominikes.* There was buried in the Church and Churchyard of Yarmouth, in one yeere 7052 men and women . . . This plague continued sometime in one place, sometime in another, untill the yeere of our Lord 1357 . . ."[121]

This was the Black Death. The sensational account of its progress from the East comes from monkish chronicles, but the figures of Norwich and Great Yarmouth casualties came from the towns themselves. It is difficult to say how hard the Lophams were hit for there were no registers of burials in those days. In the neighbouring parish of Fersfield, however, Blomefield records that "the great Plague reached even this obscure Village, for in the Court Rolls, a Year or two after, the Deaths of many of the Tenants are presented, and 'tis said, that they died in the great Pestilence . . ."[122] In the nearby village of Shelfanger three new priests were instituted successively in 1347, 1348 and 1349,[123] and this may mean that mortality was high in that parish also. The rectory of Lopham changed hands in 1349 and 1351,[124] perhaps because of death, but we cannot be sure that all the priests whose names we have were resident in their cures. From later wills of the fourteenth and fifteenth centuries it seems likely that there were a good many "chaplains", the curates of those days, whose services in the Lophams are unrecorded but who may have perished visiting the sick of the plague.

An active resident priest, who was liked by his parishioners, carried a deal of weight in a mediaeval village. He was respected or feared for his supernatural powers, and admired for whatever education he might possess; perhaps the only literate man with whom most villagers ever conversed. In a time of crisis, such as the Black Death, he might become the leader of his community, but in ordinary days he was not his own master. Apart from his ecclesiastical superiors and competitors, visiting clergy, monks or friars, he had to keep on

* i.e. Friars

good terms with the patrons of his living and their representatives. During the Bishop's visitation of Norwich diocese in 1499 the rector of Lopham, Richard Darby, was listed among absentee or non-resident incumbents, the reason being that he "served the duchess of Norfolk".[125] This was the last Mowbray duchess, a Talbot by birth, who lived a good deal at her manor of Kenninghall and used Darby for economy or personal preference as her chaplain. In his will of the same year, after a number of bequests to local good causes such as the still-unfinished tower of Lopham S. Andrew's, Darby concluded:

". . . And furthermore I in humble wyse beseeche the Ryght hygh and myghty pryncesse the Duchess of Norff. if yt wyll please her to do so myche for her powre Chapleyn as to survey* thys my p(re)sent poure testament for the love of god & in the way of Charyti . . ."[126]

But a parson who depended neither on high society nor on the alehouse could still be a dominant figure in village life. The churches were social as well as religious centres, where the priest could teach as well as preach; give family advice as well as news of the outside world; and enjoy good fellowship withal. The churches of Lopham, for example, were partly supported by gilds, small societies of men and women named after a saint or a sacred symbol and pledged to keep lights burning before the object of their devotion. By the fifteenth century there seem to have been three gilds in North Lopham: S. Andrew's, S. Peter's and S. John's;[127] while at South Lopham there were four, belonging to the Cross, the Trinity, S. Nicholas, and again S. Peter.[128]

In addition to their devotional exercises these gilds had charitable and social functions, if we are to judge from other parishes, and both their religious and their secular meetings probably took place in the church. William Aleyn, who left money to all the North Lopham gilds by name in 1500, refers to each of them as "in the Pewe",[129] meaning perhaps that there were screened chapels or oratories for each image, places where the gild-members would meet. These gilds were prosperous, two of them being endowed with lands known as

* i.e. supervise.

S. Peter's Acre and S. John's Acre,[130] and there was a Lamp Acre which belonged perhaps to S. Andrew's gild.[131]

At South Lopham also the gilds received bequests, for example from Marion Yongs in 1511, who bequeathed "one kowe to the trinitie gild to be praid for . . ."[132] Subsequent bequests make it clear that it was Marion, not the cow, who needed their prayers, but it was nowhere prescribed that the cow should be sold to pay for masses for her soul. Since Marion Yongs was one who followed the genial custom of providing

"At my buryeng brede & Ale & chese . . .",[133]

she may have expected the beef to be eaten in her memory.

For one of the most popular activities of the gilds was the organization of "church-ales". These were feasts, at which you paid for admission, held sometimes in the church itself, sometimes in a "church-house" close by, the ancestor of the parish hall or church room, in which this history is being written, and the descendant of the churchyard shelters prescribed by S. Gregory the Great to maintain the festive rituals of the newly-converted heathen.[134] Church-ales were used to raise funds for the maintenance of the church and its fabric, much as church fêtes are used today.

Early churchwardens' accounts, from which we draw most of our information about the mediaeval church gilds, do not survive, apparently, for either North or South Lopham. In consequence we may have lost details of one of the earliest forms of amateur dramatics. Fifteenth century churchwardens' accounts for S. Peter and S. Paul, East Harling existed, or are said to have existed, until recently, shewing that village's well-known interest in cultural occasions to have been awake four hundred years ago. The relevant entries have been quoted as follows:

"1452. Pd. for the original of an Interlude played at the Church gate ...
1457. Pd. for bread and ale when Lopham Game came to this town xii^d^
For bread & ale to Garblesham Game vi^d^
1463. Item in expenses, when Keningale Game came to town at Wrights vi^d^
1467. Bred & ale to ye Keningale Players vi^d^"[135]

"Interludes" were early forms of comedy or farce, often

performed in the intervals of much longer miracle or mystery plays on religious subjects. One of the most famous surviving manuscript collections of mediaeval mystery plays used to be known as the "Coventry Cycle". During the last forty years, however, research has shewn that the language of the manuscript is East Anglian, and scholars have recently placed the main scribe of the collection in "the neighbourhood of Harling".[136] Since it appears that the greater part of the manuscript was transcribed in 1468 we are faced with the interesting possibility that the Lopham, Kenninghall or Garboldisham players were concerned in these very plays.

On the other hand it is just as possible that these "Games" or plays were mummeries peculiar to May Day and Whitsuntide, sometimes featuring Robin Hood, Maid Marian and their friends; sometimes S. George and the Dragon; but always accompanied by music and dancing. Morris dancing was an associated frolic, and an account, by a puritan, of such frolics invading the church, survives from 1585:

"... Then march this heathen company toward the church and church-yard, the pipers piping, their drummers thundering, their stumps dancing, their bells jingling, their handkerchiefs swinging about their heads like madmen, their hobby-horses and other monsters skirmishing amongst the throng: and in this sort they go to the church (though the minister be at prayer or preaching), dancing and swinging their handkerchiefs over their heads in the church, like devils incarnate, with such a confused noise, that no man can hear his own voice. Then the foolish people, they look, they stare, they laugh, they fleere,* and mount upon forms and pues to see these goodly pageants solemnized in this sort. Then after this, about the church they go again and again, and so forth into the churchyard, where they have commonly their summer-halls, their bowers, arbours, and banqueting-houses set up, where they feast, banquet, and dance all that day, and (peradventure) all that night too ..."[137]

We cannot say whether this was the impact of the Lopham Game upon S. Peter and S. Paul, East Harling, but at least their visit seems to have caused twice the normal consumption of bread and ale.

* i.e. mock.

CHAPTER TEN

Lopham Developments 1350–1570

Whatever the mortality in Lopham may have been, the social and economic effects of the Black Death were felt throughout Norfolk. There was a severe shortage of labour. The holding of land by service to the lord of the manor, in the style of *Domesday Book* tenancies, had been much diminished between the eleventh and fourteenth centuries by the commutation of services for payments in money and kind.* After 1350 it became necessary to reduce these rents if the lands of the manor were to be kept in cultivation. Moreover, the lords must pay higher wages for labour on their own demesnes, and it became very difficult to prevent labourers from deserting the manors to which they belonged in search of better-paid work elsewhere.

By 1399, when the surviving membranes of court rolls begin, Lopham had become a manor like many others, where the demesne was surrounded and interspersed with common land and some freehold plots, but mainly with the lands of copyholders, tenants by copy of court roll. A copyholder who wished to convey his holding to another person, for example his heir, had to "surrender" his copyhold to the court, where the lord or his representative would regrant the holding to the

* As late as 1841 Mrs Frances Bridgman, whose Lopham inheritance is discussed in Chapter Nineteen, held a house and a cottage in two acres and half a rood of land on Craneholme Street, South Lopham, "by the rent of Two Hens, twelve Eggs and the Custom of Nine pence by the year".[138]

heir, subject to the payment of the feudal dues. It was this practice which kept the manorial courts alive until 1894, when the last of a series of Copyhold Acts made it possible for all such tenants to acquire the freehold of their lands. The last Court Baron of the manor of Lopham seems to have been held on March 27th, 1912.[139]

The devolution of manor lands into the control of freeholders and into the virtual possession of well-to-do copyholders must have led in many places to the building of substantial farmhouses. For reasons discussed below, however, it seems likely that this development was delayed in the Lophams until the late sixteenth and the seventeenth centuries. The most important new buildings of the fourteenth century seem to have been in Lopham S. Andrew the chancel, the south aisle and porch; in Lopham S. Nicholas the chancel and south aisle. The building of the chancel at South Lopham was attributed by Blomefield to Nicholas de Horton, who was rector from 1361–1380 and who had been "a Monk of *Thetford*".[140] Presumably he means a monk of Thetford Priory, which may suggest some continuing interest in the Lopham living on the part of its former patrons. In principle the rector was responsible for the maintenance of both chancels but perhaps he was assisted by the Priory in these considerable building works. On the other hand, the architectural style of the same works and the labour and expense they must have cost, suggest that they were begun well before the Black Death rather than just after it. Perhaps it was the consecration rather than the foundation of the chancel of S. Nicholas which took place in the time of Nicholas de Horton. So far as rectorial finances were concerned, there was a predecessor of Nicholas de Horton, William Vigerons, perhaps an agile pluralist,* who held the livings of both Lopham and Fulham between 1336 and 1341,[141] and who may have been better able to pay for the two chancels.

It was an ancient custom to leave money to your parish church: "for tithes negligently forgotten"; to the high altar; for lights to be kept burning before particular shrines and images; for masses to be said for your soul; and for maintenance, repair

* i.e. a holder of more than one living.

N. Lopham Church: lettering on south face of tower.

and improvement of the building. In the last category the will of Edmund Clerk in 1375, may refer to work then in progress at S. Nicholas's.[142] In the rest of the fourteenth and in the fifteenth centuries money continued to be left by parishioners, chaplains and rectors to both churches, but in the 1470s special attention began to be paid to the new bell-tower or "steeple", as it was often called, at North Lopham.

We should be able to read much of the history of this tower from the inscriptions on its southern face. At the foot we may see its foundation in the names of probably the Trinity, the symbol being a crowned "T"; of Mary, Queen (of Heaven), with a crowned monogram of "MR" ("Maria Regina"); and of S. Andrew, the patron saint, with a crowned "A". It may be noted here that the latest inscription, which was to be added at the top of the south face some forty or fifty years later, appears to be a combination of the "MR" monogram and the "A". This would match the names of "S. Mary's and S. Andrew the Great's", by which Thetford Priory was known at that time.

The decorative panel between the "T" and the "MR" shews a circle containing a small shield or escutcheon over three quatrefoils. No sign of carving now appears on this shield but it may have been painted originally.

The inscription above the foundation stones, commemorating the founder and first subscriber perhaps, is in four insets of highly abbreviated Latin which Blomefield expanded into a sentence meaning "Pray for the souls (sic) of John Kailli".[143] Possibly he had in mind the Cayley (or Kailli) family of Hilborough and Denver, whom he had recorded at Old and New Buckenham, and who are known to have used the spelling "Kally" in twelfth century charters. For in fact the surname in the existing inscription reads "kallī". Since the last of the Norfolk Cayleys in the male line appears to have died in 1317 however,[144] it does not seem likely that any of them would be named in this late fifteenth century inscription at North Lopham.

The name of John "Calyors" or "Calyons" appears in Lopham court rolls of the early fifteenth century,[145] and possibly it was a member of this family who founded the tower. The dash over the last letter of "kallī" was a recognised sign of abbreviation and could stand for the last syllable of this surname. It may also be read as a sign of continuation. Perhaps we are told to pray for souls in the plural because the first builders wanted to encourage future benefactors with the thought that any inscriptions would be read upwards, and that everyone who was commemorated on the ascending tower would earn our prayers. Unfortunately the commemorations are incomplete and the initials which do appear have been difficult to identify.

Thomas Jente, the first known benefactor by will, does not now appear among the initials on the south face. In 1479, having left his soul to God Almighty, the blessed Andrew, his Mother (that is, Mary, the Mother of God), and to all the saints; and his body to be buried in the graveyard of the church of S. Andrew of North Lopham, he bequeathed "to the making of the bell-tower of S. Andrew eight (?) marks . . . to the church of S. Nicholas of South Lopham two nobles . . ."[146] A noble was half a mark and therefore the equivalent of six shillings and eightpence in the money of those days.

The first group of initials above the inscription to John Calyors (?) is in a column, reading from top to bottom: "i b/m b/r b". The first of these may stand for John Barker of South Lopham, whose will of 1486 provided a legacy for "the building of the new bell-tower of North Lopham".[147] The second might be Marion Busshe "of Lopham", who made no specific bequest to this building in 1460, but desired to be buried in the churchyard of S. Andrew's and appointed executors to dispose of all her property for the good of her soul and the souls of her friends, in whatever way they thought best. Since one of the three executors was "Sir John Halybbott, Chaplain" of North Lopham, he may have pointed at the unfinished bell-tower as the nearest and most obvious good cause.[148] The initials "r b" may stand for Robert Bolle of North Lopham, recorded by Blomefield for his gift in 1500 of "a Rood and Half at *Willbush*, to repair the Church for ever",[149] or possibly for Richard Bosse whose gift of Shelfanger lands for the same purpose, early in the 15th century, is discussed in Chapters Seventeen and Nineteen.[150]

Above this group stand the letters "W A" on their own. It

seems likely that they refer to William Aleyn of North Lopham, whose bequests in 1500 to the "pewed" gilds in S. Andrew's church have been quoted. He also bequeathed "to the makyng of the stepill . . . ix^{s} iii^{d} . . . (and) to the r(e)par(a)c(i)on of the said church ii^{s} . . ." His will mentions another William Aleyn, who was a priest, perhaps at North Lopham. He himself was a bit of a sheepmaster: "Item I woll that Margaret my wyff shall have xx Ewes xx lamb and x wethers . . ."[151]

What seems to be the uppermost group of benefactors' initials, below the "MRA" dedication (?) symbols, reads "PD RD". The writer has not found any likely candidate for "PD" and it is just possible that the group of letters should be interpreted as "Patro dedicavit Rector dedicavit", referring to dedications of the tower by the patron of the living and the rector. Sometimes, as at Kenninghall about a hundred years later, the initials of the current churchwardens are found in such a situation, as though to mark the completion of a job under their supervision. There is a benefactor whose initials would fit the "RD": the rector Richard Darby, whose courtesies to the Duchess of Norfolk have been quoted. His will of 1499 bequeaths "to the stepull of saynt Andrew x^{s} and a combe of malte. Also I bequeth to the Repar(a)c(i)on of the Churche of Saynt Andrew x^{s} and a combe malte . . . Also I bequethe to the Church of Saynte Nicholas x^{s} & a combe malte . . ."[152]

Apart from Thomas Jente there were a number of other benefactors whose initials do not appear. These include William Skowle of Woodrising, probably a relative of a contemporary North Lopham family, who left money for the "repair" of the bell tower in 1481;[153] Katherina Turnour of North Lopham, whose legacy of 1498 shews signs of either impatience or improvidence:

". . . I bequethe to the makyng of the stepulle x^{s} and more yf yt may be borne & p(er)fermed . . .";[154]

and Richard Warne of Lopham S. Andrew, who left three shillings and fourpence towards the building of the bell-tower and six shillings and eightpence towards the repair of the church.[155]

The word "steeple" which appears so often in these

Monograms on south wall of South Lopham Church.

legacies should not be misunderstood to imply that a spire was once intended at S. Andrew's. The proper meaning of "steeple" is "a lofty erection attached to a church, chiefly to contain its bells".

About the same time as the foundations of North Lopham tower were laid, S. Nicholas, South Lopham was given a clerestory over the south aisle, and on the outside of it there were set between the windows four panels of dedicatory initials, comparable to the foundation stones at S. Andrew's. The first of these is a monogram, "IS", probably standing for "Jesus Salvator" ("Saviour Jesus"). The second is the "Maria Regina" monogram we have seen at S. Andrew's; and the third, a crowned "T", almost certainly invokes the Trinity. The last, a monogram of "AT" (?) is less easy to interpret. It is not unknown for prayers to be inscribed in carved stone or in flushwork on the outside of East Anglian churches of this date. The monogram "AT" might be an abbreviation for "a(udi)t(e) (nos)", or "hear us", and the whole inscription an echo of the prayer of consecration when this part of the church was completed:

"O Saviour Jesus, Mary, Queen of Heaven, and Blessed Trinity, hear us!"

Alternatively "AT" might stand for "accipite", with the meaning of "accept (this building)".

More by sound than sight, devotion to "L'Incoronata", the Crowned Mary, is also proclaimed from within the belfry of S. Nicholas. "South Lopham fifth" was cast by William the Founder at Aldgate before the fifteenth century began, with a superscription which may be translated:

"I am called the bell of the excellent Virgin Mary!"*

Every letter of the Latin words was crowned. But while the crowns on the inscription outside the church are undefaced, every crown over the bell letters was maimed.[156] This may have happened in 1552 when all the "church goods" of S. Nicholas were inventoried for removal and sale or destruction, and only one bell, possibly this one, was reserved.[157] Or it may have happened some ninety-two years later, the skilled work of John Nun who was "paid for two Days Work" in 1644 "for taking down Glass and Pictures about the Church, and filing the Letters off the Bells" in the neighbouring parish of Bressingham.[158] Whenever the damage was done, it seems at South Lopham that the reformers held the glorification of S. Mary to be more superstitious than her invocation. Or perhaps the desecrator's hand was stayed for fear of cracking the bell?

The top of the tower of S. Nicholas, with its panelled flushwork battlements, is of late fifteenth or early sixteenth century date. The pinnacles surviving at the north-east, south-west and north-west corners of the parapet seem to be sitting lions. A "lion sejant", to use heraldic language, was not among the regular attributes of the Mowbray achievement, even though Elizabeth, the last duchess of that ilk, exhibited in Kenninghall Church windows, beside the rampant white lion of her husband, the rampant gold lion of her

* According to Francis Bond: *Dedications of English Churches*, Oxford, 1914, p. 218, this superscription is evidence that the bell was actually baptised with the name of S. Mary.

Some of the South Lopham bells in 1964 (pre-Reformation bell on left). Raymond Culley, John Sillett, Jacqueline Sillett and Richard Culley.

father and three passing red lions which he quartered for Lestrange of Blackmere. But the second and third Howard dukes, to whom the manor of Lopham belonged continuously between 1507 and 1546, were also Earls Marshal, the heralds' masters, and recked little, until 1546, how they displayed the lions and leopards of their quarterings. In any case, a lion rampant would have had a hard fight with Norfolk winters at the top of South Lopham tower; the remaining lions sejant are weathered enough.

When John Sell Cotman drew and etched South Lopham Church tower from the north west in 1819 he shewed three sentry-like figures carrying spears at the north east, north west and south west corners of the parapet.* Perhaps these were fanciful interpretations of the lions sejant and their lightning rods, or recollections of the stone watchmen on the battlements of Alnwick Castle in Northumberland. The architect Thomas Henry Wyatt, who surveyed South Lopham

* See frontispiece.

church for restoration in 1864, reported only that "The small Finials & the Parapet will I think require to be reset for they are far from being secure & a fourth Finial introduced in the South East Angle."[159]

It was probably Thomas Howard, the second duke of Norfolk who decided to move from Framlingham Castle, the ancient Suffolk fortress which his family had acquired in their share of the Mowbray inheritance, and to build a grand modern house at Kenninghall. He died in 1524 but Kenninghall Place, as it was called, was ready for the third duke to house and feed some ninety people in 1526. By moving to the head of Guiltcross Hundred, half of which belonged to the duke of Norfolk's "Liberty", the Howards had placed themselves in a central position for the administration and exploitation of their East Anglian estates. The family seat and its dependencies were kept up in princely style for some forty-five years. Even while the third duke languished in the Tower of London between 1546 and 1553, for a kind of heraldic treason, Kenninghall Place housed a real princess, the later Queen Mary I. The Lophams, like all the neighbouring villages, must have prospered from the custom of a household which in 1526 consumed, for example, 2370 eggs in twenty-six days.[160]

On the other hand it was a feudal state which the Howards maintained, and the growing independence of the villagers was threatened by the revival and extension of half-forgotten manorial privileges. A Norfolk petition to Queen Elizabeth I tells the tale:

"Notwithstanding messuages, lands etc., have been held for thirty, or forty years, or more, by copy of Court Roll, according to the custom of Manor, yet, for some little displeasure or grudge, the Lords put out the tenants on pretence that their holdings are part of the demesne. Thus the tenants cannot be certain of their inheritance, though held by their ancestors time out of mind; nor can they be certain even of holding such lands as they buy, although they duly pay their fines and yearly rent."[161]

In the duke's "Liberty" the problems began perhaps round his parks, those traditional symbols of privilege. As late as 1621 Kenninghall Park still contained seven hundred acres, forty-four of which were originally annexed by the third duke from Fersfield Green, "desiring to make his Great Park at *Kenninghall*, in which his Palace stood, every way compleat".[162] The villagers of Fersfield were still resisting this invasion when the fourth duke was executed in 1572, and they finally achieved an exchange of territory with his grandson. The Howards had another park at Lopham, of which "the Lawne", as we have seen, still extended to four hundred and twenty-three acres in 1612.[163] It had been an obvious aim of the fourth duke to join the two parks together. As the petition to Queen Elizabeth put it, ". . . these gentlemen have enlarged their parks, and made enclosures not only of their own lands, but also of the commons where the Orators" (the petitioners) "were wont to feed sheep and cattle . . ."[164]

The enlargement of parks also threatened the commons with the manorial privilege of "freebord". Blomefield explains what could happen when parks bordered upon commons, as at Winley (now Wilney) Green.

"To which *Lopham* Park joins, and had it's *Freebord* on this Common; all the Parks hereabout had that Privilege, which was to plant whatever Bushes and Trees they would against the Parks, which the Inhabitants could not cut, (as they do and always have done, all other Trees, Bushes &c. on the Commons in these Manors) but were to belong to the Lord for the Gamekeepers to kill their Game from, and for to hinder escapes from the Park . . ."[165]

The petitioners had another complaint about trees:

"If the tenants have planted on their copyholds oaks, ashes or elms which grew to timber, the Lords will not allow them to fell the trees, or to take any parcel thereof for repairs or building, or to burn in the house . . ."[166]

In the enlargement of parks, they alleged moreover the abuse of ancient privileges, one of which has been described in Chapter Eight.

". . . the same gentlemen, under cover of charter warren, maintain so many 'conies and dowes' (rabbits and pigeons) that the tenants' corn and grass are consumed and wasted . . ."[167] "Freewarren" was one of the feudal privileges with which the manor of Kenninghall, for example, had been endowed by charter since at least the thirteenth century.

Nothing is said in this petition about damage from park

deer, and the deepest grievance against the lord's livestock is reserved for his sheep:

"Furthermore, there is most commonly in every town and village a sheep's course or fold course belonging to a manor, and the Lord's sheep cannot be fed upon his own lands, but come upon the commons and the tenants' lands in summer, and after harvest in the fields of the towns (sometimes before harvest), whereby the great cattle of the inhabitants (the Shake once defiled and overcome with sheep) can have no feed. The tenants can have scarcely one sheep for their land (although the said sheep feed for half the year and more on the tenants' lands) even for money . . ."[168]

The Shake or Shack was the immediate aftermath of the harvest. The gleaners had the first pick of the ears and grain the reapers lost, but then it was the turn of the cattle in the common field. At Snytterton (now Snetterton), which was not a Howard manor, it was a bye-law in Queen Elizabeth's time that every inhabitant "shall allwaies after the feaste of St. Michaell tharchangell avoid their cattell out of the feildes of Snytterton & shall kepe no cattell there untill shacktyme come againe except they kepe them on theire owne lands where the lordes sheepe cannot come . . ."[169] The Shack Bell continued to be rung at Lopham even after the common fields had been enclosed. After the harvest of 1826 the churchwardens of North Lopham paid seven shillings and sixpence for "John Ruddock tolling the Bell for the Gleaners".[170]

The Snytterton bye-laws do not contemplate the possession of sheep by anybody except the lord of the manor. In the Lophams also, except for William Aleyn in 1500, there seems to be little evidence in sixteenth century wills of the keeping of sheep by the villagers. It may be that the petitioners' picture of subjection to the lord's sheep applied with particular force to the duke of Norfolk's manors in Guiltcross hundred. For the commissioners of the Queen's Council, appointed to inventory the fourth duke's possessions after his arrest on September 7th 1571, reported:

"Shepe cattell
The number of all the duke his graces shepe cattell
of all kyndes and in all places

within this countie of Norff. amounts to

xvi thowsand
viii hundred
odde shepe"[171]

At this rate the numbers, noise and nuisance of the Lopham flocks alone must have tried any tenant's patience with his lord.

PART ONE:

References

1. Eastern Daily Press (EDP) of ll.vii.51 and other dates. Local gossip.
2. Francis BLOMEFIELD: *An Essay Towards a Topographical History of the County of Norfolk*, Fersfield 1739, vol. i, folio, p. 157.
3. Ibid., p. 155.
4. By Mr. J. D. Alston of South Lopham Hall.
5. Admissions of Mrs. Frances BRIDGMAN at Lopham Manor Court, May 8th, 1841, penes auct.
6. R. RAINBIRD CLARKE: *East Anglia*, London (1960), pp. 18, 20, 21.
7. T. E. AMYOT of Diss, quoted by W. A. DUTT: *The Waveney Valley in the Stone Age.* Lowestoft, 1905, p. 34.
8. CLARKE, op. cit., p. 24.
9. Ibid., p. 25.
10. P. A. WRIGHT & F. J. BINGLEY: *Redgrave & Lopham Fen*. Ipswich 1970.
11. Ex inf. Mr. Hogg of High Common, North Lopham.
12. Ex inf. Norwich Castle Museum.
13. Ibid.
14. CLARKE, op. cit., pp. 94, 95.
15. Ibid., p. 101.
16. Ibid., p. 108.
17. Ibid., pp. 114–115.
18. H. C. DARBY: *The Medieval Fenland*, Newton Abbot (1974), p. 4 n. 4.
19. CLARKE: op. cit., pp. 121–122; NORFOLK ARCHAEOLOGY, xxxi, 402.
20. Eilert EKWALL: *The Concise Oxford Dictionary of English Place-Names*—Second Edition. Oxford 1940, pp. xii–xiv.
20[A]. Calendar of Patent Rolls (Cal. Pat.) preserved in the PRO: Edward III 1330–34, p. 520.
21. SKEAT, W.W.: *Etymological Dictionary of the English Language*, Fourth Edition, Oxford 1910.

21[A]. Cal. Pat. 1216–1225, p. 590.
22. Norfolk Record Office (NRO) MS. 15172. 37 B 6.
23. OXFORD ENGLISH DICTIONARY (OED), sub art. "Lope *sb*.1" and "Loup *v. Sc*."
24. Op. cit., sub art. "Lope-staff".
25. Op. cit., sub art. "Lope 3. *comb*."
26. WRIGHT & BINGLEY, op. cit.
27. W. W. SKEAT: *The Works of Geoffrey Chaucer*, Oxford 1894, vol. vi, p. 154.
28. Loc. cit.
29. CLARKE, op. cit., p. 130.
30. EKWALL, op. cit., p. 478.
31. *Norfolk Archaeology*, vii, 293, 358.
32. CLARKE, op. cit., p. 138.
33. Ex inf. Norwich Castle Museum.
34. Mr. David Self of South Lopham.
35. CLARKE, op. cit., pp. 139, 147.
36. *Monumenta Historica Britannica*, (London) 1848. (BEDE'S Ecclesiastical History), p. 141.
37. Jonathan SUMPTION: *Pilgrimage*, London (1975), p. 29.
38. *Monumenta Historica Britannica*, loc. cit.
39. CLARKE, op. cit., pp. 154–156.
40. NRO, Norwich Consistory Court (NCC), Willis, 112 HEYDON.
41. VICTORIA COUNTY HISTORY: NORFOLK (VCH), vol. ii, London, 1906, p. 235.
42. BLOMEFIELD, op. cit., pp. 153–154.
43. (John CHAMBERS): *A General History of the County of Norfolk* Norwich and London 1829, vol. ii, p. 714.
44. S. BARING-GOULD: *The Lives of the Saints*. Third ed. Edinburgh 1914, vol. xiv, p. 598.
45. C. L. S. LINNELL: *Norfolk Church Dedications*, Borthwick Institute of Historical Research (1962).
46. Ibid.
47. BARING-GOULD, op. cit., vol. xv, pp. 67–68.
48. V. H. GALBRAITH: *The Making of Domesday Book*, Oxford 1961.
49. VCH, vol. ii. pp. 101, 106.
50. H. C. DARBY: *The Domesday Geography of Eastern England*. Third edition, Cambridge 1971, p. 117.
51. F. W. MAITLAND: *Domesday Book & Beyond*. Cambridge 1897, pp. 66–67; P. VINOGRADOFF: *The Growth of the Manor*. London 1905, pp. 342–343 &c.
52. CLARKE: op. cit. pp. 164–165.
53. VCH, Vol. ii, p. 6.
54. THE EAST ANGLIAN, vol. i, p. 3.
55. See 40 above.
56. BLOMEFIELD, op. cit., p. 157.
57. Robert REYCE, ed. by Francis HERVEY: *A Breviary of Suffolk, 1618*. London 1902, pp. 7–8.

58. (COX, T. & HALL, H.): *Magna Britannica et Hibernia, Antiqua & Nova* &c., Vol. v, London 1730, p. 189.
59. BLOMEFIELD, op. cit., p. 542 and note n.
60. Ibid., p. 157.
61. Ibid., p. 158.
62. "Lopham", a copyhold rental book 1773–1840, penes the lord of Lopham manor.
63. NORFOLK RECORD SOCIETY: Faden's Map of Norfolk, 1973.
64. BLOMEFIELD, op. cit., p. 155.
65. H. C. DARBY, op. cit., pp. 138–139.
66. CLARKE, op. cit., p. 173.
67. F. BLOMEFIELD: The History of the ancient City and Burgh of THETFORD, Fersfield 1739, p. 58.
68. K. J. CONANT: Carolingian and Romanesque Art, Pelican History of Art, 1959, p. 214.
69. CALEY, ELLIS & BANDINEL: *Dugdale's Monasticon Anglicanum*, Vol. v., London 1825, p. 151.
70. Henry HARROD: *Gleanings among the Castles and Convents of Norfolk*. Norwich 1857, p. 3.
71. CALEY, ELLIS & BANDINEL, op. cit., pp. 148–149.
72. Ibid., p. 142.
73. Ibid., p. 153.
74. Ibid., p. 151.
75. Ibid., p. 147, note a.
76. NRO: TANNER'S INDEX OF INSTITUTIONS, vol. ii, p. 705.
77. BLOMEFIELD's *Thetford*, pp. 95, 135.
78. NRO. NCC Wills 142–144 PUNTYNG.
79. BLOMEFIELD's *Norfolk* vol. ii, folio, Norwich 1745, p. 699.
80. Ibid., p. 701.
80[A]. Cal. Pat. 1301–1307, pp. 190, 193; Ibid. 1317–21, p. 98.
81. Ibid., p. 153 and note (h).
82. Arundel Castle MS, PS/1.
83. BLOMEFIELD's Norfolk, vol. i, folio, Fersfield 1739, p. 155.
84. OED, Oxford 1933, *sub art*, "town".
85. P. VINOGRADOFF: *Villainage in England*, Oxford 1892, pp. 223–224 n.1.
86. NRO: MS 14890 37 B1.
87. G.E.C. THE COMPLETE PEERAGE, vol. ix, London 1936, p. 595.
87[A]. Cal. Pat. 1338–40, p. 545.
87[B]. Ibid., p. 104.
88. G.E.C., pp. 600–601.
89. Ibid., p. 609 n.(j).
90. Deeds penes the lord of Lopham manor.
91. G.E.C., op cit., p. 600, n.(n).
91[A]. Cal. Pat. 1374–77, p. 53.
92. Ex. inf. Mr. Rednall, Lodge Farm, North Lopham.
93. See 5 above.

94. Ibid.
95. At the County Hall, Norwich.
96. North Lopham Church records: MS "Survey of the Parish of North Lopham . . . 1815".
97. BLOMEFIELD: op. cit., p. 155.
98. Ibid.
99. VINOGRADOFF: *Growth of the Manor*, pp. 19–36.
100. British Library (BL) Add. Rolls 66805–66816.
101. BLOMEFIELD, op. cit., p. 153.
102. BL. Add. Rolls 66816. 20.iii. 1652.
103. R. HINDRY MASON: *The History of Norfolk*, London 1884, p. 26, col. ii, lines 25–28. Writer's translation.
104. Ibid., p. 30, col. i, lines 13–14.
105. John STOW: *Annales of England*, London (1605), p. 247.
106. Ibid., p. 249.
107. Ibid., p. 247.
108. Ibid., p. 249.
109. Ibid., p. 250.
110. Ibid., p. 231.
111. Ibid., p. 387.
112. Writer's version of tale reported from Mr. H. P. STYLES of South Lopham in EAST ANGLIAN DAILY TIMES of March 19th, 1921.
113. MASON, op. cit., p. 104.
114. Ibid., p. 77.
115. See 5 above.
116. Will of Bartholomew WADE of South Lopham, 1567, NRO, NCC Wills 6 ADAMS.
117. South Lopham Inclosure Award, 1815 (SLIA), p. 4.
118. STOW, op. cit., p. 305.
119. Ibid., loc. cit.
120. Op. cit., p. 338.
121. Op. cit., pp. 384–386.
122. BLOMEFIELD, op. cit., p. 75.
123. Ibid., p. 76.
124. NRO TANNER's Index, loc. cit.
125. C. HARPER-BILL: "1499 Visitation of Norwich Diocese" in JOURNAL OF SUFFOLK INSTITUTE OF ARCHAEOLOGY & HISTORY, vol. xxxiv, part I, 1977, p. 42.
126. NRO, NCC Wills 32 SAVYE.
127. NRO, NCC Will of William ALEYN, 1500. 201 CAGE.
128. NRO, NCC Wills of Marion YONGS, 1511: 97–98 JOHNSON; Richard DARBY, 1499: 32 SAVYE. N. Archdeaconry Will of Richard WADE, 1466: 152 GREY.
129. See 127 above.
130. BLOMEFIELD, op. cit., p. 154.
131. Loc. cit.
132. See 128 above.
133. Loc. cit.

134. See Chapter Four.
135. NORFOLK ARCHAEOLOGY, ix, 338, quoted on the dubious authority of J. Payne COLLIER's *History of Dramatic Poetry*. But also quoted by J. Charles COX, with one variation, on p. 268 of *Churchwardens' Accounts*, London (1913). He cites no authority except, by implication, the original.
136. Messrs. Angus McIntosh and Michael Samuels, quoted by Stephen SPECTOR: *The Provenance of the N-Town Codex* in the LIBRARY 6th Series, Vol. I., no. 1, March 1979.
137. Philip STUBBES: *The anatomie of abuses*, London 1585, pp. 92–93.
138. Deeds penes auct.
139. LOPHAM MINUTE BOOK April 1828–May 1855 penes the lord of Lopham manor.
140. BLOMEFIELD, op. cit., p. 156.
141. Loc. cit.
142. See 40 above.
143. BLOMEFIELD, op. cit., p. 154.
144. NORFOLK GENEALOGY, Volume Six: *Norfolk Pedigrees*, 1974, p. 39.
145. BL. Add. Roll 66805.
146. NRO. NCC Will of Thomas JENTE, 1479: 204 BRIGGS.
147. Do. NCC Will of John BARKER, 1486: 290–291 ACASTON.
148. Do. NCC Will of Marion BUSSHE, 1480: 207 BROSYARD.
149. BLOMEFIELD, op. cit., p. 154.
150. Loc. cit.
151. See 127 above.
152. See 128 above.
153. NRO, NCC Will of William SKOWLE, 1481: 95 ACASTON.
154. Do. Will of Katherine, TURNOUR, 1498: 146 MULTON.
155. Do. Will of Richard Warne, 1502: 195 POPY.
156. John L'ESTRANGE: *The Church Bells of Norfolk*, 1874; J. J. RAVEN: article under the same title in MASON, op. cit., pp. 594–595.
157. H. B. WALTERS: *Inventories of Norfolk Church Goods (1552) Hundred of Guiltcross*, NORFOLK ARCHAEOLOGY, xxx, pt. III, 1951, pp. 218–9.
158. BLOMEFIELD, op. cit., p. 46.
159. NRO PD 120/22.
160. Richard HOWLETT: *The Household Accounts of Kenninghall Palace in the year 1525* (sic), NORFOLK ARCHAEOLOGY, vol. xv.
161. MASON, op. cit., p. 156.
162. BLOMEFIELD, op. cit., p. 62.
163. See 82 above.
164. MASON, op. cit., p. 157.
165. BLOMEFIELD, op. cit., p. 63.
166. MASON, op. cit., p. 156.
167. Ibid., p. 157.

168. Ibid., p. 156.
169. Snitterton &c. Court Rolls 1604 plus, penes auct.
170. North Lopham church records: MS "Churchwardens Book 1813".
171. Public Record Office (PRO), State Papers (Domestic) Elizabeth 81.fo.194.

PART TWO

Social and economic changes in the Lophams between 1570 and 1900

CHAPTER ELEVEN

Tudor Lopham

The fall of Norfolk's last prince and the feudal pretensions which went with him were not the only event to shake Lopham in the sixteenth century. There had been the king's supplanting of the Pope, the dissolution of the religious houses, and a bewildering series of religious changes. There had been the Norwich rebellion of 1549, starting at Attleborough and led by two Wymondham men.

At home the most shocking signs of the times may have been experienced by the church congregations and gilds. The splendid images of God and his Saints to which they had turned for so long, the inheritors of who knows how ancient an idolatry, came under official disapproval as objects of superstition as early as 1538. Twelve years later an act of Edward VI's first parliament condemned them to destruction, and although a few escaped for a time it is likely in this reign that Saint Andrew with his saltire cross or his fish, and Saint Nicholas with his three boys or three purses both vanished from their pedestals at North and South Lopham. Many other glories would disappear: paintings, painted glass, embroidered robes and altar-cloths, a "pair of organs" at South Lopham,[172] even the ornamented tombs, all seem to have been among the victims of intolerance and greed in the Reformation or the Great Rebellion. There survived at S. Andrew's in Francis Blomefield's time a "Bishop in his *Pontificalibus*", his episcopal robes, "in the South Window of the Chancel . . . represented as dead, lying along".[173] Perhaps this was post-Reformation stained glass, a memorial to John

Salisbury whose career is described in Chapter Fourteen, the only rector of Lopham who was at the same time a bishop.

At the church of S. Nicholas "a beautiful bit of the old Chancel or Rood Screen (9 Panels) painted white & Red & gilt in places, 18 ft. long", and "some fine old specimens of Perpendicular Carved Bench ends (about 22)" still survived in the building in 1864, according to Thomas Henry Wyatt's report.[174]

North and South Lopham "church goods" were not inventoried until September 1552[175] and perhaps some were saved by the next régime. For great events began at Kenninghall Place on July 9th, 1553,[176] when a Popish queen successfully declared herself against a Protestant pretender. But this had brought little joy: a Spanish king; burnings of Norfolk people by John Hopton, the Bishop of Norwich, once the Lady Mary's chaplain at Kenninghall Place; the loss of our last foothold in the kingdom of France; high prices and bad money. Then there had come the accession of Queen Elizabeth and England had begun to seem herself again. *Semper eadem*, said the queen's motto: "Always the same".

But no-one in the Lophams could really feel the same after so many strange happenings, and after so much provocation to think for yourself. Some reflections of the changing times survive. To begin with religion, there is a striking contrast between the testaments of two successive parsons of Lopham: Andrew Jenney in 1507[177] and John Graveley in 1545.[178] They start in much the same ancient style:

"In the name of God, Amen: the 23rd day of October in the year of our Lord God 1507. I Andrew Jenney, clerk, parson of Lopham and Canteley" (a pluralist: he had been presented to the living of Cantley in 1477 and to Lopham before 1507) "being in my good mind make my Testament in this form following: first, I commend my soul to Almighty God, our Blessed Lady Saint Mary, and all the holy ('holly') company of heaven, and my body to be buried in the chancel of the church of Saint Nicholas of Lopham . . ."

"I, John Graveley of Lopham in the county of Norfolk, clerk, being of good mind and whole remembrance, thanks being to God, make my testament and last will in this manner and form following: First that I bequeath my soul unto

Almighty God, to Our Lady . . . Saint Mary, and to all the holy ('holly') company in heaven; my body to be buried in the chancel of South Lopham before the high altar . . ."

But then the contrast begins. Andrew Jenney left money firstly for the repair of the two Lopham churches and to the church of Filby; secondly to his sister "Dame Keteryn Jenney", who was a nun, to her prioress and all her sister nuns; thirdly to the abbot and to canons of Langley Abbey to say a "dirige"* and mass for his soul; fourthly to the nuns, prioress and priests of Carrow for the same purpose; fifthly to two other religious houses in Norwich, one of them another nunnery, to pray for his soul; sixthly to Norwich Cathedral; and seventhly he left two chalices to the church of Cantley.

John Graveley on the whole was more concerned for the things of this world. Certainly he leaves money to the parish priest of Redgrave to pray for his soul, and a handsome bequest of eight marks sterling and his best gown to Robert Nuham, another priest,† for "one year service" of prayer. But they are to pray both for his soul and for "all Christian souls". In the same altruistic vein he leaves twelve pence to each of his godchildren not yet married and more substantial sums to the "poor people" of Redgrave, Garboldisham, Kenninghall, Fersfield and Bressingham. There are legacies to all the lazar-houses‡ of Norwich and to Thetford lazar-house, and the residue of his estate is left to the disposition of his executor, William Hugheson, clerk, "in such good deeds of charity as he shall think best and see where most need is to pleasure of Almighty God and the health of my soul".

There are also separate bequests: a large one to his sister Anne, who seems to have been old or ill; particular gifts of cattle to friends; a handsome provision for Margaret Sewall, perhaps his housekeeper; and "to Mistress Cooke my silver piece". John Graveley would be cheerfully remembered for at least one old custom he kept:

* From which we derive the word "dirge". "Dirige" is the first word of the Latin version of Psalm V. 8, and this verse was used in the church service for the dead.

† Vicar of Kenninghall 1557–1571.

‡ "Lazar-houses" were originally leper-houses but the disease of leprosy had virtually disappeared from England during the fifteenth century and the objects of Graveley's charity were the hospitals of his day.

"I will that every one of my parishioners of Southlopham and Northlopham have twopence apiece, man and woman and child, and meat and drink honestly at my burial day."

The custom still flourished thirty years later, when Francis Reade of South Lopham added to his testament:

"I will that there shall be provided at my burial day bread, drink and other victuals necessary for them that come for it, at the only costs & charges of . . . Edmonde Reade my son . . ."[179]

The wills of the parishioners reveal the differences of belief in those times. Nicholas Barrett of South Lopham, making his testament under Mary, avoided any commendation or dedication of his soul in 1557, and reduced his preliminary bequests to the essentials:[180]

". . . Item, I give to the high altar for my tithes negligently forgotten twelve pence: Item, I give to be distributed among the poor three shillings and fourpence; Item, I give to the highways twenty pence . . ."

John Gysyer of the same village, who described himself as a "labourer" but was a prosperous man of his hands, stuck to the old religion in the same reign on April 10th, 1558:[181]

". . . First I bequeath my soul unto Almighty God and unto our Blessed Lady Saint Mary and unto all the holy ('hollie') company of heaven and my body to be buried in the Churchyard and holy ('hollye') sepulchre of Saint Nicholas of South Lopham . . ."

Whereas Matthew Ringbell in the same year and village avoids the saints:[182]

"First I commend my soul to God the Almighty, the Father, and the Son and the Holy ('hollye') Ghost and my body to be buried in the churchyard of Southlopham . . ."

Other people had other worries. In 1561 Queen Elizabeth was still calling in the base coinage permitted by her stepsister, and Robert Sherwyn[183] of North Lopham was concerned about the risks of devaluation. He left ten pounds apiece to each of his six daughters, "Provided where there have risen a great rumour that money shall fall I will if there shall happen any such fall of money, as I believe there shall not, that then every of my said daughters to have but eight pounds of lawful money to them paid by my said Executrix at the days and times in manner and form before limited so the said fall happen before the feast of Saint Michael the Archangel* next coming after the date of this Testament . . ."

Then there were troubles domestic. There was the generous Nicholas Pye[184] of North Lopham who was buried, as his will directed and as the parish register records, in the churchyard there on July 22nd, 1559. By the same will he gives

". . . to Christopher Aldred my great white mare ('meare') that I bought of him; Also one bay nag . . . Item, I give to every household within the parish of North Lopham twelve pence; Item, I give to every of my godchildren that be named Nicholas two shillings . . ."

Perhaps one more Nicholas had been expected, for his bequests begin:

". . . Item, I give to the child of Katheryn Dalton if she be with child my house and my land . . . Item, I give to Katheryn Dalton abovesaid ten pounds to be paid her within three days after my decease . . ."

The parish register records no child of Katheryn Dalton in 1559 or 1560 and, despite her ten pounds, it seems, alas, from her father's will some thirty years later that no-one would marry her. But Henry Dalton,[185] who was buried in the same churchyard on May 5th, 1589, made careful provision for her future, including in certain circumstances . . .

". . . my little house by the gate and twenty shillings a year every year . . ."

These are the wills of the well-to-do and nearly all of them, like Parson Graveley, leave money or goods to the poor. In 1544, the year before Graveley's death, John Levold[186] of North Lopham left

". . . to the officers of the township of North Lopham six acres of land . . ."

A member of the same family, Thomas Levould,[187] "bachelor", describing himself as "servant unto the Right Reverend Father in God my Lord the Bishop of Norwich" (probably John Hopton, the persecutor), left a residue of his property to be divided

* Queen Elizabeth I's first proclamation devaluing the base coinage had been on Michaelmas Eve, 1560.

"one part thereof to Loppon Church and the other part thereof to the poor people of the same town of Loppon . . ."

Thomas Levould's will, like other Elizabethan testaments, also distributes his clothes and bedding to his friends and relations. But a more remarkable catalogue of this kind appears in a will of the same year made by John Cowell,[188] who was buried at North Lopham on November 13th, 1559. His initial bequests were in the mediaeval tradition of votive offerings.

". . . Item, I give and bequeath unto the Churches of Northeloppham and Southe Loppham five shillings apiece; Item, I give and bequeath unto Gunwell" (i.e. Gonville) "and Caius College a great gilt spoon for the use of the Master at feasts and otherwise."

He went on to provide for his second wife, Elizabeth:

". . . one cassock" (meaning a long loose cloak or gown) "of sheep's colour cloth, edged with cony" (i.e. rabbit fur) "and a kirtle of the same;

one Russet" (a cheap woollen cloth) "frock guarded" (i.e. laced) "with velvet;

an English gown of velvet cloth;

a velvet neckerchief ('neckerchoff');

a kirtle of Russets;

a petticoat (of) scarlet, all the laps, letters and other" (i.e. a scarlet skirt with lappets and trimmings of the same colour);

"a round silk hat and my felt hat;

all my linen belonging unto my late wife's body;

a little bearing sheet" (i.e. christening robe);

"a . . . sheet to truss gear in;

my late wife's cloak, her saddle and bridle and all other things belonging unto it;

my mail" (i.e. portmanteau)

"the old ambling mare ('meare') and a horse to carry the gear with; she will choose one silver spoon, and four pounds in money."

It seems that the second Mrs. Cowell was expected to leave the house. To Robert, presumably his eldest son, Mr. Cowell left

"my best gown of cloth sewed with satin;

my best velvet coat;
my blue linsey coat;
my shirt of mail and a morion" ('murryon', i.e. helmet);
"my yellow velvet coat;
a chest bound with iron;
two silver spoons;
all my written books and my desk."

To his son John:

"my second velvet coat;
my morning gown with the hood and cap;
my coat and cloak of new coloured cloth;
my worsted gown, my worsted doublet, a pair of hose;
(a) black chest bound with iron;
two silver spoons and all my printed books."

His daughter Isabell was married perhaps, for she was left only

"a gown of Russells" (woollen cloth) "faced with marten or foins" (i.e. pine-marten or stone-marten fur) "and odd (?) silver spoons."

Mary, his goddaughter, did better with

"my late wife's broad silk hat;
a piece of cloth uncut to make her a cloak;
one silver spoon and forty shillings in money to buy her a gown withal."

He had two daughters called Margaret, not an uncommon family situation in days when the expectation of life was short. Each of them got one of the silver spoons, and Margaret "the elder" was left "a cassock of new coloured cloth faced with cony with sleeves of tawny satin belonging to it . . ." Margaret the "younger the fourth daughter" also went in fine, if second-hand, raiment with "my wife's best gown delivered to her beforehand", and was to be given "ten shillings in money to buy her necessaries withal". Had there once been a set of Apostle spoons? If so, the last went to daughter Elizabeth. Perhaps she was the youngest and the smallest of the family for her legacy comprised no more than "half a kirtle of grosgrain" and "a purse of crimson satin laid on with parchment lace of gold". (This was a kind of lace which had a parchment core.)

Next Henry Downing and his sister, whose relationship to

the Cowells is not explained, were each left "a calf of one year old". Then the testator's "sister Buller" was to receive "a pair of linen sheets to be delivered by the discretion" (at the choice) "of mine Executor".

Finally there were the servants and a nearly forgotten godson: "Item, I give and bequeath unto Rose, my maid, an old cloak for a remembrance, and for the chief relief of her necessity I refer it unto the discretion of my Executor as shall seem unto him meet" (i.e. proper) "whose conscience I burden before God in this behalf;

Item, I give unto my maid Johan two shillings and threepence and besides her wage;

Item, I give unto James, my servant, a fustian" (i.e. coarse cloth) "doublet, a cap, two calves' skins ready tanned, a pair of old hose and a shirt;

Item, I give to John Partrydge, my godson, a single coat of Russell, two calves' skins ready tanned, a blue coat, a cape, a shirt, a crown (?), a calf of the last year;

Item, I give to James's brother a calf's skin."

John Cowell did not describe his class or calling in his will, and from the lavish descriptions of clothes, some of them apparently new, the references to ready tanned calfskins and to pieces of uncut cloth, it might have been supposed that he was a tailor. But there are pointers in other directions. His benefaction of a ceremonial silver-gilt spoon to Gonville and Caius College "for the use of the Master" suggests acquaintance with that famous and wealthy physician, John Keys of Norwich, latinised as Doctor Caius, and for the last ten months head of the foundation he had himself re-established in 1557. The historian of the college records a John Cowell who proceeded Bachelor, then Master of Arts in 1553 and 1556 from what was still Gonville Hall, and who was nominated by Caius as a Fellow of the new college under the royal charter of 1557.[189] Perhaps it was in acknowledgement of this honour conferred upon his second son, John, that John Cowell senior presented the spoon. Perhaps he was himself an unrecorded student and contemporary of the sometime John Keys at Gonville Hall. There is a faintly academic flavour about the bequests to his second son of all his "printed books" and his "morning gown with the hood and cap". But what were the "written books" which went with his desk to son Robert? Were they what his heir would need to carry on a family business?

On the other hand the possession of a coat of mail and a helmet—together with a shield and a lance—was an obligation laid upon every holder of a "knight's fee", that is, a piece of land held by that form of military service, from the days of Henry II right up to John Cowell's last years under Philip and Mary.[190] Perhaps he was a gentleman who had conveyed his landed property to his heir before he made his will. There is a record of a David Cowell of Norfolk who was described as of gentle blood in 1500,[191] and Arthur Womock, rector of Lopham, in his will of 1607[192] refers to a "Robert Cowell gentleman deceased" who may well have been John Cowell's eldest son.

CHAPTER TWELVE

The Beginnings of Lopham Linen

The fame of Lopham linen dates from the nineteenth century when it won recognition as a quality product made for the Quality. But linen manufacture had been a home industry in the Lophams for at least three hundred years. As early as 1400 one of the manorial courts of Lopham recorded John of the Moor as a "webster".[193] Perhaps "the Moor" may be related to a place in South Lopham which was still called "Morland" in 1841.[194] We do not know what kind of web John wove, but by the middle of the sixteenth century there was more than one linen-weaver in the Lophams. John Bylnye of South Lopham, "weaver", who was named in a kinsman's will of 1567,[195] was almost certainly a linen-maker. John Fenne[196] and William Partriche[197] of North Lopham, both of whom made wills in 1586, described themselves by occupation as "linen weavers".

John Fenne was a prosperous man who left a house and lands to his wife and four children, including "one piece of ground called the Grove lying by the Park pale". Two fields in such a situation, north east of Park Farm, were still called "The Grove" in 1815, although the woodland had gone. In 1586, however, substantial timber remained, perhaps from Margaret Marshal's days, and John Fenne was able to provide for his son Roger

". . . to have four of my best oak trees now growing in my said Grove with free egress and regress into and from the same Grove to fell, hew, cut and carry away the said trees towards the maintaining and repairing of the . . . house before to him given, when, and at such time and times as he shall think most requisite to be bestowed about the said house, one or more in a year . . ."

That linen-weaving could be combined with other occupations is shewn by the will of Richard Cotnye in 1600.[198] He described himself as "linen-weaver of Sowthlopham" but he seems also to have been a dairy farmer. He had five surviving daughters but no sons, and first of all he left a series of milchkine to be delivered to the girls at progressive intervals as each of them reached a marriageable age. Then he said:

". . . Item, I do give and bequeath unto Edwarde Poole, my godson my weaving looms and slays;* Item, I do give and bequeath unto every of my said children, Anne, Mary, Alice, Joane and Frances, a pair of sheets to be delivered unto each of them at their days of marriage . . ."

It is reasonable to suppose that these pairs of sheets were homemade and that some of the Cotnye daughters had taken part in their manufacture. It is a bequest which features in a number of Lopham wills of that period, such as John Cowell's, and no doubt much of the linen was locally made. The Lophams, however, were only two among many Norfolk and Suffolk villages where linen was woven in the sixteenth century. The manufacture had been encouraged by Acts of Parliament in 1533 and in 1563, when it was prescribed that every person occupying sixty acres of arable land in Norfolk or Suffolk should sow one acre with flax or hemp seed on pain of a five pound fine. Such acts were easier to proclaim than to enforce, and thirty years later, after it had been shewn that not all lands were fertile in flax or hemp, the statute was repealed. To judge from the various "Hemplands" recorded in the Lophams, however, and the "Flaxlande" or "Flaxlonde Furlong" which lay "between the Churches"[199] in 1589, both crops flourished in this part of Norfolk.

Thomas Tusser (*c.* 1524–1580), who taught agriculture and housekeeping in doggerel verse, learnt his "Five Hundreth

* The slay or reed was a weaver's instrument for separating the threads of the warp and beating up the weft. The surname of Slaymaker was current in North Lopham until 1930.

Pointes of Goode Husbandrie united to as many of Good Huswifery" (1573–85) by trial and error, mostly the latter, in Norfolk, Suffolk and Essex. His teaching was much admired, like that of another unsuccessful East Anglian farmer two hundred years later, Arthur Young. Tusser described the cultivation of hemp and flax as woman's work:

> "Good flax and good hemp, to have of her own
> In May a good huswife will see it be sown;
> And afterwards trim it, to serve at a need,
> The fimble to spin, and the carl for her seed."[200]

In our ancestors' eyes the weaker hemp plant, with the shorter fibre, was the female or "fimble", while the stronger and longer was the male or "carl". Unfortunately for Tusser's male chauvinism John Ray shewed as early as 1686 that these plants had been sexed the wrong way round.[201] Perhaps it was a judgement on the men for leaving this work to their womenfolk, as it seems they did in sixteenth century Lopham.

Robert Saunder of South Lopham in 1551[202] left

"... unto John my brother one tenement* called Andrew's, containing a rood, provided always that Isabell my wife shall sow a peck of hemp seed in the foresaid tenement on the which side she will ..."

William Hobbarde[203] of the same village, yeoman and perhaps Calvinist, left ten shillings to the poor of Lopham in 1565, and in his bequests to his wife seems to suggest that he was the dressmaker in a household where husbandry was shared between them:

"... Also I give and bequeath unto Jone my wife all the goods and chattels ('cattalls') which were hers at that time when I married unto her, with the apparel which I have made her since ... Also I give unto Jone my wife five combs of wheat and five combs of maslin ('meslinge')† the wheat to be of that where" (wheat is) "lying upon her own chamber ... Also I wish that my wife shall have sufficient feed both of hay and straw to winter her three bullocks and her horse until the winter be fully gone ('goone'); Also I will that my wife shall have all her hemp that was her(s) before I married with her,

* i.e. holding.

† Maslin is a mixture of grain, chiefly wheat and rye.

Lopham girls at the loom in Lopham Week, July 1951. At the looms: Mary Nolleth, Janet Baker, Rita Crowe, Gladys Demoore, Olga Aves, Averill Frost. Behind: Mrs. E. Witton, Mrs. E. Farrow, unidentified, Mrs. A. A. Crook, Mrs. Crook senior, Mrs. H. Arnold. Lower right: Mark Cooksley.

and half that hemp which grew on her own land this year . . ."

July, said Tusser, was the month for culling the hemp crop:

"Ripe hemp out cull,/From carl to pull./Let seed hemp grow/Till more ye know."[204]

More explicitly, he enjoins with his usual masculine prejudice:

> "Wife, pluck fro thy seed hemp, the fimble hemp clean,
> This looketh more yellow, the other more green:
> Use t'one for thy spinning, leave Michell the other,
> For shoe-thread and halter, for rope and such other."[205]

The words "leave Michell the other" mean "leave the carl until Michaelmas", for it was in September that Tusser directed:

> "Now pluck up thy hemp, and go beat out the seed,
> And afterwards water it, as ye see need;
> But not in the river, where cattle should drink,
> For poisoning them and the people with stink.
>
> Hemp huswifely used, looks clearly and bright,
> And selleth itself by the colour so white:
> Some useth to water it, some do it not,
> Be skilfull in doing, for fear it do rot."[206]

The last seven lines refer to "retting". This was the stage at which flax or hemp plants were prepared for the separation of the fibres from their woody rind either by exposure to the weather, "dew retting", or by steeping them in water. In East Anglia "hempits" were often set aside for the latter process, and their use had to be regulated to control, for example, that bad old smell of the good old days recorded by Tusser. At the manor of Snetterton, a few miles north west of the Lophams, a bye-law of 1571[207] required that

"no inhabitant within the precinct of the parish of Snyterton shall at one time lay above one load of hemp in the common hempit in Northorpe upon pain of six shillings and eightpence to be forfeited unto the lord of this manor for any offence contrary to this ordinance . . ." The penalty for fouling another man's water was six times more severe:

". . . Also that no Inhabitant shall water any hemp in any

other man's several" (i.e. separate or private) "water without the license of the owner upon pain of loss of forty shillings."

Where were the "common hempits" in the Lophams? Among the various ponds remaining or recorded in place-names the most obvious probability in North Lopham, considering its central position, is Letchmere or "Leech Mere", as the 1958 Ordnance Survey reports it. An ancient meaning of the verb to "letch" or "leach" was to "water" and hence to "soften by soaking". Legend has it that Letchmere was once used for ducking scolds and drowning witches, and when the pond was dredged between 1930 and 1940 there was an unsuccessful search for human bones. But any ill odour this pool may have had in the sixteenth century is more likely to have been the result of retting flax and hemp than of torturing unpopular people to death.*

Letchmere and the Chestnut Trees in 1927.

Once the hemp had been retted it was carried in "baits" or sheaves to the barn for "breaking". There the baits were bundled together and beaten with a wooden "swingle" to break the rind from the fibre. This part of the process was completed by "scutching". The scutcher or "swingle-hand" was a long, flat and narrow piece of wood with a sharpened

* For its ill odour in more recent times see Chapter Twenty-Three.

edge, used to separate the fibre from the broken rind. The dried-out rind or "hemp-offal" made good fuel.

The tangled fibre was now ready for "heckling". This was the task of splitting, straightening and combing out the various grades of fibre till they were fit to spin into yarn. The heckle, hackle or hatchel was a piece of board set with iron teeth, fine and short or long and coarse, according to the type of fibre required. Heckling was skilled work and in times to come a man would describe himself as a heckler by occupation, or "Hickler", as Jonas Keeble registered at the age of seventy in the North Lopham census return of 1851.[208] But in the sixteenth century it was just one of the housewife's multifarious arts.

John Skelton, who was rector of Diss from 1498–1529, wrote of countrywomen paying in kind for the ale of Elynour Rummyng:

> "Some laid to pledge
> Their hatchet and their wedge,
> Their heckle and their reel,
> Their rock, their spinning-wheel;
> And some went so narrow
> They laid to pledge their wharrow,
> Their ribskin and their spindle,
> Their needle and their thimble."[209]

A "rock" was a spindle; a "wharrow" a grooved pulley in a spinning wheel; and a "ribskin" probably a leather apron. We begin to have a picture of a one-woman linen-factory: heckling the hemp which no doubt she had sown, reaped and retted; spinning the results into yarn which perhaps she wove at the loom in her leather apron; and hemming the sheets with her needle and thimble.

That the Lophams produced linen of various qualities for different purposes seems evident from the will of John Cowell and from other sixteenth century testaments, such as that of Michael Richardson of Lopham, joiner, in 1575.[210] He left to his brother and executor, Roger,

"... one pair of sheets, one cushing" (i.e. cushion) "cloth,* one velvet nightcap, one fair bearing sheet ..."

* Presumably a cushion cover.

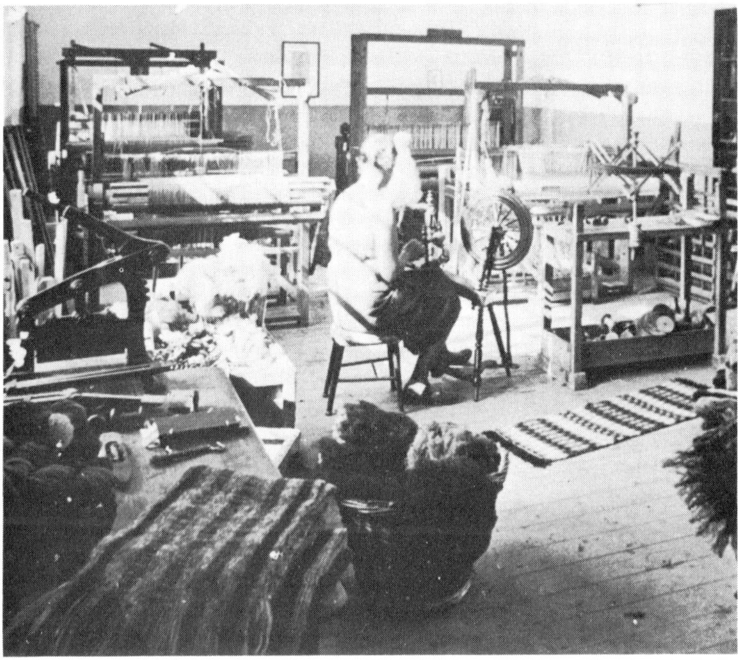

Mrs. Rita Beales at her Norwegian spinning wheel in The Limes weaving shed, *c*. 1927. By courtesy of Mrs. Rita Beales.

The last item was probably a christening robe, as in Cowell's will. The duke of Norfolk's linen store at Thetford in 1571[211] may offer a fair illustration of the range of linen manufactured in Lopham and other villages in his Norfolk and Suffolk Liberty. It included:

". . . old fine sheets of two breadths . . . linen sheets of three breadths ('breeds') . . . livery" (i.e. servants) "sheets of a coarse sort . . . plain tablecloths . . . plain cupboard cloths* . . . plain towels . . . one diaper towel . . . six old tablecloths of diaper . . . plain arming towels† . . . six dozen . . . of napkins striped with three blue stripes at each end . . . one dozen of coarse napkins . . . four pillowbeers" (i.e. pillowcases).

These types of linen may be said to bear a remarkable

* i.e. sideboard cloths.

† Rather than towels worn under armour, these may have been a protection against babes in arms.

resemblance to the range offered by Messrs. T. W. & J. Buckenham of Lopham in their nineteenth century heyday. But there is one notable exception: damask linen. "Picture cloths", as they were sometimes called, do seem to have been available in England as early as the sixteenth century, and at Wortham Hall eighty years ago the last of the Betts of Wortham still possessed a hand-made damask linen table-cloth apparently of Queen Elizabeth's reign. It was said to display a large portrait of the queen, "bordered with patterns of pelicans and the royal arms, and the words 'Qvene Elizabeth God save the Qvene'."[212] It is possible that such a work of art was made by one of the immigrant weavers from the Low Countries, or it may have been imported from abroad. It is not likely that damask linen was produced in the Lophams until the reign of Queen Victoria.[213]

But linen of the types described in the Thetford inventory of 1571 probably continued to be made by home industries in the Lophams throughout the seventeenth and into the eighteenth centuries. Such Lopham families as the Sanders or Saunders and the Wades were still weaving linen in the reign of King James I.[214] It remained a cottage industry, whose products were marketed locally, and the trade was not important enough to be mentioned by either of the topographers who wrote about the Lophams in the early eighteenth century: Thomas Cox in 1724[215] or Francis Blomefield in 1736.[216] Nevertheless we have records of linen-weavers Valentine Harte[217] of South Lopham, who made his will in 1633, John Greene[218] of North Lopham in 1640, Lawrence Rust[219] of the North in 1663, Robert Francis[220] of the same in 1689, Edward Vynor[221] of the South in 1703, James Johnson[222] of the North in 1707, and John Adamson[223] of the South who seems to have been "in the loom" from 1726 until about 1760. There is also record of William Bayes,[224] a "whitster" or bleacher, who made his will in 1661. The Francis family had branches in both villages and Robert Francis of North Lopham seems to have prospered both as a linen-weaver and as a farmer. He is known to have owned and hired "linen-land" in his lifetime, and in his will of 1689 he left 230 clews of linen yarn, valued at £22.10s, together with "things belonging to the weaving trade" worth £63. At the same time he left lands and cattle; all his South Lopham property going to his wife, Sarah,

". . . during the full time and term of her natural life without any manner of waste, and keeping my houses and fens in tenantable and good reparations . . ."

The property was then to go to his son, John, subject to legacies to his two daughters, Sarah and Mary,

". . . both payments to be made in or at the porch of the parish church of Northlopham . . ."[225]

This antique sanction, requiring the public fulfilment of financial obligations, need not have been a personal reflection on a heartless son. But perhaps the brief will of a less wealthy weaver, Lawrence Rust, suggests a happier family:

"I give unto my brother John Rust All my estate what soever desiring him to pay my debts and let no man be wronged."

During the seventeenth century efforts were made by both Parliament and private enterprise to encourage the English manufacture of linen, but while it prospered in Scotland and Ireland it remained a minor industry in this country. Legislation even in those days could prove to be self-defeating. One Act of 1678, for example, intended to help both the linen and the woollen trades, provided that every English corpse should be buried in "sheep's wool only", on pain of a five pound fine. There survives "An account of Buryings in the Parish of South Lopham since the late act entituled an act for Burying in Woolen from October the 12, 1678".[226] It contains sixty-five entries, the last being dated November 7th, 1682. The law was not repealed until 1814 and though it was often broken, we may suppose that it put an end to the Lopham manufacture of linen shrouds.

CHAPTER THIRTEEN

New Times, New Thoughts and Old Inclinations

The dangers into which their duke was falling may have been rumoured in the Lophams even before his first imprisonment in 1569–70. Perhaps there were some sympathisers there in December 1569 when a rising was attempted at Kenninghall in the duke's defence. Henry Sporle, a sawyer of Bunwell, one of the agitators, seems to have escaped punishment on that occasion, and fourteen years later he appears to have been living or hiding in Lopham. On September 13th, 1584, Nicholas Bacon of Redgrave, Justice of the Peace, later to become the premier baronet, wrote an order which survives in the manuscript collections of the British Library:[227]

"To the Constables of Lopham and to every" (i.e. each) "of them give these."

The constable, headborough or tything man was a manorial court official directly descended from the reeve, described in Chapter Eight, and he remained the village executive of law and order until 1842. It is unlikely that there were more than two of them in the Lophams when they perused the following.

"These are to command, and in the Queen her Majesty's name straitly" (i.e. strictly) "to charge you and every of you that to-morrow by eight of the clock in the forenoon you do carry before Mr. Bassingbourne Gawdie" (of West Harling) "Henry Sporle to answer to such matters as shall be objected against him. And hereof fail ye not at your peril . . ."

But the fall and execution of their local king in 1571–2 must have been a shock to both his loyal and his restive subjects. Inside "Park-hall" at Kenninghall his family and his household were prepared for the worst, and when the commissioners of the Queen's Council came down to inventory his possessions in September, 1571, they found a great number of "packs" already "trussed to be carried to Walden".[228] Audley End, Saffron Walden, was to be the new establishment of the duke's children, with a reduced and selected household. Among the Park-hall dependencies it must have seemed an earthquake in his palace, his parks and his pastures. The Steward, the Marshal, the Clerk Comptroller, the Clerk of the Kitchens, the gentlemen, the officers, the yeoman, the master of the children of the chapel, the schoolmaster, the master of the horse, the cook, the butcher, the saddler and the grooms, all were to go. It is said that some sixty servants, who were not wanted at Audley End, were sent to their houses on the Norfolk lands or told to find homes with their friends.[229] There was one last flicker of glory in 1578 when the young Earl of Surrey wasted his substance in entertaining the queen and her court, on progress through Suffolk and Norfolk, at his Kenninghall and Norwich houses. But afterwards the gates were shut and Park-hall became a hollow place of caretakers.

Lopham Lodge, which the duke had recommended to his children for economy's sake in a draft will of 1571,[230] was let about 1574 to Christopher Coote, gentleman, who died there in 1606. He had lived in South Lopham, perhaps at the old hall, from 1563 to 1573, begetting eight children, all of whom were baptised at S. Nicholas's.[231] Seven following children, beginning with Eustas, born in 1575, were natives of North Lopham and were baptised at S. Andrew's.[232] The philoprogenitive Christopher presumably belonged to a junior branch of the Cootes of Semere-Hall, Blo' Norton,[233] and his patient wife, Barbara, according to Blomefield, was a Harvey.[234] One of their South Lopham sons, Francis, (1566–1589) seems to have become a Gentleman-Usher to Queen Elizabeth and to have been buried like his parents in S. Nicholas's church.[235] One of their North Lopham daughters, Anne, married John Sheringe or Sherwyn, gentleman of

North Lopham, to whom she bore a son, John, in 1602.[236]

Sir Nicholas Coote, one of Christopher's near relations, was, according to Blomefield, "a Retainer of the" (4th) "Duke of Norfolk's, & upon his Cause, happened to strike the Attorney General, for which he was fined 20,000 l." (i.e. pounds) "& laid in prison for it a long time . . ."[237] Christopher does not seem to have been affected by this connection and was evidently not among the duke's Roman Catholic friends, the "recusants", or those who "refused" to attend the Elizabethan Church of England.

The only Lopham recusants reported in 1586 were described, with fines in mind, as of "mean and uncertain estates".[238] They were Elizabeth, the wife of Thomas Bowell or Vowell; Elizabeth, the wife of Thomas Cowell; and Katheryne Wylton. The names of Bowell and Cowell may be found at Lopham under various spellings as far back as the early fifteenth century.

Sticking to the religion of your forefathers was not the only reason for refusing to attend the services of the recently-founded Anglican establishment. As Chapter Eleven has shewn, new beliefs were abroad in the Lophams. William Hobbarde of South Lopham, whose will of 1565 was quoted in the last chapter,[239] may have come under Calvinist influence in the days of King Edward VI. "I bequeath my Soul," he says, "into the merciful ('marcifull') hands of Almighty God, the Father, the Son and the Holy Ghost, three Persons and one God, trusting faithfully to be saved and redeemed through the Merit and Passion of our Saviour Jesus Christ, beseeching Him of his merciful goodness to pardon me and my offences, and that it may please his Divine Majesty to accept me to be one of the elect number that shall enter his eternal glory."

Two years later the will of Bartholomew Wade, yeoman of the same village, spoke of "the Holy Ghost, the comforter of me and the elect people of God".[240] It was probably in South Lopham also that Michael Richardson, the joiner, in 1575 left his brother Roger "one bible of the Geneva translation".

Against this background it is not surprising that records of Archdeaconry Visitations in 1590–92 reveal symptoms of dissent in South Lopham. Andrew Gibson was examined there for denying the validity of infant baptism, but apparently withdrew his opinions on October 22nd, 1590, to preserve the stability of the Queen's Peace.[241] William Charlton was interrogated for walking out of S. Nicholas's "irreverently and impiously" when the sermon began on June 1st, 1592. He promised future reformation but whether religiously is left in doubt, for the next entry concerns the sin of William Saunder "in playing at Skalbones" (knucklebones?) on the same date during the hours of evening service for the feast of the Ascension.[242]

There must be some doubt also about the motives of Mrs. Christopher Toftwood, who was reported to the Archdeacon for refusing to come to church at Lopham, "affirminge that she will not come theare at all, do what yow can". On February 17th, 1591, it seems that responsibility for her future good behaviour was laid upon Mr. Toftwood, at his expense.[243]

There is no mystery in the case of Oliver Eure of North Lopham who was summoned for keeping a house of eating and drinking during the hours of divine service on April 22nd,

Stumpy Howard of the North Lopham Bell; Jack Shaw at the reins; Joe Glover, M. Glover, Whippleshaw Emms and "Tip" Ludbrook, *c.* 1912.

1591.[244] Was he a landlord of the "Bell" who opened his doors too soon?

North Lopham also had its Elect, and one of them, Richard Murrell the elder, yeoman, in his will of 1596 shewed that he could combine new beliefs with firm old fashions.[245] He left

"the use and occupation of my houses where I now dwell in Northlopham"

to his widowed daughter-in-law, Katherine Murrell, but he stipulated

"it is my will and mind that all my hanging and stained" (i.e. painted) "cloths shall always remain unto my said house undefaced and untaken away as now they are at the day of my death."

"Painted cloth" was the cheapest and most popular form of wall-hanging at this time and Shakespeare makes Falstaff refer to its pictures:

"a pretty slight drollery or the story of the Prodigal or the German hunting . . ."[246]

It seems likely that Mr. Murrell would have preferred the second of the three and that the old puritan was more concerned about the maintenance of moral lessons on his walls than the preservation of works of art.

Outside his house the scene was changing fast from the feudal picture of small villages overshadowed by large parks to a landscape of progressive husbandry. When did the deer go? Christopher Coote of Lopham Lodge in his will of 1606[247] left

"Edward Barnes, my servant, a steel bow" (i.e. crossbow) which he doth usually shoot in . . ."

and Sir Bassingbourne Gawdie recorded the receipt of a *fee buck* or *fee doe* from Kenninghall, Lopham and Winfarthing parks each year between 1600 and 1603.[248] Yet a deed of June, 1610, giving a lease of the manor of Lopham "with all its appurtenances" to Thomas Plumstede and John Gooch of London, gentlemen, makes no reference to deer,[249] nor is there any sign of them in the 1612 map of Lopham Park described in Chapter Seven. It is unlikely that the various lessees and their subtenants were interested in the maintenance of a private deer park, and although King James I, whose favourite recreation was hunting, bought a house at

Thetford to pursue the sport, there is no evidence that he rode as far as Kenninghall, Lopham and Winfarthing. Thomas Martin, in his history of Thetford, says that James stopped visiting there because he "was affronted by a farmer in the neighbourhood who threatened his Majesty with an action for riding over his corn". The story may be more symbolic than authentic, foreshadowing Norfolk's general attitude towards the royal prerogative as Charles I tried to exercise it.

Lopham Park was destined for agriculture, which is incompatible with deer. No doubt many of them fell victim to the time-honoured rural crime or craft of poaching, in which the Lophams and their neighbours have been famous for their skill. The official record goes back at least to June, 1281, in the days of the last Bigod earl of Norfolk, when his king, Edward I, granted a commission to enquire who hunted in Roger's parks at Lopham, Earsham, etc.[249A] In another June, three hundred and forty-one years later, The Privy Council of the first James gave warrant to Sir John Hare, to take care of the game of Norfolk for the sport and recreation of gentlemen and persons of quality who "are much abused by mean persons keeping lurchers and poaching dogs".[250] The Lopham fens must have provided sport for the poachers and perhaps one of their favourite haunts is commemorated in the name of Pantshorne Lane. In the mid-eighteenth century Penterhaugh[251] or Panter Hall[252] or Paynters[253] Lane still led to a place called Painters hirne.[254] "Panter" is an old word for snare,[255] while both haugh and hyrne can mean a nook or corner.[256] Perhaps the lane once led to a good place for traps in the fen.

The disappearance of a resident lord of the manor increased the self-confidence and independence of both Lophams and brought into the light of day a rivalry which may have existed for generations past. It was in the reign of Charles I that arguments about their respective liabilities for taxation led to the drafting of an "Indenture" or treaty between North and South Lopham which determined the existing boundary between the two parishes. The document, of which a 1685 copy survives in the Norfolk Record Office,[257] was first drawn up on November 2nd, 1628, when it was signed and sealed by Robert Wade, Francis Marsh, Will(ia)m

Some Lopham hunters: William Womack of The King's Head with his dog Ponto, and Baker Womack of Tann's Lane Mill, *c*. 1913.

Goodman, Robert Rush, Lau(rence) Womocke (the rector), Will(ia)m Carlton, Mary Heasell, Math(ew) Nun, John Beers, John Locke and Thomas Marsh. But there was no cease-fire, even among the signatories:

". . . notwithstanding this Agreement thus confirmed there is some difference between some of the Inhabitants of South and Northlopham concerning the division of the said parishes, notwithstanding some of them hath agreed ... under their hands and seals ..."

The issue was therefore referred to arbitration by two squires who presumably owned no lands in the Lophams. On March 30th, 1631, John Dix, Esquire and John Havers, Esquire

"did as absolutely determine that this Indenture should stand good and should be the guide of all the provings for the matter of rates and for the division between the land allotted to the benefit of the one and the other p(ar)ishes ..."

Nevertheless in 1685 the parish of North Lopham felt it necessary to add some sixteen riders to the agreement, describing the outlying territories of the village, including

"one pightle ('pictell') lying near Portway in Southlopham ..."

As for the immediate effects of this treaty, it is interesting to observe that in 1636, when all Norfolk was assessed for King Charles's unfortunate "Ship Money", North Lopham was rated at £9-8-3 and South Lopham at £9-8-9.[258]

Whether there was any political difference between the two villages during the civil war is uncertain. In the court rolls, which deal with both North and South Lopham, there is an entry somewhat oddly expressed for its date:

"The general Court with the Leet* there holden upon Wednesday in the fourth week of Lent, viz. the twelfth day of March in the year of our Lord God according to the computation of the Church of England One thousand six hundred and fifty by Robert Morse, gentleman, Chief Steward there ..."[259]

The Church of England had been virtually in suspension since 1646 and her "Supreme Governor" had lost his head on January 30th, 1649. But in the Lophams she maintained her sway. Laurence Womack or Womocke, as he signs his name in the parish registers, did not die or resign in 1642, as some would have us think; his entries and signatures continue in the Lopham registers until February 25th, 1653, and his will was proven in 1656.[260] He had been rector of Lopham since 1607,

* A particular kind of court of record held yearly or half-yearly.

exceeding the reign of his uncle and predecessor, Arthur Womock, in the same office by seventeen years. His parishes seem to have remained Anglican, at least in their marriages. There was only one wedding recorded at North Lopham church between Laurence Womocke's probable death in 1656 and the Restoration of Charles II and the Church of England in 1660. This was on November 26th, 1657, when Arthur Womocke, "Clerk", married Stephen Parke of one of the Forncetts to Anne Williamson of North Lopham "in the presence of Henry Hill gentleman & John Whitinge & divers others".[261] There was a similar care for the "Church by law established" at South Lopham. The "intruder" rector, Thomas Ellis, had arrived there by November 17th, 1654, when he took part in the choice of John Spinke to be "*Register* for our said Town of South Lopham".[262] In accordance with the Commonwealth Act of Parliament of August 23rd, 1653, the Register published "an Agreement of Marriage between Charles Muskett of South Lopham widower and Margaret Spincke of Garboldisham widow & of full years in the parish church of South Lopham August 9th, 16th & 23th being 3 several lord's days together".[263] But Mr. Muskett and Mrs. Spincke "were joined together in Marriage" at Garboldisham on October 22nd, 1657 by "Arthur Womocke Clerke", and with witnesses.[264]

Arthur was Laurence's eldest son and had received from him in 1642 the rectory of Fersfield, which his father had held in plurality with Lopham since 1609. Arthur himself became a pluralist in 1668, holding the rectory of Quidenham in addition to that of Fersfield until his death in 1685. In Lopham he may have officiated at baptisms as well as marriages during the "intrusion" of Thomas Ellis, since the latter was deprived of the living in 1663 "for holding Anabaptistical Errors, and refusing to baptise Infants".[265] Apart from his acceptability as a Womocke of the third generation and an Anglican, Lopham may have liked Arthur for less admissible reasons under the Commonwealth. In 1658 two parishioners of Fersfield and one of Diss informed against Womocke as a Royalist together with two of his friends. According to Blomefield, the rector of Fersfield "was particularly charged with speaking these Words,

'Here is a Health unto his Majesty,
pray God confound his Foes,
And the Devil take all Round Heads,
For we are none of those.'

And also that he abused the Government thus,

'Hey-ho! for a Two-penny Halter,
When you are hang'd you shall have good Quarter,
Oh! 'twould be, a brave Sight, to see,
All the Round-heads, hang on a Tree.
Oh! yee Rogues, Ye must All come to it'."

Arthur Womocke and his friends were committed to Ipswich Gaol but the informers confessed eventually to false witness and "after much Trouble and Expence" the three accused "were at last freed".[266] We shall never know if there was any truth in the allegations but we may feel sure that if these songs were sung at the "King's Head", North Lopham, Arthur Womocke got some of the credit.

It was during this period of emancipation and self-assertion in the last quarter of the sixteenth century and the first half of the seventeenth that most of the oldest surviving inns, farm-houses and substantial cottages of North and South Lopham were built or rebuilt, such as Grange, Chestnut Tree, Noddle (now Dairy), Church, Poplar Tree, Oxfootstone, and Oak Tree Farms; and a number of cottages both in the village centres and on the commons, such as Willow Tree Cottage. Perhaps the finest surviving exterior of the sixteenth century is the eastern wing of Oxfootstone Farm, with its high gable, double hexagon chimney stack, bold chequer of blue bricks on red, and brickwork transomed and mullioned windows (both blocked up).

No doubt there are many vestiges of older buildings to be found inside much later casings. Outside the churches there may be little ancient masonry, but woodwork, despite the dangers of fire and rot, can live to a great age. As many old Norfolk householders have found for themselves, the older the oaken beam the more iron girderlike it gets, and it would not be at all surprising if the trees bequeathed to Roger Fenne in 1586 were upholding his old Lopham property today. Not

Mr. Jesse Green at Church Farm, North Lopham, *c*. 1930.

that the face of his cottage need look in the least Elizabethan. Wattle and daub or clay lump are easily faced or replaced, and the shapes of windows and doors can be manipulated to the breadth of the householder's figure or tastes, and the height of his head—so long as there is no amputation of the wooden anatomy within the walls.

By commonsense and compromise the English have kept their houses reasonably safe, fairly comfortable and passably modish without peril to the ancestral roof-tree. At Trennel House off North Lopham street beams of some age have been installed downstairs to support an early nineteenth century ceiling, while upstairs the building's ancient skeleton rises waist-high above the floor. Sometimes it may seem that beauty as well as strength have kept a beam in use, for example the splendidly moulded supporter of the living-room ceiling at Chestnut Tree Farm, comparable to one of the beams surviving from Park-hall in Kenninghall Place Farm kitchen. Perhaps in the late seventeenth century, a balustered staircase was added to the back of Chestnut Tree Farm, but the original outer wall was preserved together with a wooden mullion window of the sixteenth century. There is a comparable addition at the back of Walnut Tree Farm, South Lopham, but there the staircase has acquired a rustic Queen Anne style. At Brook House in South Lopham as at Willow Tree Cottage and other places, there are vestiges of the hole through the ceiling which once gave ladder access to the upper floor, but in the rafters of Brook House there is a soot-encrusted relic of earlier days when the smoke from an open hearth in a one-storey building had to find its own way through a louvre in the roof. At Poplar Tree Farm on Great Common a seventeenth century builder seems to have adjusted a beam to avoid a fire risk. Instead of carrying it

16th century wall & chimney at Oxfootstone Farm, South Lopham.

through the great fire-place to the outside wall, the cause of many conflagrations in other places, he has rested the beam-end on a bracket of bricks projecting from the chimney breast.

As Chapter Two suggested, the sites of village inns can be of respectable antiquity. The unprepossessing front of South Lopham's White Horse conceals hindquarters of sixteenth and, it is said, fifteenth century date. The present management moreover remembers in 1951 an inn-sign which bore no chocolate-box horse but a prancing beast with a leafy branch in its mouth. The white horse mouthing a spray of oak had been a badge used by Henry, the last Fitzalan earl of Arundel, and some of his forebears. It was brought to Kenninghall and Lopham by his heir, Philip, Earl of Arundel and Surrey, the last Howard to inhabit Park-hall. S. Philip Howard, canonised in 1970, is renowned for his sufferings, sanctity and charity as a political prisoner in the Tower of London. In these parts, however, he was celebrated in his salad days, before his conversion, for the party he gave to the queen in 1578 at Kenninghall

"... where for divers dayes he lodged & feasted not only her self, & all her family" (i.e. household), "the Council, Courtiers, and all their company, but all the Gentlemen also, & people of the Country, who came thither upon that occasion, in such plentifull, bountifull, & splendid manner, as the like had never been seen before in those Countrys."[267]

It seems fitting that such hospitality should be commemorated by village inns at both Kenninghall and South Lopham.

At the back of South Lopham's White Horse there is a wooden mullioned window which might have been produced by the very carpenter who worked at Chestnut Tree Farm, and there is a spiral staircase of solid oaken steps, a sixteenth century feature which seems also to have existed at the old Bull in North Lopham. The handsome fireplaces in the main stack of North Lopham's King's Head appear to belong to the time of the first Arthur Womock, whose story follows.

CHAPTER FOURTEEN

Some Lopham Names and Fames

The name of Womocke or Womack, as it is most frequently spelt today, has more than a local fame. The Lopham branch of the family seems to have been established there first by Arthur Womock, as he signed himself in the parish registers, rector from 1578 to 1607. He came of an East Dereham family already known for its churchmen; his uncle, James Womocke, and his great-uncle, James Wamuke, having been rectors of Whinbergh and Yaxham respectively.[268] He was presented to the living by William Dyx, of Wickmere, Esquire, and William Cantrell of Norwich, gentleman, two of the late duke's surveyors, who acted as feoffees, or trustees, of the Earl of Arundel and Surrey, his son's, Norfolk estates, and who then or later granted the advowson to Womock himself. Womock was well-to-do and had the respect and trust of his parishioners; his name appearing as a witness to both North and South Lopham wills, such as that of Richard Cotnye, quoted in Chapter Twelve,[269] and as "supervisor", for example in the testament of Richard Bryant of North Lopham in 1592,[270] where his help was sought in the distribution of ten shillings to the "poor people of Northlopham aforesaid where most need shall require".

His nephew Laurence seems to have been a Bachelor of Divinity aged thirty-one when he succeeded his uncle in 1607, not on the presentation of Edward Carell and John Holland of Wortwell,* Esquires, the current Arundel trustees, as Blomefield records, but at the hands of his aunt Avice Womock, to whom her husband had left the advowson for this purpose.[271] One of his brothers, Thomas, settled in South Lopham where he had descendants; another, Henry, had been rector of Fersfield since 1595, a living to which he united the rectory of Great Ellingham in 1601.[272] Uncle Arthur, in his will of 1607, describes his favourite nephew as "Lawrence Womocke of Fersfield . . . clerk" and it may be therefore that Henry had moved to Great Ellingham and that Laurence was serving as his "locum" at Fersfield. In 1609, no doubt by some family arrangement, the Fersfield living was transferred to Laurence, to be held in union with Lopham. Perhaps Henry knew already that he was to be presented to the comfortable living of Attleborough, which he held in union with Great Ellingham from 1614 until his death in 1627.[273]

Laurence Womocke of Lopham married twice and had five surviving children: four sons and one daughter.[274] The career of Arthur, the eldest son, has been described in the last chapter. The second son, another Laurence,† was born at Lopham in 1612, and graduated from Corpus Christi College, Cambridge in 1632. He was ordained in 1634, and soon won esteem for his preaching. He was an ardent supporter of Church and King, and became well-known for his writings against the dissenters. One quotation from his "Pulpit Conceptions, Popular-Deceptions" of 1662, an attack on the misuse of extemporary prayer, may be enough to shew his mettle:

". . . I am satisfied that *occasional* Ejaculations and Prayers of a *private* Conception are not unlawful . . . But when they are set up in competition with a well-digested Liturgie, prescrib'd and establish'd by Authority for public use, I am at a stand . . ."[275]

* An important stage in the transformation of the Hollands of Wortwell into the Hollands of Quidenham is commemorated in the first surviving volume of the North Lopham parish register. This is bound in the remains of a vellum deed whereby Sir John Holland of Quidenham, baronet, in 1676, conveyed Wortwell, with certain exceptions, to John Cooper of Suffolk, yeoman. Sir John was the grandson of John Holland of Wortwell, esquire.

† Who spelt his name both Womock and Womack.

He was well-regarded by "Authority", and was appointed archdeacon of Suffolk soon after the Restoration. By 1663 he had become a Doctor of Divinity by royal prescription, a prebendary of both Hereford and Ely cathedrals, and, in keeping with the family traditions, the incumbent of two Suffolk rectories.[276] In 1683, during Charles II's last four years of unparliamentary government, he published perhaps his last political pamphlet, "A Short Way to a Lasting Settlement". This is full of warnings against the interested parties who have made it impossible for kings and parliaments to retain their dignities at one and the same time. Womock warns "all Loyal Gentlemen and Freeholders" in particular to

"Take heed of such as are *Discontented* at their *Disappointments* in pursuit of their designs of Avarice or Ambition . . .[277]

In November of the same year he was consecrated Bishop of S. David's in the archbishop's chapel at Lambeth. Having realised the ambition of becoming a bishop, however, he does not seem to have gone into residence at his see before his death in 1685. He was buried in S. Margaret's, Westminster, where there is a memorial to him and his only child, Anne, who died at the age of nineteen.[278]

His heir was his nephew, Laurence Womack of Mautby, gentleman, whose grand-daughter, Mary Womack, married Francis Blomefield, the historian of Norfolk and the rector of Fersfield and Brockdish.[279]

Whether from the Bishop's uncle Thomas in South Lopham, or from his younger nephews, Robert of North Lopham, and John of South, the Womack descent flourished in both villages, as farmers, linen-weavers, and in other trades. The Census of 1851 enumerated eleven Womacks as heads of households in North Lopham and two in South Lopham. These included six farmers, a miller, a baker, a wheelwright and two linen-weavers.

Looking back in history, the Lophams had one rector who was already a bishop when he was appointed to the living. This was John Salisbury (1500?–1573?), who must have held more benefices at one time than any other Lopham rector, a man to whom the Vicar of Bray's career would have seemed unenterprising. He was born a Welshman, of the Salusbury family, and after graduating at Cambridge in 1523 he became a Benedictine monk of Bury S. Edmund's. From there he went to Oxford University, where he won more degrees but was suspected of Protestant leanings by Cardinal Wolsey, and was sent to prison for a year. He returned to Bury under a cloud, but somehow became known to Henry VIII, presumably after Wolsey's disgrace and death in 1530. However it came about, he rendered the king some peculiar services during the dissolution of the monasteries. First, in 1534, Henry appointed him prior of Horsham S. Faith's, whereupon Salisbury persuaded the remaining five monks in that Benedictine house to subscribe to the Act of Supremacy and to resign the priory to the king. He was rewarded with fees and an annuity, then proceeded apparently to perform the same disappearing trick in Hampshire. This time he became the abbot of Titchfield, a house of another order,* only to surrender the abbey to his grateful monarch. Henry had newly revived and regulated by act of parliament the institution of suffragan bishops, and in 1536 Salisbury was consecrated as the first suffragan bishop of Thetford. During the next three years he was made archdeacon of Anglesey and first a canon, then Dean, of Norwich Cathedral. In the last capacity he obliged the king once more by signing the decree of 1540 which annulled the royal marriage with Anne of Cleves. He collected numerous other church preferments and his last reward from Henry VIII seems to have been his presentation to the rectory of Lopham in February, 1547.[280] It was a week after the advowson had been forfeited by the third Howard duke, on his attainder for high treason; and five days after the king's death.

The only new benefit Salisbury seems to have acquired during the reign of King Edward VI was a wife, a member of the Barrett family of Norfolk. She was perhaps a South Lopham girl, related to the Nicholas Barrett of Chapter Eleven, but she proved to be a disadvantage when Queen Mary I restored the old religion. In 1554 Salisbury, the married man, was deprived of his suffragan bishopric, his deanery and all his other preferments. He must have had a way with

* The Premonstratensian Canons.

him—Thomas Tusser, who had served him as a singing-man in Norwich Cathedral, calls him "the gentle dean"[281]—and he seems to have been able to charm most people, even Mary the Queen. For in the very same year he was re-presented to the rectory of Lopham by the old duke, whose attainder had been reversed in September 1553. Back in Kenninghall Place, the duke bore him no ill will but, according to Blomefield, "had a great Value for him", and "procured him the Rectory of *Diss*, to which he was instituted the same Day", holding it in union with Lopham.[282] Still in 1554, Salisbury was installed Chancellor of Lincoln Cathedral.

We do not know what happened to Mrs. Salisbury but we hope that she was allowed to rejoin her husband after Queen Elizabeth's accession in 1558. Salisbury's career accelerated: he was restored to the archdeaconry of Anglesey in 1559; to the deanery of Norwich in 1560; and between 1554 and 1567 he acquired six additional rectories in Lincolnshire and Norfolk. It should not be thought, however, that he tried to please everybody, and after a quarrel with the Bishop of Bangor, another acquisitive Welshman, he was deprived for a time of his Anglesey archdeaconry, probably and not unreasonably on grounds of non-residence. He was also suspended from his deanery for a sermon to his Norwich congregation in which he "inveighed too sharply against the vices of the gentry and clergy and seemed to prefer the popish" to the reformed religion.[283] But he made a satisfactory explanation from the same pulpit and was re-instated. Salisbury reached his summit in 1571 when he was appointed Bishop of Sodor and Man, and was given a dispensation by Archbishop Parker to hold his deanery, archdeaconry and two rectories at the same time. One of the rectories was Diss; he seems to have resigned the rectory of Lopham in 1560, but in what circumstances remains unclear. Before he achieved his independent bishopric in 1571 his only voluntary resignation of a Norfolk rectory seems to have been Creke in 1541, after reserving a life pension to himself from the stipend. He handed over what was left to a son of Sir Roger Townsend, who forthwith presented him to the rectory of Claydon in Suffolk. Salisbury seems never to have visited his diocese of Sodor and Man, and died at Norwich.[284]

To return to the inhabitants of Lopham, some of their oldest surnames on record seem to refer to the situation of a man's dwelling; to the place he hailed from; to an occupation; or to a nickname. In the first class the surnames of John *delepol*,[285] John *de moor*,[286] and John *Underwood*[287] are redolent of the fen, the waste and the forest. There were Underwoods in the Lophams for at least four hundred years, recalling the days when "this Town was most Wood". Names of the second class in the court rolls of King Henry IV's time may be John *Hauylye*,[288] perhaps from a Norman Hauville, perhaps from Haughley in Suffolk; John *Fynchyngham*,[289] perhaps from Finningham in Suffolk, perhaps from Fincham near Downham Market; and *Burgonys*,[290] perhaps a far foreigner from Burgundy. Carpentry may have given *Boorde*[291] and *Wryght*[292] their names; and *Barker*[293] could have been a shepherd or a tanner. *Bolle*[294] and *Bowll*[295] seem likely to connect with the *Bowles* and *Bowells* of later days and all might derive from the Norman French nickname of "*boule*" for a round-bodied man.[296] John *Cowl*,[297] perhaps a forebear of the *Cowells* and *Cowlles* of the next two centuries, may have borne a nickname also, since a cowl or cowel in the Middle Ages could be a large tub with two ears sticking up to be carried on a cowl-staff.[298] *Savage*[299] could have been another nickname, or simply descriptive of a "wildman" from the backwoods. *Hoggison*[300] was probably not as rude as it looks but just an early form of the common "son of Hodge". More mysterious are *Baldry*,[301] still a well-known name in Norfolk, and *Oryell.*[302] Some relate the first to an Old German "Baldric", meaning "bold rule"[303] and perhaps to be compared therefore with the "eight bold reigners" of "Green Grow the Rushes O"? Oryell has been related to an Old German word of even obscurer meaning: "Orieldis", that is, "fire-strife".[304] The origins of the English word "oriel" are difficult enough to discover:[305] perhaps it would be easier and wiser to think of the meaning of the word when we are considering its application as a surname. The thought of a "projecting" piece of architecture,[306] or just a bulge in a building suggests immediately the inveterate English habit of personal remarks, and thus another nickname.

In the same group of Lopham surnames in the earliest

surviving court rolls there are repeated references to *Fulmerston* or *Fulmerstone*,[307] presumably a version of the place-name Fulmodestone, near Fakenham. The Fulmerstons were a leading family in the Lophams during the fifteenth and sixteenth centuries, but Sir Richard Fulmerston, one of the third duke's retainers who did not turn against him and the Earl of Surrey in 1547, and whose prosperity under the fourth duke enabled him to refound Thetford School, belonged to a Suffolk branch and was apparently born in Ipswich.[308]

CHAPTER FIFTEEN

Eighteenth Century Lopham

Although the Restoration of 1660 also restored the title of Duke of Norfolk to the great-great-grandson of the Thomas Howard executed in 1572, and the Howards had repossessed themselves of most of their Norfolk estates, the feudal days of the "Liberty" were over. Kenninghall Place had been pulled down about 1650, except for a fragment which served as the Steward's house and a farmhouse. According to Blomefield, "the Materials sold for a Trifle, with which great Numbers of Chimneys and Walls in the Neighbourhood are built, as is evident from the *Mowbray's* and *Arundel's* Arms which are upon the Bricks". Both coats of arms shewed rampant lions such as may be seen built into the outside walls of the Greyhound Inn at Diss. Bricks and stone were in short supply in this region of wattle and daub, and perhaps some of the Park-hall building material may yet be found incorporated in Lopham houses.

Even Norwich House, which the sixth duke had begun to rebuild and glorify as "The Duke's Palace" in 1662,[309*] was in decay by 1710. Blomefield says that it was pulled down by the eighth duke, another Thomas, "on Account of the ill Behaviour of *Tho. Havers* then" (1708) "Mayor &c towards him, in not permitting his *Comedians*" (play-actors) "to enter

* Fifteen years before he suceeded to the title.

the City with their Trumpets &c from which time it hath been neglected . . ."[310]

In the Liberty the parks had all become farmland, as we may read in a survey of the eighth duke's Norfolk property in 1720:[311]

". . .	acres	roods	perches
South Lopham Hall Farm	327	1	10
North Lopham Lodge Farm	613	3	23
Farsfield Hall Farm	422	2	20
Farsfield Lodge Farm	339	2	27
Kenninghall Place Farm	719	1	24
Boyland Hall and White House	522	3	25

. . ."

The owning of sheep was no longer a privilege of the few, and the flocks which grazed the eighteenth century commons of Lopham were perhaps branded as well as shepherded. For the breed of "Old Norfolk Sheep", a "long-legged, horned animal, with black face and black legs",[312] were described as "wanderers and never satisfied, except with a great range of pasture. They will break through almost any fence, and jump over any hurdle; these disqualifications have brought them into disrepute . . ."[313] However, this was a verdict of 1829, when most of the commons had been enclosed: in the eighteenth century the Norfolk Sheep was still esteemed for other qualities, such as "clothing wool, the third in the kingdom for fineness . . . Mutton 18 lb. a quarter equal to any in the world in cold weather, and yields an uncommon quantity of high coloured gravy".[314]

A great encouragement to sheep-breeding was the introduction of the turnip. Where and when this first occurred in Norfolk seems to be as much a matter of dispute as the burial-place of Boadicea. It may be safe to assume, however, that the common field turnip came in during the 1730s, while the Swedish Turnip, possibly from the benevolent hands of the Reverend Dr. Miles Beevor of Mulbarton House,[315] arrived some fifty years later. By the end of the century Arthur Young reported that "Norfolk farmers are so wedded to turnips that they sow them almost indiscriminately on all soils",[316] a practice of which he did not approve. At the same time he recognised the hard work devoted to the cultivation of the turnip.

"The turnips in Norfolk are universally twice hoed; the operation is every where well done, except, I think, in one respect, that of being set out too thin, which with *dashing* hoers is a common evil."[317] And he acknowledges "the great additional advantage secured of supporting great flocks, and herds of sheep and cattle."[318] In 1829 T. S. Norgate, esquire of Hethersett, declared that:

"The basis of Norfolk farming is the TURNIP; it is mainly to the extensive culture of this inestimable root and its congeners, that we have succeeded in fertilizing a soil naturally barren, and have made this county produce not only corn and cattle sufficient for our own multiplied and multiplying population, but likewise that we have made it one of the largest export counties in the kingdom, for these articles."[319]

Apart from the cultivation of turnips, in which we will hope that Lopham did not exhibit too many "dashing hoers", the larger farms in the two villages are likely by 1750 to have concentrated their labour and their fertilisers on the "Norfolk Four Course Shift",[320] a rotation of crops generally producing turnips, barley, clover and wheat. On the surrounding and intermixed smallholdings, and on outlying portions of the large farms, however, there was a competitive crop, hemp. The cultivation of hemp required a disproportionate amount of manure: Arthur Young reported Norfolk farmers to be applying between ten and thirty cartloads of farmyard dung to the (hempland) acre.[321]

What were the advantages? Because of wars in Europe, particularly the Seven Years' War of 1756–63, and the consequent restriction on imports of foreign linen, the English linen industry enjoyed great prosperity in the third quarter of the eighteenth century. Exports increased. According to the *Annual Register* of 1773, exports of British linen, excluding Irish linen, rose from over a million yards in 1757 to over four million in 1771. This led to an expansion of English hempland, particularly in south-western Norfolk. Andrew Somerville, a Scotsman who toured Yorkshire, Lincolnshire, Norfolk and Cambridgeshire in 1773, estimated that nearly one tenth of all the hemp grown in England was produced in Norfolk.[322] The bulk of the hempland lay in the south of the county and at the end of the century Arthur Young was told that "most hemp" was grown in the Lophams, Fersfield, Bressingham, Kenninghall, Winfarthing, Garboldisham, Palgrave, Banham, the Buckenhams and Diss.[323]

These were all villages or towns in which the skill or at least the tradition of hemp production could have survived from the sixteenth century when in some of them the craft of linen-weaving also had been practised. In the Lophams there are good grounds for believing that both skill and craft had continued to be exercised for more than two hundred years. Chapter Twelve has shewn how hemp-growing and linen-weaving continued as complementary home industries in Lopham from the seventeenth into the early eighteenth centuries. The overlapping careers of John Adamson of South Lopham and William Womack of North Lopham suggest that these industries continued throughout the 1700s. John Adamson was a "Linnen Weaver" when he took part in an indenture of June 23rd, 1726, and was still so described at his death, shortly before 1761.[324] William Womack, a descendent of the bishop's brother John, was born about 1729, and as "farmer and linen weaver" was rich enough to buy property in Kenninghall and elsewhere in 1771.[325]

The cultivation of hemp in the neighbourhood of Diss seems to have reached its peak about 1780. But what Somerville saw in 1773 was the beginning of overproduction, and by the end of the decade depression was setting in. The value of linen exports fell from £28,000,000 in 1758–63 to just over £15,000,000 in 1766–71,[326] while foreign imports recovered their strength from less than nineteen million yards in 1762 to the tune of some twenty-eight and a quarter million in 1771.[327] The war with France, which began again in 1778, soon made wheat a more valuable crop than hemp.

When Arthur Young, as Secretary of the Board of Agriculture, visited the "vicinity of Diss" at the turn of the century he reckoned that about two hundred acres of hempland were still in cultivation and remarked "there is scarcely one-tenth grown of what there was some years past: this is chiefly attributed to the high price of wheat".[328] But there were other

18th century hand-loom from North Lopham Limes. Now at Bankfield Museum, Halifax. By courtesy of the Calderdale Museums Service.

threats to the Norfolk linen industry in the last quarter of the eighteenth century. One was the progress of mechanisation. Hargreaves had produced his "Spinning Jenny" in Lancashire in 1764. Further advances by Arkwright, Crompton and Cartwright led to the development of the power loom in the 1790s. How the Lophams survived these threats is discussed in Chapter Eighteen.

CHAPTER SIXTEEN

Disaffection and Dissent

The depression in the weaving industry was felt with most severity in the cities and towns, such as Norwich, Wymondham and Diss. But there were other reasons for discontent throughout the county. In the 1790s bad harvests and too much exportation of wheat caused sharp rises in the price of bread. At Yarmouth in 1792 law and order were overwhelmed for a time by mobs rioting for a cheaper loaf. Troops were moved into Norfolk but there were fears that they too might become disaffected. Colonel Vyse of the Dragoon Guards refused to make Norwich his headquarters in 1792 because he considered it

"... one of the very worst places for young soldiers—a place where the most daring and dangerous publications were in daily circulation—a place where the most destructive principles were openly avowed—where houses of resort were open for the public discussion of those principles ..."[329]

One of the "dangerous publications" was no doubt the recently-published *Rights of Man* by Tom Paine of Thetford. News of the French Revolution had certainly aroused feelings of sympathy and even competition in some Norwich and Norfolk hearts, feelings which were not dispelled by the war with France between 1793 and 1802. In 1798 Charles Howard, the eleventh duke of Norfolk, was deprived by King George of all his offices for giving a toast at a political banquet:

"Our sovereign's health—the majesty of the people!"[330]

How were his tenants behaving in Lopham? At South Lopham, in July, 1800, a reward of £30 was offered for discovery of the authorship of an "incendiary paper" which had been posted up in the parish.[331] Its contents do not seem to have survived but we may guess at their style from an example found in the parish of S. Peter Mancroft seven years before:

"English men—Behold a Despotic Whelp, by some called a King, sitting on the Throne of England, making unavailing excuses by Declarations and such like Nonsense, for this unjust and ruinous War, which so distress and burthen the Sovereign People. Be advised: suffer this Villinous proceedings no longer, but this instant Rise in one body, and overthrow this Damn'd Infernal Constitution . . . Be sure not let the Members of the Corruptible House of Commons ever meet again to vote away the Liberties of the People. Amen."[332]

There is some evidence that this kind of propaganda was put about by visitors from Norwich to the villages, but we must suppose there were some villagers prepared to post it up, and perhaps more to read it. The "Amen" could have been meant to catch the eye of those who were at least disaffected towards the Church of England. There were plenty such in North Lopham and perhaps some in South Lopham, if Baptist traditions had survived there.

For it would be misleading to suggest that the history of dissent in the Lophams began in the eighteenth century. We have seen in Chapter Thirteen the Calvinist influence which appears in some sixteenth century wills, with their hints of predestination. We have read of Andrew Gibson at South Lopham, who denied the validity of infant baptism in 1598.[333] There is no reason why such unauthorised beliefs should not have continued and increased there in the first half of the seventeenth century, considering the strong Puritan influences then abroad in Norfolk. The long reign of the rector, Laurence Womocke, may have enforced a high degree of Anglican conformity in the churches of S. Nicholas and S. Andrew, but this would not prevent Lopham men and women thinking and talking for their non-conformist selves, nor of walking for themselves to hear the various lecturers and preachers of those stirring times. Norwich, which had known Lollards in their days, was still a centre of reform and was only twenty miles away. There were other dissenting prophets closer at hand: for example, the rectors Jeremiah Burroughes of Tivetshall and William Greenhill of Oakley, both of whom were deprived of their livings in 1636 for their Congregationalist errors.[334]

In the Lophams themselves, after the departure of Laurence Womocke in 1653, Thomas Ellis occupied the rectory for about nine years and, to judge from his sentence of deprivation in 1663, preached some form of the Baptist beliefs expressed by Andrew Gibson in 1598. The size of his following in either Lopham is unknown but it seems unlikely that his doctrines would be soon or wholly forgotten by any parishioners whom he baptised or rebaptised as adults. Some three generations later, in the last thirty years of the eighteenth century, there are several adult baptisms and some rebaptisms of children recorded in the North Lopham parish register. There may be various explanations for these entries: it is possible that some of them refer to Baptists entering or re-entering the Church of England. A Baptist chapel seems to have been established in South Lopham by 1840.

It was the Methodists who took the strongest hold at North Lopham in the second half of the eighteenth century. John Wesley does not record any visit to the village, but he came close enough in November, 1758, for Lopham folk to have heard him preach at Kenninghall.[335] Perhaps they went to hear him there again on Boxing Day of the same year.[336] For when a Leicester Methodist, Thomas Glover, came to stay at North Lopham in 1770, he had, as he may have expected, a friendly reception. This was in contrast to the lot of his colleague, Thomas Lee, who brought Methodism to Diss in the same year and was mobbed. Glover invited the preachers of the Norwich Circuit to visit North Lopham, and their first station was under an ancient ash tree by King's Head Lane. They had no pulpit, and one of them, remarkable by his velvet cap, always preached from the saddle. Another horse came into the story when one of the Womacks, a scoffer, brought his nag to the preaching, "saying it would do the animal as much good as it did him". But it was the rider who became perhaps the first Methodist Womack before he died.[337]

By 1775 the society was meeting in the kitchen of one of the Gooches in Tann's Lane, but three or four years later George Wharton linen weaver and for many years innkeeper of the King's Head, became a convert. It was not until October, 1792 that George Wharton transferred his copyhold of more than six acres of land, together with the inn, a weaving shop, a stable and a "firing house", to Charles Woods "of Thetford in the County of Norfolk Common Brewer", and when he did so it was with considerable reservations. Woods was to have only the south side of the King's Head yard "from the hanging post of the Gate leading from off the Green in a strait line westward to the brow of the Ditch of the Gardens belonging to certain Cottages of the said George Wharton". At the same time George reserved to himself, "his Heirs and assigns free ingress Egress and regress with servants Horses Carts and Carriages at all times to bring and carry Corn Hay or any other things whatsoever through the said Gateway leading off the said Green over and through the pump yard . . . unto and from a barn of the said George Wharton (*then used as a preaching House*)* situate between the said Stable and firing House". Finally he provided for similar access by the owners or occupiers of his cottages, whether to use the pump and well or to store firing and building material. He and his tenants would bear "one half part of the expence of keeping the said pump and well in repair".[338]

It is not known when the King's Head barn first became "a preaching House". George Wharton established himself at the King's Head in 1754[339] but according to Wesleyan tradition it was at Grange Farm, North Lopham, before 1780 that he made his ample kitchen available to the Methodists, and that Samuel Bardsley, a minister from Norwich, applied for the necessary license for preachings.[340] The Grange Farm kitchen, in which the society met, could be entered in those days by a door in the great chimney. This curiosity has now disappeared, but it was once listed among the *Seven* Wonders of Lopham![341] Through it there passed a number of famous

* Writer's italics.

Chimney door into Grange Farm kitchen, North Lopham, *c.* 1935. Unidentified man with the halter, V. Woodrow, W. Yeates, Eric Reeder.

preachers, among them the learned Dr. Adam Clarke (1762?–1832), who is said to have found on the Norwich Circuit of 1783 that

"A kind of invincible ignorance and brutal depravity marked the state of the mass of the people . . ."[342]

The Circuit was an arduous task, comprising twenty-two towns and villages on a monthly journey of not less than two hundred and sixty miles, most of them on horseback, through Norfolk and Suffolk.

It needs to be remembered that John Wesley's disciples presented no challenge to the doctrines of the Church of England. As late as 1790 John Wesley himself asked for permission to preach in Diss parish church and was given the express approval of both the rector and Dr. George Horne, the bishop of Norwich.[343] The bishop's biographer remarked on this occasion that Dr. Horne was "always more ready to encourage than to hinder any good work".[344] The "good work", as Wesley saw it, was the revival of personal religion in the search for salvation by methodical worship and moral discipline. For these purposes regularity and organisation became Wesleyan characteristics, especially in the system of "Class-meetings for Christian fellowship".

The Methodist "classes" bore no relation to the social class-structure, for Wesley preached universal redemption, regardless of wealth or rank. They were bands of selected men and selected women who met under the supervision of appointed leaders to examine and improve the state of their souls together. The effect of such a system on the village life of North Lopham must have been considerable. For whatever Dr. Clarke may have felt about other parts of the Norwich Circuit, ignorance in the Grange Farm kitchen proved by no means invincible and the North Lopham society flourished. Seats were installed in the King's Head Barn and George Wharton junior fitted up a gallery for singers. There was an attentive congregation and ultimately the chapel was provided with a pulpit. By 1809 the Methodists found that they needed more room. George senior had died at the age of eighty in 1808[345] and bequeathed his barn to the society. They sold it for £40, bought some land for £19, and raised enough money to start building the present chapel, which was opened on December 2nd, 1810. It had cost them altogether £639-0-1 and their debts were finally cleared in 1886.[346]

There seems to have been little opposition to Methodism during its establishment at North Lopham. This may have been due in part to the fact that from 1770–1801 there was only a curate in charge of the parish, John Smith.[347] The latent hostility of the minor country gentry to the classless society of the Methodists may be seen in the story of Mrs. Porter, the wife of another well-to-do North Lopham farmer, Samuel Porter senior. During a dangerous illness in 1780 she had been visited by Jonathan Coussins, a Methodist minister, and was converted. After her recovery she provided the travelling

Lopham Wesleyan Chapel and school, N. Lopham, *c*. 1920.

preachers with hospitality. Her husband's grandfather, a High Churchman, Mr. Porter of Snetterton Hall, could not bear the thought that the Methodists should be entertained by any of his relatives, and rode over to North Lopham to demand if what he heard was true. Mary Porter replied that she had entertained them; that she would continue to do so; and that if they were expelled the house she would follow. "Seeing her fixed determination to remain a Methodist, the old man mounted his horse, never again to trouble her about the matter."[348]

Weavers and farmers were the backbone of the society. George Wharton had been both and the "Gooch of Tann's Lane" was probably Thomas Gooch, the linen-weaver. Thomas Glover, who was for some time the leader of the Class at North Lopham, used to conduct its meetings in the house of Robert Leeder, a member of another linen-weaving family.

But the Wesleyan Methodists were not to have it all their own way. The musical George Wharton junior broke with them in 1822. "Like his Father, he was a genuine specimen of the old Norfolk yeoman, his great aversion was pride in any form. The Wesleyans were moving with the times and this did not suit" (George Wharton II) "who preferred the old ruts. He believed in the old camp meetings and original Methodism."

About the time of his break he handed over Grange Farm to his son, George Wharton III, and retired to "a house opposite". As an ardent musician with spare time he now "spent most of it playing the violin. This appears to have annoyed his wife who was not a lover of music—at least not the way George played it. So he built a shed near the road and used to go there to play his violin . . . (He) invited the Primitive Methodists to come and preach in the building and for a long time services were held there. Ultimately he built a chapel on one side of the dwelling house and leased it to the Primitives." He also built them chapels at New Buckenham and Wortham, and he is believed to have been the donor of the old Primitive chapel in Guildhall Street, Thetford. By his will of February 14th 1837, he devised the North Lopham chapel to his son John.[349] By 1951 it had been sold and converted into a bungalow, Bourne Cottage, but the "Ranters" and their camp meetings are still remembered with affection by people in North Lopham who as children enjoyed their open air performances.

In October, 1837, the churchwardens of North Lopham laid out the sum of £2 "for 32 Hymn Books for the use of the Church".[350] Even if we allow each book to be shared between two singers it does not suggest a large congregation from a population numbered at 807 in 1836.[351] In 1851 the Whig Government ordered a count to be made of all persons attending a public place of worship. It is said that the rector of Lopham, the Rev. James Barrow, a strong Tory, refused to comply with the order and that no return exists for South Lopham. A return was made for North Lopham however, perhaps by the parish clerk, Coleby George Cobb, son of the weaver master, Coleby Cobb:

"Church 80, Chapels (2) 173 and 130."[352] The total population of the village recorded by the Census of the same year was 832. North Lopham had become a stronghold of dissent.

CHAPTER SEVENTEEN

Property and Poverty

Not all the farmers of North Lopham were dissenters. In January, 1813, when the earliest surviving churchwardens' accounts begin, the Churchwarden was Samuel Porter, probably the eldest son of Mrs. Mary Porter, and who owned more than 130 acres of arable and pasture in North Lopham.* His colleague, "the Townwarden", from 1814–1821 was Nathaniel Cooke, tenant of the Duke of Norfolk, but, with some 355 acres, the largest farmer in the parish. James Mornement and Christopher Betts, who succeeded for Church and Town in 1822 and 1826 respectively, continued to support the establishment from the largest farms, Betts until the 1870s.

Both large and small farmers in both Lophams were advantaged in 1815 by the "Inclosure Awards", which followed the "Act for Inclosing Lands in North Lopham and South Lopham, in the County of Norfolk", passed by Parliament in 1812. Rationalisation in the holding and the use of land had advanced rapidly in East Anglia during the last twenty-five years, and the enclosing of open fields and commons ended the days when it could be said of one Norfolk village:

"There were 41 houses that had a right of commonage over all the open fields after harvest, which totally prevented the use of turnips and clover . . ."[354]

But the same writer had remarked in 1771 that

* He was bankrupted before 1828 in the hard times following the Napoleonic wars.[353]

"In lieu of rights of commonage, the proprietors of a parish inclosed, generally divide it amongst themselves, and give the poor no indemnity . . ."[355]

It was to be hoped that the Lopham Awards would embody the experience of the more enlightened landlords. Kenninghall, for example, which had undergone enclosure in 1801, was comparable to the Lophams in the large extent of its commons, and had adopted a system of exchanges whereby the allotments the "little commoners" received in lieu of commonage were laid as near as possible to their cottages.[356]

The maps of the 1815 Awards shew that the Commissioners for the Inclosures may have tried to follow the Kenninghall solution but that they had a more difficult problem on their hands. North and South Lopham had always been joint Commoners on Commons which, as Blomefield said, contained "as much land as the whole Towns beside . . . *Great* or *Mill-Common*, *North-Green*, *North-Common* and the *Fenn Common* . . ."[357] With all their powers, the Commissioners could not move the fens, and in a judgement of Solomon they appear to have cut Lopham Fen into three parts, allotting the central section of some 103 acres to the Poor of North Lopham, and the two sections on either side of it, each of some 61 acres, to the Poor of South Lopham. At this date the fens provided not only grazing but fuel, and these allotments involved the regulation of peat-cutting. In South Lopham a charity was established in 1815 to give "poor persons legally settled and resident in the Parish authority to cut peat from the Great and Little Fens".[358]

An entry of June 6th, 1813, in the North Lopham Churchwardens' book shews that they had already laid out ten shillings "To wrighting many notices & sending em about, & many Stakes & painting em for the Fen". On April 16th, 1814, the book shews that there had been "P(ai)d for Ditching the Town Land £10-17-3d". This considerable sum in the money of those days probably represents the cost of the "Division Drain", which is shewn on the Inclosure Map and recorded in the Award as the eastern boundary of "the Allotment of Fen Ground, set out by us for the use of the Poor Persons in North Lopham . . ." According to an entry of December 22nd, 1814, £222-18-7½ was paid to Thomas

Ruddock "For Town Barn on the Allotment",* and on June 15th, 1815, there is an entry of £3-11-8 paid for "Ditching 86 Rod on Town Fence". This refers probably to the fence between the northern edge of the allotment and the private property beyond it. The Award prescribed that such fences "shall consist of Ditches four Feet and an half wide at the Top, and three Feet Deep, perpendicular; and of Banks adjoining to such Ditches and formed of the earth taken from the same; and that the Banks of such Fences shall be planted with White-thorn-layer in a proper manner, and that Half-hurdles or Thorns shall be set on the Summit of such Banks . . ." On May 11th 1815 the book records a payment of sixpence for "1 P(ad) Lock for Fen Gate".

The maps and the written notices of allotment shew drastic changes in the Lopham landscape made by the stopping up or enclosure of footpaths and lanes. Many of these were the tracks by which mediaeval tenants of the manor had made their way to the scattered strips of land they had cultivated after the fashion described in Chapter Eight.

The names of these lost or half-forgotten paths survive in records and some Lopham memories. In South Lopham there was the Broadway,[359] a 'Common way' which lay near Craneholme or Cranesholme Street[360] abutting on the Botesdale Road. There was also Bird's Lane[361] which still joins the Botesdale and Blo' Norton Roads. Eastgate Street[362] and Nethergate Street[363] may be less easy to trace, and Fit Lane[364] had been enclosed before 1792. Fenstrete was named in a will of 1486[365] but where was Goryeway?[366] The 'heyways called N'ordale Lane' and 'Narrowe Nordale'[367] in 1576 may be related to old glebeland called North Dele and North Dale,[368] lying south of the Garboldisham Road. 'An ancient Lane called the Packway'[369] still runs from the Diss road past the old Crown Inn and the Baptist Chapel across Low Common and over Red Bridge into the Botesdale road. Another 'ancient Lane', Hatch Lane,[370] was a tributary to the same route. There was a Watry Lane,[371] a Water Gate[372] and a Sokkiswishwell[373] in South Lopham.

* The same book records that this expensive Town Barn was burnt down in February 1846. Perhaps only the roof was lost for in 1847 no more than £88-18-0 was paid for "Rebuilding Town Barn and Cartin".

North Lopham had a Berry (Bury) Way,[374] a Churchgate Street[375] and a Churchweye[376] in 1596. In the following century there was a Blowland Way[377] running across Blowland, and a Brysettway[378] near Overwell-Meer.[379] Conney Lane[380] was part of the boundary between the two parishes, but Foldway[381] and the modern-sounding Common Market Footway[382] lay to the north. Howard Way[383] and Portway[384] ran across common land but Hall Way[385] was part of 'the King's high Way'. The Race-ground[386] presumably disappeared in the enclosure of North Lopham Common where it stood, but who can say what happened to Stelestock or Pykards Stile,[387] a sixteenth century landmark in the same village? 'Stele' is an old form of stile,[388] and 'stock' can mean a stump.[389] Could it be that this 'stump-stile' was the long-lost Selfgrown Stile, the first of Lopham's Wonders? There is still a "Shop House" in North Lopham, marking perhaps the site of "Shopehowse yarde" in 1593. Sallowbushweye,[390] Calvegate,[391] Stangate[392] and Wickgate[393] all seem to have been fieldpaths in unenclosed North Lopham."

The memory of unenclosed Lopham survived well into the second half of the nineteenth century, and it is recalled in "W.J.G"'s poem, *The Legend of the Oxfoot Stone*, first published in 1893:

"These pastures in the good old days
Were own'd by one and all
No narrow path to mark the ways
Where certain feet should fall.

No thickset hedge, to keep the bounds
From every point 'twas free
For ramblers on their pleasure rounds
Whoever they might be . . ."

The wide green roads into which some of the pathways had grown, before enclosure, were a waste of land in terms of modern farming, but they had long been used by the little commoners and "Poor Persons" as free grazing for their scanty cows, sheep and geese.

These people were altogether in hard case. The allotments granted to little commoners in lieu of commonage rights were

Shop House, North Lopham, *c*. 1925.

too small for such grazing, and the cost of the prescribed fencing, hedging and ditching could be so much beyond their means that they had to sell the land. Cottagers who paid yearly rents for their dwellings were given no compensation for rights they had only enjoyed as tenants. Squatters who had built on wastes or commons but failed to make their titles good were simply evicted.[394]

For such folk in the Lophams, and in many other Norfolk villages, the Inclosure Acts brought not only poverty but a painful loss of liberty and dignity. They must have felt that they were losing their last shreds of independence when they were forced to exchange a relatively free life at the subsistence level for service in a cash economy. There was some resistance. In April, 1815, William Mason, Edmund Chilley, Thomas Brock and Ann Rush were indicted at the Norfolk Assizes for wilfully and maliciously damaging a fence erected after the pronouncement of the Lopham Awards. Such an offence was punishable by death[395] but, according to the *Cambridge Chronicle* of April 7th, 1815:

"MASON addressed the court as champion of the rights of

the poor, whose property he said the commons were. The Judge stated distinctly to the prisoner and to the Jury, however, that the poor had no such right as was asserted by the prisoner."

It was adduced that in this Inclosure some 200 acres had been allotted to the poor of Lopham, presumably with reference to the 225 odd acres of the Lopham Fen allotment. According to the *Norwich Mercury* of April 1st, 1815, Mason,

"his case being more aggravated from the part he took in the transaction was sentenced to *twelve months imprisonment*, and the three other prisoners were sentenced to *three months imprisonment* each."

The North Lopham churchwardens, reflecting perhaps on the need for law and order, paid one shilling and ninepence in April, 1815, for "1 Fancy Pad Lock for Stocks". They had many other responsibilities: the upkeep of S. Andrew's; the small school held apparently inside the church; the roads of North Lopham; the Townhouse or workhouse; the management of charitable endowments in "town lands" and stock investments; and the administration of charities.

Between 1813 and 1837 North Lopham church had to be furnished not only with hymn-books, as the last chapter records, but with a regularly washed "surplus" in good repair; with "pesses" (hassocks); with a new "Violoncello", which cost three guineas; a new parish register; brushes, brooms, "dwiling", and an "Iron Duspan" to clean the floors; a lock for the "Church Door", costing 3/3; new glass for the windows @ £5-15-4; new tiles for the roofs; repeated whitewashings; repairs to the aisle; money for the singers; money and beer for the bellringers on Guy Fawkes Day and other Royal occasions; gravel for the churchyard; nails for the churchyard pales; and two ounces of gunpowder @ 2½d, perhaps for clearing birds from the church.

Churchwardens were answerable to the bishop for the condition and equipment of both church and churchyard on the occasion of his periodical visitations. They could be required also to answer questions put by him regarding the conduct of their clergy, and to bring to the discipline of the ecclesiastical courts certain moral and religious backslidings of the laity.[396] Offenders, as we have seen in Chapter Thirteen, were commonly cited to appear before the archdeacon on his annual visitations. Expenditure on "Visitations" and "Journeys to the General" or "to Generals" continues to be entered throughout the period 1813–1861 covered by the surviving North Lopham "Churchwardens' Book". In the earlier years there are also frequent entries for "Citations", at a shilling a time but with no particulars of the subjects. General visitations of the Deanery of Rockland, to which Lopham belonged, seem to have been held at Attleborough for the most part, though the variety of the not ungenerous travel expenses which the churchwardens allowed themselves shews that they were sometimes called to other places. Many of the citations may have been no more than orders to a churchwarden to appear at a particular time and place.

Then there were the schoolmaster and the schoolmistress to be paid: equal pay, at one guinea each every quarter; new schoolbooks: "6 Testaments, 6 Vyses Spellings, 6 Reading Made Easy", at a total of 19/6, but how many children to each book we cannot say; and a childrens' excursion to Diss, perhaps for Confirmation, which, with man, waggon and horses, cost altogether two pounds.

The upkeep of roads and bridges had been one of the many secular responsibilities superadded by Queen Elizabeth and King James I to the ecclesiastical work of the churchwardens. It was probably under this heading that on June 17th, 1813, the North Lopham wardens entered the sum of ninepence "P(ai)d for mending Harling gate", presumably a folgate or cattle barrier where the Harling Road crossed the parish boundary. "The word "fall-gate" was recorded in 1795 as Norfolk dialect for a gate across a public road.[397] Before the Inclosure Award of 1815 took effect in South Lopham there was a locally-named "Folgate" across the Botesdale road opposite the old Chequers.[398] The Award shews that two other "Falgates" remained in the West Fences of Great and High Commons at the parish boundaries with Blo' Norton. More expensive items of highway maintenance appear, for example in the "Carriage 3 Loads Gravel from Banh(a)m" and "4 do. do. from Keninghall", entered on July 2nd, 1816 @ fifteen and sixteen shillings respectively.

The Townhouse, later known as Workhouse Row and now as Weavers' Cottages, stood presumably on the site of the

Schoolchildren in North Lopham Street, *c*. 1929. "Weavers Cottages", formerly the Townhouse, in the background.

original "Tenement called the Town-House", which was given together with "a Croft of one Acre"[399] by Katharina Turnour, who died about 1498.[400] When it acquired its sometime top-lighting for looms* is unknown, but the churchwardens of the early nineteenth century had to look after its reed thatching and other repairs. There was also clothing to be provided for the inmates, especially the children. The principal workhouse tasks seem to have been hemp dressing, spinning and making clothes. The parish paid for the tools and materials.

The income from Town Lands and stock investments was £185-8-11¼ in 1813–14, and £186-17-11½ in 1814–15. The parish paid the land taxes and poor rates on the land they let to farmers in Lopham and Shelfanger. The Town Lands in Shelfanger amounted to more than fourteen acres, granted in 1412 by the lord of the manor of Vice de Lou (Wolf's Face) in that parish to Richard Bosse and his heirs to be held "by the

* Comparable to the windows surviving in the weaving-shed behind "Linden", farther up the street, and at other places.

payment of a Red Rose, every *Midsummer-Day*". Bosse settled these lands to the use of North Lopham "to repair the Church for ever".[401] By 1815 the red rose had vanished from the transaction but there seem to have been some gaieties when the lease was auctioned at Shelfanger and 18/7 was paid in "Expences at the Public House".[402]

There were other compensations in the churchwardens' life: a degree of patronage in the distribution of jobs for which no tender was asked, and a comfortable conviviality in the settlement of bills. There was the annual tenants' dinner at the Bell, and other affairs were discussed over a drink at the Bull, the King's Head or—perhaps when there was a need for extra-parochial discretion—at the South Lopham White Horse. On one occasion in May 1830, business cordiality seems to have led through genialities to charity. It all began when Churchwarden James Mornement repaid Town Land tenant Charles Dodd £1-8-0 Land Tax and one shilling for the repair of a gate. Accordingly Mr. Mornement "Spent with Mr. Dodd at the Bull" two shillings, but not satisfied with this demonstration of good will he then "Relieved a Man at the Bull having a loss at Sea" with 2/6. But by one of those strange coincidences it seems that another shipwrecked mariner had landed at North Lopham that May afternoon, and the next entry reads: "another the same 2/6d."

A number of seafaring men, one "with a pass by recommendation of Justices", and another with a "petition" were given relief as they passed through North Lopham, perhaps on some cross-country track to the sea. In the present century there were still traditions of a "smugglers' way" leading to the Bell from the coast.[403] Other wandering strangers were given help, once, in May 1827, "by order of the Magistrates" to the tune of five shillings. But the most frequent and substantial charities began of course at home.

There was the 1696 bequest of (Miss) Mary Williamson of Garboldisham, providing the churchwardens with rents from two meadows in her parish "to bind out a poor Child every Year to a Trade, and if there be no poor Child in the Parish, then they are to lay it out, to cloath the poor People of the said Parish".[404] This charity was still functioning as late as 1865 when William Lovack, described as "Deserted by Parents" and "Left in workhouse" was apprenticed either to a ship or to a shop.[405] Although there was never a lack of "poor Children" in nineteenth century North Lopham the churchwardens' book shews that apprenticeships were by no means granted yearly. On the other hand Miss Williamson's apprentices seem to have been well looked after in the supply of clothes, and her alternative of "clothing the poor People" was certainly not neglected, whether or not the money for this purpose came from her bequest.

Some of Norfolk's hard times in the first half of the nineteenth century have their reflections in these North Lopham accounts. 1826 was a year of particular distress in the weaving industry. There were 12,000 unemployed weavers in Norwich and their troubles spread into the countryside. Lopham seems to have escaped, for reasons discussed in the next chapter and perhaps aroused the jealousy of Shelfanger, for on May 27th, 1827, the churchwardens recorded the payment of three guineas for "Repairing the Gates on the Shelfanger Town Land which were broken all to peices by some illdisposed person or persons unknown . . ." The agricultural distress which set in during the 1830s perhaps lies behind a curious entry of October 16th, 1830:

"paid ½ part of 25/- to redeem the Base Violl from G. Kemp . . . 8(s) 4(d)"

Presumably the bass viol, when not in pawn, played alongside the violoncello in the North Lopham church gallery. More earthly signs of need appear in 1832:

"Gave the Widow Atkings for Cloathing for her Family . . . (£)11-0-0 . . . Poor Families towards Cutt(in)g Turf . . . (£)9-17-0"

Presumably this was relief work and they may have been cutting peat for fuel at the Townhouse.

But the book is altogether silent about a report in the *Norfolk Chronicle* of April 3rd, 1830:

". . . Last month a number of persons left North and South Lopham in wagons on their way to embark at Liverpool for the United States of America. Between 100 and 200 persons are emigrating from these parishes, a considerable sum of money having been borrowed on security of the rates to defray the expenses of their passage (about £6.10s per head) and to furnish each family with the clear sum of £5 on their landing at New York."

The only reference to this subject in the North Lopham churchwardens' book is an entry of 1835:

"Expences Conveying Rob(er)t Davy & family to America . . . (£)25-0-0"

South Lopham Charities, as will be seen, did provide occasional assistance for emigrants, but unfortunately their churchwardens' records for this period do not survive and no light has yet been thrown in either parish on the story of borrowing upon the rates. No confirmation of the major exodus of March, 1830, has been forthcoming from Lopham family records. The population figure quoted for North and South Lopham together in 1825 and 1829* was 1562. White's Directory of 1836 gives 1536, a reduction of only 26 inhabitants, and the 1851 Census shews the total to have risen again to 1563. It is at least a coincidence that the Vestry records of Stradbroke, over the border in Suffolk, shew a decision in April, 1830, to fund a scheme for emigration by instalments, and that the first of these, consisting of 42 men, women and children sailed in the "Preston" from Great Yarmouth the same month. The *Norfolk Chronicle* of April 3rd, 1830, which carried the story of the Lopham exodus, also contained an advertisement of this emigrant ship, giving notice that she would sail on April 15th. It is another coincidence that according to the Stradbroke records the cost of a singleman's passage and maintenance in the "Preston" was reckoned at £6-10-0.[406] Why should the alleged host of pilgrims from the Lophams go to the trouble and expense of travelling by wagon to Liverpool when the Yarmouth passage was so close at hand? Newspapers of the early nineteenth century were at least no more reliable than newspapers of today.

Whatever the truth about emigration, there need be no doubt concerning dearth in North Lopham in the 1830s. The Hungry Forties came early to North, and presumably also to South Lopham. From 1837 to 1846 there are continual entries in the churchwardens' book of payments to people "in

* By a local directory and Chambers's *General History of Norfolk*.

great distress"; "in Case of a very havey afflict(ion);" and "in need". At the same time there are increasing amounts of food and clothing dispensed to the poor, with benefit to home production. In 1833 Elizabeth Womack, probably the daughter-in-law of the William Womack mentioned in Chapter Fifteen, received £14-17-0 "for 27 pairs of Sheets for the Poor at 11s a pair". J. Womack, possibly the father of the miller and the baker mentioned in Chapter Thirteen, may have received as much as £114-18-10 for flour and bread for the Poor between 1837 and 1846. Individuals were given a helping hand in various directions. On December 10th, 1835, there is record of a pound "Paid the Lads, Brock and Ruddock to go to Yorkshire", presumably seeking work. J. Cable was given three pounds in 1836 "toward lors(s) 4 Donk(ey)s." In 1844 "Ludbrook Towards buying A Donkey" was given a pound, whereas Jonah Cable, perhaps because of various favours already received, got only half a crown "toward Donkey". But "Larances tire for Ludbrooks weels" cost 2/7¼. Perhaps the happiest occasion for all the hard-up in those difficult days was "A Treat to the Poor on Coronation Festival", which cost the parish £8-4-9. Queen Victoria was not crowned until June, 1838, and the North Lopham peal seems to have been rung at the proper time, but the feasting took place in 1837, the year of her accession.

South Lopham was more richly endowed with charitable bequests than the northern parish, and it is to be hoped that their poor benefited accordingly in those hard times. Their principal asset in Blomefield's day had been

"an Estate of 30 *l.*"(£30) "a Year at *Wortham* in *Suffolk* which was given by one *Purdy* for the Repairs of the Church, and if there were any Overplus, to charitable Uses, such as the Feoffees would apply it to, for the good of the Town, the Houses and the greatest Part of the Farm is Freehold . . ." Blomefield shewed a proper spirit of historical criticism in his comment on this benefactor:

"Tradition has it, that *Purdy* was a *Wortham* Man, and a Leper, and gave his Estate to this Town, because they were willing he should be buried among them, which *Wortham* was not; but this being a common Story in most Places where there are Gifts of this Nature, I look upon it as Tradition only."[407]

By the eighteen-fifties "Lopham Town Farm", as it came to be known, consisted of sixty acres and one rood of land in Wortham and Redgrave, and was let for £80 a year.[408] South Lopham also possessed over fifty-six acres in various parcels within its own parish, including, we may suppose, what remained of some sixteen acres with a Messuage and Barn settled, according to Blomefield, at some unspecified date "to repair and beautify the Church for ever". There were also fourteen acres of freehold estate at Dickleburgh, a provident investment made by the parish in Blomefield's lifetime, and then let for eight pounds a year.[409] By the eighteen-fifties this had become twenty-one pounds.

With all this property to administer it would be surprising if there were no muddle or mismanagement in succeeding years. About 1850 there seems to have been an action in Chancery regarding the charities of South Lopham, wherein the Attorney-General was the "Informant" and the "Defendants" were rector James Barrow and others.[410] The outcome was a "Scheme" prescribed by Chancery in accordance with the Charitable Trusts Act of 1853. After providing for an initial outlay of fifty pounds from rents received up to Michaelmas, 1854, "in or towards repairing the parish church of South Lopham", the appointed trustees were to pay to the churchwardens every year one fourth of the net proceeds of the whole charity estate, and the churchwardens were to apply these funds to the repair of the church "and for such other purposes . . . for which church rates are now legally applicable".

The next and most interesting provision of the Scheme required the trustees to provide

". . . a new school-house, containing a suitable school-room for boys, and a school-room for girls, and a playground and a residence",

according to plans to be approved by the court of chancery, using the balance of the funds now in hand and borrowing, if necessary, on the credit of the charity estate. The trustees were to appoint "a master, or mistress, or both" at salaries of no more than sixty pounds a year for the master and fifty for the mistress. The school was to be open

"to all the children of the inhabitants of the parish of South

Lopham, of the age of five years and upwards, and who are not afflicted with any infectious disorder."

Each child was to pay a weekly sum to the school, not exceeding fourpence a week, and their instruction was to be

"in the principles of the christian religion; reading, writing, arithmetic, sacred and profane history, geography, astronomy, general English literature, and such other branches of education as to the trustees may seem expedient."

While the orientation of the school was firmly directed towards the Church of England, Chancery was not intolerant of other opinions. Religious instruction was to be given by the master or mistress on orthodox lines to all children "whose parents or persons standing in loco parentis shall not object to their receiving such instruction". There was to be regular attendance at South Lopham parish church with master or mistress in charge of each crocodile, "but no child shall be compelled so to attend church whose parents or persons in loco parentis shall express, in writing to the trustees, their objection thereto on conscientious grounds". The sons and daughters of dissenters, it seems, were not to be regarded as "afflicted with any infectious disorder".

The school prescribed by this Scheme was not built until 1863, as Chapter Nineteen records, but in 1861 there was already a school on or near the site of the present building, apparently without residence or play-ground.[411] The conduct of the first school may have followed the lines of the scheme; the second school seems to have developed organised connections with the church and the diocese.

Finally the trustees were instructed to

"apply the annual surplus of the rents and profits of the charity property", after provision for debts and interest, "amongst the most deserving poor of the parish of South Lopham, who have not for the time being been in receipt of parochial relief for six calendar months, in clothes, coals, or apprenticeship fees, but not in money, except as an assistance to emigrate, or in such manner and at such times as they shall think fit."

The poor of North Lopham were also given relief work of various kinds but it is not easy to determine whether one long series of payments between 1813 and 1852 were made with charitable intent or in response to an ancient racket. These were payments for "Birds", "Sparrows", "Sparrows and Hedgehogs", given to Messrs. Pratt (1813–*c.* 1830), Eaton (*c.* 1830–1834), Horne (1835–1840), Porter (1842–1847), and Green (1847–1852), amounting in all to £156-4-5d. In origin these rewards went back to an Act of Parliament of 1566,[412] when Queen Elizabeth assented to the revival of an Act of 1533, designed to reduce the numbers of "rooks, crows and choughs", which did daily breed and increase throughout this realm, and devour wonderful and marvellous great quantity of corn and grain of all kinds in the sowing, as also at the "ripyng and kernelynge" of the same. The same birds were also charged with the marvellous destruction and decay of the covertures of thatched houses, barns, ricks, stacks and suchlike. Queen Elizabeth's parliaments, with no fear of conservationists before their eyes, went further. They prescribed that in every parish the churchwardens, with other parishioners, to the number of six persons, should tax every owner of land or tithes, and that the money so raised should be placed in the hands of "two honest & substantyall persons" in each parish, who should be named the "dystributors of the provision for the dystructyon of noyful" (harmful) "fowells & vermyn". These distributors were authorised to pay a penny to every person who brought to them three crows', choughs', pies', or rooks' heads, and a penny for every six eggs or young birds. The same sum was to be paid for every twelve starlings' heads. Many other kinds of bird were added to the list: martins, various hawks, cormorants and hen harriers at twopence a head; herons and ospreys at fourpence; green woodpeckers, jays, kingfishers and bullfinches at a penny each. Sparrows were at a premium of a penny a dozen by 1612. Among the "noyful" animals, foxes and badgers were prized at twelve-pence a head; polecats, weasels, stoats and wildcats at a penny; hedgehogs and otters at twopence; and a penny was paid for the heads of three rats or twelve mice. Records in various parts of the country show that the Act was obeyed with considerable slaughter during the seventeenth and eighteenth centuries. In Norfolk the parish accounts of Pulham S. Mary the Virgin shew that the killing of sparrows was still being rewarded in 1838 at rates perhaps comparable to those paid at North Lopham.[413] In October, 1830, at the latter village, £7-7-5½ was paid "for 7078 Sparrows", and at Easter of the following year £1-15-5½ was paid for "Mr. Eaton's Bill of 1702 Sparrows." One cannot help wondering how Mr. Eaton—the "Mr." suggests that he was not one of the Poor—authenticated his account. In Pulham there were black stories of the exhumation of sparrows so that they could do duty a second year. Hedgehogs disappear from the North Lopham record after 1827 but it is not known why the villagers had cherished such a vendetta against them. Perhaps there was a lingering belief in the ancient slander that hedgehogs suck the udders of sleeping cows.

CHAPTER EIGHTEEN

One Green Oasis

The troubles of the Norwich weavers, to which the last chapter referred, were a by-product of the Industrial Revolution, and continued to worsen as the construction of power-looms improved and increased throughout the British Isles. In 1839–40 a Parliamentary Commission enquired into the situation of the hand-loom weavers, and James Mitchell (1786?–1844), one of the sub-commissioners, reported on conditions in the East of England. He said that

"The men and women of Norfolk are an exceedingly fine race, probably not surpassed by any in the world . . . The city" (of Norwich) "is in a plentiful, well-cultivated country, producing an abundance of provisions of the best quality. There is a fresh and healthy appearance in the complexions of the working people; of all these advantages the weavers participate and as a body, generally, their physical condition appears better than that of the weavers of London.

There are however effects produced on the human constitution by the operation of weaving which may be partially mitigated, but cannot be totally obviated by any situation whatever . . ."

In blunter words, hand-loom weaving was unhealthy, wherever you plied the trade. Mitchell described the occupational diseases as "dyspepsia and consumption, causing the usual symptoms of debility and indigestion . . ." He added that

"The children inherit the feeble constitution of their parents, and where diseases break out, there is a greater mortality among them. Take them in general, the weavers, after a generation or two, are weaker and smaller in stature than other men . . ."[414]

Like Arthur Young, nearly seventy years before him, Mitchell remarked on the hard drinking among Norwich hand-loom weavers. By all accounts it was a common habit in the craft, and it is hard to believe that it had no direct connection with dust from the warp and the woof. One highly temperate craftsman has gone so far as to admit to the writer that "weaving could be thirsty work", and Mitchell might have painted a truer picture if he had attributed some of the drinking he observed to an occupational craving.

On the economic problem Mitchell came to the same gloomy conclusion as other commissioners that *in general* the only salvation for hand-loom weavers was to find a different kind of employment. But when he reached North Lopham he reported:

"It is delightful at last to have met with one green oasis in the vast desert of discontent in which the inquiries of this Commission have been conducted."[415]

This poetic beginning may have been stimulated by the hospitality with which, as the writer can bear witness, Lopham is accustomed to receive well-meaning, if ignorant, enquirers. Mitchell continued:

"Three of the operatives, Messrs. Christopher Land, Michael Barman, and George Shaw, who were sent for to the inn, on being asked how trade was going on with them, at once replied, 'Pretty middling; we are pretty well off here. We are not as they are in many parts.' These men, like the other weavers of North Lopham, were engaged in making shirting, sheeting, and table-linen. They stated that their net wages, after deducting expenses, were on the average 10/- a week. The hours of labour are twelve hours, out of which two are to be deducted for meals, leaving ten hours in the loom. This length of time they declared to be the utmost that men in general could endure for a permanency. Occasionally, when an order was received, which must be executed by a given day if taken at all, the men, to oblige the master, worked even 16 or 18 hours; but such work rendered it necessary to have corresponding relaxation afterwards.

When inquiry was made of the number of weavers, they went over the names of every one in the place, and they amounted to fifty.* The number of masters was in like manner found to be nine, and one in London. Two of these masters, Messrs. Coleby Cobb and George Shaw,† joined the party and all seemed happy and sociable together."

According to a descendant of one of the ruling families among the weavers of North Lopham in those days, this happy and sociable party was mainly the creation of Coleby Cobb, who saw to it that the sub-commissioner was told no more than the weavers wanted him to know. There were Cobbes in South Lopham in the sixteenth century and Colebys in the eighteenth, but by the 1840s Coleby Cobb was well known as a North Lopham man. He had been a "master" or "Linen Manufacturer" there since the 1820s, and his eight resident competitors named to Mitchell were probably George Shaw, Jeremiah Beales, John Bowen, William Womack, Jonas and Thomas Coates, Henry Jolly, the butcher, and Thomas Gooch, the innkeeper. The master who was away in London must have been the richest of them all, Thomas Buckenham. The subject on which Cobb and his companions seem to have remained totally silent was the existence of another oasis, a mile away, called South Lopham.

At South Lopham there were eight contemporary masters or independent men. First of all there was the other half of the Buckenham business, the John of "T. W. & J." Then there were Friday Bowell, who had married a Buckenham; Ephraim Bowell, John Dove, Henry Huggins, Richard Downing, Thomas Pitcher and John Witting.[416] As for the journeymen weavers, there were probably few less than the number in North Lopham.‡ Coleby Cobb's reasons for the mystification are not clear: hostility towards his southern neighbours was probably the strongest, but no doubt he was also delighted to hoodwink a Scottish official from London.

* In 1851 the number in North Lopham was forty-five.

† In 1851 there were four Shaw households in North Lopham and three of them contained linen weavers. One of these was headed by a George, aged 39. In 1840 perhaps there were two George Shaws, one of them a master and the other a journeyman.

‡ In 1851 the number in South Lopham was twenty-eight.

He succeeded: there is no reference to South Lopham in the Commissioners' published report.

The core of Mitchell's report, nevertheless, probably held good for both the Lophams:

"The material employed is hemp, which is raised in the counties of Norfolk and Suffolk. Some beautiful specimens of very fine thread were shown. It is spun by the hand in the neighbouring county, and the masters expressed regret that they could not get enough of it spun, and that they were obliged to get some from Yorkshire." (This was possibly flaxen yarn from the Leeds spinning mills.) "The bleaching is done in the grass, and all parties entertained a very primitive horror of the employment of chemical compounds." (The source on Coleby Cobb could remember the linen in the 1890s laid out in the sun on the meadow behind the North Lopham "Limes", and the weavers walking to and fro to water it with watering cans.) "The race of weavers is kept up by the fathers teaching their sons. Lads accustomed to the looms, and to winding quills, and handling the yarn from their early youth, readily learn weaving, but a man from field labour would be difficult to teach." (Eleven years later, the 1851 Census return shewed eight cases of the son taking after the father to the loom in North Lopham, one of them apparently a grandson taught by his grandfather; and four cases in South Lopham, one of them where the son was eleven years old and still a "Bobbin Winder". But there were a good many more families where the sons of linen-weaving fathers seem to have preferred agricultural labour.) "The masters said that if they were asked to take an apprentice they would not do it under 20 *l*., and it would be necessary besides to pay 50 *s*. to the journeyman who taught the apprentice, to make up for his loss of time. This expense saves the trade from overwhelming ruinous competition."[417]

After completing his notes on these opinions, James Mitchell seems to have strapped up his memorandum book and emerged from the Bell for a breath of fresh air. He has left us an attractive snapshot of the village street.

"The houses of North Lopham are distributed along both sides of the road, at some distance from each other, and frequently back in the fields. There is a neat and cheerful air about the place, which is pleasing to behold. The men seemed to be in a fine state of health."[418]

We do not know whether he visited any of the weaving sheds or any more of the houses of call. But it does seem that he remembered North Lopham as a place where drink was taken. Perhaps he would never have admitted his oasis to have been a mirage, but in his more sober conclusions, where he attributes "the comfortable condition and content of the weavers of North Lopham" mainly "to the regularity of their employment", he shews no faith in their providence or temperance. If their income were subject to large fluctuations, ranging from sixteen shillings to eight shillings and to nothing at all; "even if under these fluctuations the aggregate amount had been greater than now, the weavers would have been comparatively wretched and would have been full of complaints. At the time when 16 *s*. a week were earned not one halfpenny would have been saved; the 6 *s*. earned above the ordinary present average would have been spent in additional drinking, to the injury of the constitution and deterioration of the moral habits of the weaver."[419]

Mitchell's general conclusion in 1840 was that:

"The weavers in most of the fabrics made of hemp and flax, as compared with the silk-weavers and the Norwich weavers, are in a greatly preferable condition; and they are protected by not being liable to competition from women and children; and their numbers are prevented from rising rapidly beyond the average amount of employment on the occasion of a great demand, by the dificulty of learning the trade."[420]

Although he is still talking in terms of a cottage industry, we can see how the conditions of Lopham linen-weaving had changed since the times described in Chapter Twelve. It was no longer woman's work—though there was still one unmarried woman of twenty-eight, Elizabeth Green of North Lopham, who described herself as "Linen Weaver" in the 1851 Census. It seems also that little hemp was now being dressed and spun in North Lopham. This is borne out by the contemporary churchwardens' accounts which shew no signs of such employment at the Townhouse; but since the weavers admitted that hemp was still being raised in Norfolk as well as Suffolk, it may be that Coleby Cobb and his friends were concealing the production of hempen yarn in the rival village. Profitable corn-growing during the Napoleonic Wars had much reduced the hemplands of southern Norfolk. In 1846 there remained 20 enclosures in North Lopham with the name of "hemplands" and with a total area of 14 acres. The corresponding figures in South Lopham were 43 and 55.[421] But for most of these small pieces the name was no more than commemorative: it was only in South Lopham that the Buckenhams may still have used home-grown hempen yarn. Then although it was still worked by hand and foot the techniques of the loom had become more difficult to master. While there were still some who combined linen manufacture with farming and other occupations, the bigger masters were specialists.

Most of the changes had set in towards the end of the eighteenth century when the surviving predominance of the Lophams in the quantity of hemp produced in the Diss neighbourhood suggests that they had also established a name for quality. If some Lopham man, or better, family were to shew enterprise at this juncture the consequences could be considerable. The Buckenhams rose to the occasion. The family seems to have settled first in South Lopham in the first half of the seventeenth century,[422] but a hundred years later they were in both villages, farming and then linen-weaving as well. The brothers, Thomas of North and William of South Lopham made a joint venture about 1800 by setting up weaving sheds and "trade houses" at their home addresses in each village. Confusingly, but perhaps in demonstration of family unity rising above village rivalry, both addresses were "The Limes".* This was the first step towards factory organisation instead of the old methods—which seem to have continued nevertheless until the very end of Lopham linen—by which yarn was farmed out to individual cottage looms.

This step led to larger and more regular production and a systematic "export drive". From the early nineteenth century Lopham weavers seem to have peddled their linen round the

* "The Limes", South Lopham, came into the tenancy of William Buckenham, Weaver, in 1810. From 1752 until about 1800, and perhaps earlier, it had been an inn, "The Six Bells" on Spicer's Hill at the Cross Ways.[424] It was renamed "The Court" in the late 1940s.

The Court, South Lopham (formerly "The Limes"), behind the Green, the War Memorial and the Jubilee Cedars, 1979.

neighbouring shires from donkeys, then, as we saw in the case of "Ludbrooks weels", from donkey-carts. It is said that a common practice was to weave as a day-labourer until you had saved enough to buy yarn of your own; then to weave your own donkey-load, hawk it, and drink the proceeds. But the Buckenhams were businessmen and went about their marketing with a van, advertising the name, as may be seen in the early nineteenth century picture at the Bridewell Museum in Norwich:

"WILLIAM BUCKENHAM,
LINEN MANUFACTURER
South Lopham Norfolk."

These respectable proceedings helped to build up good connections as far away as London, and it is said that William's son, Thomas, who was born in 1796, was already supplying linen to the Royal Household at the time of Queen Victoria's accession in 1837.

(By courtesy of the Norwich Bridewell Museum).

Export enterprise by the Buckenhams of N. & S. Lopham about 1800. S. Lopham Chequers ("Last Drink in Norfolk") and Folgate to the right. The wild mountains of Suffolk in the background.

On November 29th, 1837 "*Thomas Buckenham*" of N. Lopham was "sworn and admitted" into "the place of Manufacturer of Diaper and Huckaback Table Cloths in ordinary to Her Majesty".[422A]

By this time the Buckenhams were producing a variety of damask table linens, ranging from their well-known diaper pattern napkins to a table-cloth of 1825, measuring eighty-four by sixty-three inches, with a large vase between two peacocks in its centre.[423] Thomas II, if we may call him so, took the third important step for his firm when he met the Victorian demand for florid designs by importing a Jacquard loom from Scotland, together with a Scottish craftsman to teach the Lopham weavers how to use it. This was David Strachan—not James Strachan as he is sometimes mistakenly called—". . . Who Died at North Lopham Nov: 27th 1881 age 66 yr—he was Borne at Dumfermline" (sic) "Employed for thirty years in the works of Mrs. Buckenham Linen Manufacturer and Much Respected.", as a North Lopham contemporary records. Strachan had arrived by the night of March 30th, 1851, when he was a lodger at the house of Samuel Porter, "Carrier & Baker", of North Lopham, and declared himself to be a bachelor of thirty-six, a Hand Loom Weaver of Linen, hailing from Scotland. If Lopham respected Strachan, Strachan liked Lopham. He is said to have married a Lopham girl, Sarah, "Who Died at North Lop:—Aug 18th 1898 age 74 years".[425] According to Percy Beales, who was well acquainted with one of his pupils, Albert Tyler, Strachan also liked Lopham beer.

The vans of T. W. & J. Buckenham were adorned after 1837 with the Royal Warrant of "Linen Manufacturers By Appointment to the Queen", and on December 6th, 1857, their weavers, from both villages, recognised the achievements of Thomas II by the presentation of a silver cup "engraved with emblematic representations of their craft", and inscribed "To Mr. Thos. Buckenham, by a body of linen weavers as a token of faithful respect to their kind master and employer".[426] He died five years later, but not before he had seen the success of his innovations, especially in the supply of custom made patterns to particular clients. His first Jacquard loom was known as the Travellers' Club Loom,[427] because of the design of shamrocks, thistles, acorns and oakleaves, surrounded by the name of the club, which it produced on the great table-cloths made for that institution.

Banqueting cloths were made up to ninety feet long, and

there were carving cloths to protect their grandeur from the careless carver. The designs on Buckenham's Lopham linen ranged from borders of dancing children with garlands of flowers, to horns and bugles; sporting scenes such as cricket, hunting and horse-racing; and innumerable flowers. There was even a carving cloth, designed no doubt for Anglican rather than Dissenting dinners, displaying a crown and sceptre resting upon a bible, surrounded by roses, thistles and shamrocks. Names and arms could be incorporated to order, but one name appeared always in the selvedge of the best: "Thomas Buckenham, Linen Manufacturer to the Queen. North Lopham. Norfolk."

It was to a queen that this linen dynasty now descended, for Thomas III succumbed to the weaver's failing in 1867 only five years after his father's death, and control passed into the hands of his childless widow, Mrs Georgiana Elizabeth Buckenham. Her cousin by marriage, Thomas Buckenham of South Lopham, was but a secondary figure in the firm, and by 1900 described himself only as "Farmer and landowner".[428] He died at the age of eighty in 1907, earning from a neighbour the unbusinesslike, if companionable, epitaph:

"The more untrueths you told him the bether he loved you."

Georgiana was thirty-eight when she succeeded her husband, and she reigned for thirty-eight years with the help of her two sisters, Elizabeth Susannah and Louisa Ellen Bale. They divided their time between "The Limes" at North Lopham and the house and office which Thomas II had established at 65, Berners Street, London. In his time Thomas Buckenham had driven his own wares to Windsor Castle and Buckingham Palace in his proudly emblazoned van. In Georgiana's time, according to Ellen Bale, Ladies of the Bedchamber would call at 65, Berners Street—"A house, my dear. Not a shop. You do understand that."—and examine samples of linen by courtesy of their hostess.[429]

It should be remembered that Lopham linen had as great a name for fine sheets and underclothes as ever it had for the splendours of damask. Royal sheets, for example, woven by the Buckenhams on custom-built wide looms so that each sheet could be of one piece, were made from exceptionally fine yarn, in the tradition, if not the reality, of home-grown and homespun Lopham hemp. It is said that the weavers' wives used to compete for the waste from these sheets to make into baby-clothes.

With such a reputation it is not surprising that the name of Lopham linen should be exploited in sales to the retailers. In the 1890s, for example, John Murton of North Lopham, who had turned from linen manufacture to farming, continued to stock linen for sale. Some he had bought from the Buckenhams but some from "elsewhere". By the 1900s, first at Whitebread Farm and then at Chestnut Tree Farm, North Lopham, his linen rooms were said to be piled high with Irish linen.[430] By this date the demand for Buckenham products much exceeded the supply and Murton may have profited from the shortage of "genuine linen from Lopham". But, if so, was his ruse a new one? An entry of May 13th, 1816, in the North Lopham churchwardens' book records the payment of £2-16-4 for thirteen yards of "Super Irish" @ 4/4 the yard. A purchase of 1½ yards of the same material at the same price is recorded on October 7th, 1817. It is difficult to identify this material except as Irish linen, and when Newcastle imports coals there must be a peculiar reason for it. Is it not probable that this linen was bought to be made up at the Townhouse into sheets and pillow-cases, or something of that kind, and that it was afterwards made to pass, for whatever reason, as genuine Lopham Linen?

There is nothing to suggest, however, that the Buckenhams ever adulterated their wares, and the business continued to flourish under Georgiana between 1867 and the early 1880s. The reasons for its decline are discussed in Chapter Twenty-One. Figures survive of the numbers of parcelled consignments dispatched by the Buckenhams from their Lopham warehouses between 1871 and 1893.[431] These rose from 106 between August and December, 1871, to a total of 243 in 1883. The parcels seem to have been special orders of which more details are given below. It appears that between 1875 and 1886 vans and wagons also made general retail tours about the country, their journeys sometimes lasting three or four months. A journey might have a particular destination, such as Buckingham Palace every six months, but surplus goods would be sold on the way home, and fresh orders collected. The Buckenham vans kept up the Lopham pedlar tradition, but with more than donkeypower. The announcement of a society engagement in the East Midlands might be followed, long before the congratulations were over, by a vanload of Lopham trousseau attractions, brought to the doorstep of the future bride.[432] These travelling linen shops sometimes spent two or three days in towns like East Dereham where they were certain of a welcome. They also visited much smaller places:

"An old friend of ours who lived in Bedfordshire as a lad" (used to talk) "of the Lopham carts going through that county hawking Lopham linen. The hawkers were well known and highly respected, and were welcome visitors to the remote villages in those days."[433]

Stourbridge or Sturbitch Fair, the great annual market, which used to be held for a fortnight every September in a field near Cambridge, was another place where the "great stalls" (of) "the Lopham manufacturers" were long remembered.

Apart from the campaigns of the linen vans, selective records remain of the special orders dispatched to customers by "luggage train", "bag train", and "passenger train" between 1871 and 1875 by the Buckenhams.[434] In the surviving list it was only Arthur James, Esq., of Eton College, who required his "Truss" of linen to be sent to him by passenger train; H.R.H. Princess Mary of Teck, at Kensington Palace, was content with the luggage train, and from the quantity of her custom it is not surprising that her daughter, Princess May, afterwards Queen Mary, continued to buy Lopham linen up to the beginning of the first World War. Other distinguished customers in 1872 were the Earl of Leicester at Holkham and the Marchioness of Lothian at Blickling. The Imperial Russian Embassy had an order in 1873, and the Duke of Norfolk was supplied in 1874. The entries for 1875 shew an interesting variety. The Earl Cadogan, one of the firm's oldest customers, received a parcel, and the Commissioners for Bath and Wash Houses in the London parish of S. Giles received "3 Trusses", presumably of towelling. J. J. Colman, Esq., of Carrow Hall; Magdalene College, Cambridge; Eton and Harrow; St. James's Palace; and the Royal School of Needlework were also supplied; but there is an ominous sign in the dispatch of parcels to bleaching works in Yorkshire and Nottinghamshire. Were the Buckenhams departing from Lopham standards and trying a chemical bleach?

In 1875 there were still other linen manufacturers besides the Buckenhams in North and South Lopham. Coleby Cobb of the Green Oasis had died before 1851,[435] and his son, Coleby George Cobb, although he was trained as a weaver, gave up the business. He declared himself in that year to be "Schoolmaster & Cl(er)k", and in later years became a baker. But Robert Beales still carried on an old family concern, and John Womack junior combined theirs with farming. Thomas Chamberlain was a small farmer who had taken up linen manufacture, and Christopher Land was a weaver turned master. Finally there was Edward Murton, the grandfather of John whom we have seen diverting *sub rosa* from linen manufacture to the land. In South Lopham the Bowells and the Doves were still in business. Thanks to the reputation which the Buckenhams had won for Lopham linen there was probably more than enough for all these smaller firms to do. But they were faced with an increasing shortage of skilled labour as the old weavers died, leaving hardly a son prepared to work in the loom.

CHAPTER NINETEEN

Ructions

Discord between the Lophams was of ancient standing. The territorial dispute which flared up in the early seventeenth century arose from an older division of kin. There had been occasional intermarriages between the intercommoners, but no more, apparently, than there had been with such neighbours as Kenninghall, Garboldisham, Blo' Norton and Bressingham. Sometimes an intermarriage would result in the removal of a North Lopham family to the South village, or vice-versa; and very occasionally families like the Womacks or the Buckenhams developed branches in both parishes. But in general the records exhibit two separate groups of kith and kin. Between 1558 and 1601, for example, some of the most common surnames in one village are virtually unrepresented in the other: Bylnye, Peerse, Reade and Rush in South Lopham; Bowell, Mallowes, Murriell and Ruddock in North Lopham.[436] Turning to more recent times, the Census of 1851 shews that out of a population of 731 in South Lopham only 26 originated from North Lopham; and that in North Lopham's population of 832 only 20 originated from South Lopham.

After the disappearance of intercommonage in 1815 there were only two obvious links between the two villages: the high road and the rector. The former fared better than the latter. The rector's position had been prejudiced during the interregnum between Borlase Wingfield (1760–68) and Richard Littlehales (1801–22), when the curate, John Smith, seems to have surrendered North Lopham to the dissenters. Since by all accounts Methodism had a particular welcome from the weavers it may be that South Lopham also lost churchgoers to the North Lopham chapel.

Trouble between North Lopham and the rector, on whatever grounds, was not a new phenomenon. Some six hundred years before, in July 1225. Nicholas, who seems to be the first Lopham rector on record, went to law as "parson of Luppeham church" against Robert de Northluppeham about the rights to a house and two acres of land in North Lopham.[436A]

It could have been the right-wing rector James Barrow (1824–61) who first identified the weavers with dangers to the Establishment. Certainly by the time his successor had been installed his office was not loved among the looms. The new rector, John Fitzherbert Bateman (1861–95), was a man of property. He was even able to buy the advowson of his own living (sold by the eighth Howard duke of Norfolk between 1713 and 1732),[437] on condition that he, a sometime Fellow of S. John's College, Cambridge, his heirs and successors, would continue to present Fellows of the same college to the living. It is a misfortune of the well-to-do that they are so often suspected of trying to do better for themselves, and the weavers' suspicions were exhibited in verses called "The Parson's Idol", formerly pasted on the loom of "Coby" Cobb, the weaver-clerk-schoolmaster-baker, which is now in the Thetford Museum:

"Money's my creed, and I'll not pray without it,
My heaven is closéd 'gainst all those that doubt it,
For this is the essence of parson's religion,
Come reg'lar to church and be pluck'd like a pigeon.
Fools sometimes ask what I do with this money.
They might just as well ask what bees do with honey.
I answer them all with a wink and a nod:
I keep three thirds myself and give praises to God.
In the cool silent earth I may soon be laid low,
To sleep with the blest that went long ago;
I shall slumber in peace till the great resurrection,
Then be first on my legs to make a collection . . ."[438]

This particular abuse, although much quoted, was not home-made, whereas "The life of a tricky Parson"[439] seems to have been the work of the North Lopham "Laureate", one of the millers. Trouble over money matters may have first come to a head in 1870–71 when, according to Bateman, there were "stormy days . . . connected with the reform of" (the) "Church and Town Lands Charities".[440] Chapter Seventeen has described the necessary reform of the South Lopham Charities decreed in 1853.

The Charity Commission, which had been set up in 1853 after the discovery of much local mismanagement, was empowered by 1870 to make orders for the regulation of local charities worth more than fifty pounds a year whenever the local trustees applied in writing for such orders. As we have seen, the North Lopham Churchwardens' Book records many charitable grants but does not identify the particular funds from which they were drawn. The rector, with the support of his two churchwardens from North and South Lopham, may have been justified in taking the initiative in January, 1870, of requesting orders from the Commission, if it was only to disentangle the purposes of the various bequests made to North Lopham over the last five hundred years. The "Scheme for the Management of the Charity Estates" of North Lopham, published by the Board of the Charity Commission on July 29th, 1870, lumped together Mary Williamson's bequest and other Town Lands, including the North Lopham Poor's Fen allotment, for general charitable purposes, but explicitly maintained the provision for poor 'prentices founded by Miss Williamson. The Red Rose lands of Shelfanger, however, were separately described as the "Church Lands Charity", and were reserved for "the maintenance and repair of the fabric of the Parish Church of North Lopham, inclusive of the Tower and" (properly "or") "Steeple, but exclusive of the Chancel" (which was the rector's customary responsibility). The fourteen-odd acres at Shelfanger at this time brought in only £23 a year, but they were good agricultural land and in those sectarian days it seems probable that some North Lopham chapelgoers objected to the allocation of so much of their "Charity Estates" to the minority Church of England. From the doggerel before the last paragraph we may guess what the weavers said.

Then something went wrong. In 1878 the Charity Commissioners "sent down their opinion" that "the past accumulations of Income of these Charities should be divided among the Church and the Poors' branches of the Charities in the same proportion as the annual income".[441] It followed that £34 out of a sum of £188 delivered in 1877 to William Gill, James Mornement's successor as Churchwarden, ought to have gone to the church. It also transpired that the Fen Account Book had been "lost". On January 27th, 1879, there was a public enquiry into the Charities of North Lopham, at which Bateman spoke on the "desireableness of always keeping a separate account of the Church Lands' Income and the Poors' Lands' Income". William Gill retired from his Churchwardenship and Christopher Betts, senior, the Townwarden, now in his eighty-ninth year, "who had behaved very handsomely in the matter", was "allowed by the Charity Commissioners to compromise his share in the responsibility for the Fen Accounts by paying down £80 for the benefit of the poor of the parish".[442]

The more serious storm of 1871 again had sectarian echoes. The early history of education in the Lophams is obscure but it seems safe to assume that at the beginning of the nineteenth century both villages had small schools attached to their churches, teaching the three Rs, as the North Lopham churchwardens' accounts suggest. The quarterly payments to a schoolmaster and a schoolmistress vanish from those accounts after January, 1822, but it is possible that lessons continued in the church buildings for some time. Meanwhile, in 1835, the Wesleyans started a daily school at North Lopham, and it was still "supported by this connexion" in 1875, according to the County Directory. The Census of 1851 shews that Alex Chamberlain of North Lopham had an unmarried daughter of twenty-seven, Mary, who was employed as "Teacher Church Day School"; and another of twenty-four, Hannah, employed as "Teacher Wesleyan Day School". Outside this tolerant household the only teacher enumerated in North Lopham was 'Coby' Cobb, "Schoolmaster & Cl(er)k", who as Parish Clerk presumably taught the boys of the "Church Day School", like his opposite number, Frederick Seakins/Seakens at South Lopham. From contemporaries we learn that Mary Chamberlain, "Who Died at North Lop. March 13th 1893 age 70 yrs", was "A Conscientious and faithful teacher of the Girls School, heald from 1.850 to the year 1.862 In the Old Vestry and from the year 1.862 to the year 1.869 In a Cottage hired by the present Rector JFB. Much loved By Her Pupils."

A plan of North Lopham Church before restoration shews the "Old Vestry" immediately to the west of the south door. Perhaps the boys were once segregated in the church porch under Coby Cobb, at least until he fell foul of Parson Bateman or was disqualified for lack of a teacher's certificate. Another cottage, or "parochial school", may have been hired for the boys of North Lopham before the School Board took over the Wesleyan Day School in 1876. In 1908 a porch-front and some remarkable "dormer windows" were incorporated in the early 17th century building then known as Noddle Farm, North Lopham and now named Dairy Farm. These additions were brought from "North Lopham School",[443] and the windows, to judge from their height, may have been designed for a schoolhouse. Possibly they came from a demolished building, but since the present school was extensively altered in 1907–8 the additions to Dairy Farm may have been parts of the original "Royal Albert National School", erected in 1871 and discussed below.

There were altogether one hundred and twenty-seven children of North Lopham, several of them infants, who were described as "Scholars" in the 1851 Census. Some may have gone to dame-schools or private schools but most would have attended the Wesleyan or the Church school. Frederick Seakens, a widower of thirty-seven, and Charlotte Kerridge, a spinster of fifty-nine, were the Master and Mistress at South Lopham Church day school, possibly in the first schoolhouse on the site of the present building. School attendance seems to have been low at South Lopham, where only sixty children were enumerated as "Scholars", some of whom may have attended the Wesleyan Day School at North Lopham.

By the middle of the nineteenth century central government had begun to promote a national system of elementary education. In 1853 "capitation grants" were introduced by the "Committee of Council on Education", the ancestor of the present Department of Education and Science, giving state aid *per capita* to village schools, subject to certain conditions. The most important of these were that each school should have a certificated teacher and that three fourths of the school-children passed a set examination.

Perhaps in order to satisfy these conditions the Wesleyan Day School of North Lopham seems to have been reconstituted in January, 1862, under a "provisionally" certificated teacher, John Fletcher. Fletcher, who appears to have qualified in 1861 at the Normal Training School for Wesleyan day school teachers, did not start a Log Book until 1864, but in December of that year he refers to a previous visit or visits by "her Majesty's Inspector".[444]

It was the strictly enforced requirement of inspection before the issue of "capitation grants" which brought to North Lopham one of England's most famous nineteenth century poets. John Fletcher's log-entries are brief and impersonal: they do not shew whether he knew whom he expected to receive in the person of "M. Arnold Esq Her M. I.". When he arrived in North Lopham Street at a quarter past ten on May Day morning, 1867, Matthew Arnold was ending ten years as Professor of Poetry at the University of Oxford. But what mattered most to him and John Fletcher at the moment was that Arnold was a dedicated inspector of schools of sixteen years' standing. From his autograph annotations in the log, and from subsequent entries, it may be seen that Inspector Arnold did not approve of a Chief Teacher who was only "provisionally" certificated. In his report, addressed to John W. Bobby, the school treasurer and a leader of Wesleyan society in North Lopham, by the secretary to the Lords of the Council, it was intimated that their lordships expected John Fletcher to take another examination.

He did so and was told in March, 1868 that he had passed. But Matthew Arnold, after his second and last visit to the school in May of the same year, still had reservations:

"The high price of food has injuriously affected the Attendance and consequently the instruction in this School during the past year"—

Had Poet Arnold observed in North Lopham as in *East London*

> "(how) the pale weaver, through his windows seen
> in Spitalfields, look'd thrice dispirited"?

"—the Rate of failure is 10 per cent higher than last year, the principal weakness being in Arithmetic. The school is very fairly disciplined—My Lords will look for general improvement in the attainments next year as a condition of the Grant then claimed being paid without reduction . . . With so high a Rate of failure they are unable to order the master's certificate to be issued . . ."

Their lordships did not look in vain. Spurred by whatever feelings towards Matthew Arnold, John Fletcher began a girls' and infants' school before the end of the year and raised his evening school attendance to eighteen by March 1869. A different H.M.I., C. Alderson, Esq., reported next May that

"The School presented for Examination have passed with Credit . . ." and in September Fletcher received his "Parchment Certificate" of "Degree 4—Upper Grade".

No Log Books for the other North Lopham school appear to survive before 1896. South Lopham school, rebuilt in 1863 according to Chancery requirements and at a cost of some £800, seems to have been ignored by Matthew Arnold but was regularly visited by other H.M.I.s, by diocesan inspectors and most of all by the recently appointed rector and patron of the living, John Fitzherbert Bateman. The site for "a School and residence" was presented by Mrs. Frances Bridgman, the widow of squire Edward Bridgman of Coney Weston in Suffolk. He had been one of the "Defendants" joined with rector James Barrow in the Chancery action of 1853, presumably because a small part of his wife's large Lopham inheritance* from her father, Thomas Fox, also of Coney Weston Esquire, was already occupied by the first school on the site. This site appears to be identical with a small field belonging to "Mr. Thomas Fox" and marked as "1st Meadow" on the 1815 map of the South Lopham Inclosure Award.

On November 15th, 1870, the North Lopham overseers† had reported to the Education department that, in an estimated population of 750, 150 were "of the class whose chil-

* In 1864 Mrs. Frances Bridgman paid the Duke of Norfolk's trustees two thousand pounds for the enfranchisement of her copyhold lands in the manor of Lopham.[446]

† The overseers at this date were the churchwardens, but after the Local Government Act of 1894 they were appointed by the parish council.

dren would attend an elementary school". There were 184 ratepayers. At the same time they reported that there were two schools in operation (the Board school and the Wesleyan day school) and one "being supplied" (the Royal Albert National School).[445] When the new building was boycotted by the villagers the North Lopham School Board must have continued to use their old premises until, presumably, they were condemned by H.M.Is. The Wesleyan day school log comes to an abrupt end on June 15th, 1874, but it was not until January 3rd, 1876, that the Chapel Trustees formally agreed to let their school premises as an "elementary school" for all North Lopham. It would be a tight fit. In 1869, when the total number of children "on the Books" had been 87, John Fletcher had estimated that there was room for another 30. The dimensions of the "Principal Room" were then 52′ × 16′ and 15′ high, and of the "Class Room" 32′ × 11′ × 9′.

The crying needs of North Lopham for a modern boys' and girls' school to replace the old "Church Day School" accommodation seem to have found their first response in the heart of Mrs. Buckenham, the "beloved employer" of so many Lopham weavers. Not long after her husband's death in 1867 she became the principal fund-raiser for the "North Lopham Royal Albert Memorial School", a name authorised in a letter from the Queen herself.[447] It was to be more than a school, for it was to embrace a reading and recreation room for the weavers, a refuge from their otherwise alcoholic evenings. She collected from "people who honoured the memory of Good Prince Albert and who were interested in Lopham and its linen manufacturers". She presented the site for the the building and the presentation shewed a change of name. The cover of a brass-bound purple-velvet-lined box, which still survives, is inlaid with a plate engraved:

NORTH LOPHAM
DEED OF GIFT
OF THE SITE OF
The Royal Albert National School.
1870.

But the key and the original contents are missing. The ebony-framed glass inner lid now reveals a document inscribed:

"Mrs. F. Bridgman to the Trustees of Lopham Charity/ Deed of Gift of site for School &c in South Lopham. Dated 25th Novr. 1862." Presumably Mrs. Buckenham handed over the box and its key when she placed the subscriptions, together with a hundred pounds of her own, in the hands of the Royal Albert National School trustees. These were *ex officio* the rectors of Lopham and Quidenham. We do not know how much the latter, the Honourable and Reverend E. G. Keppel contributed or what practical interest he took in the project, but the former, who was also a trustee of the "Lopham Charity", maintained his leadership in the parish with a subscription of one hundred *and five* pounds. The school and master's residence were built in 1871 at a cost of £700.

But there was no Reading Room. According to a descendant of another weaving family, the Buckenhams' nearest rivals and successors, Bateman had foiled Georgiana's plans "by a piece of ecclesiastical trickery the shame of which and the resulting bitterness" remained until a common village hall was built between the two parishes in 1931.[448] He alleged in 1960 that

"The parson"(was)"horrified at the greater independence it" (the Buckenham deed of gift?) "gave to the weavers—he could see no alternative but that they should come to church where he had them under his control. So to make sure on the point of scrapping the Reading Room addition he had the lawyer draw up a document to this effect. *Without reading it* Mrs. Buckenham, assured by Bateman that her signature was needed to the document & it was all in order just signed it—& away went the Reading Room. The village folk, tho' a school was badly needed, boycotted the school entirely & it stood empty for years. Later on it was taken over by the Educational authorities & its status altered & so it has been under Norwich Educational Committee ever since . . ."[449]

This story of a signature induced on false pretences reads like part of a serial in a Victorian magazine. Unlikely though it may sound, however, the next instalment was certainly true, and the Albert Rooms, as they came to be known, were not occupied as a school until 1899. But the requirements of the Elementary Education Act of 1870 are unlikely to have been met by the existing church school, and in 1876, when another act made such education compulsory, the local School Board had to hire the Wesleyan Day School. The minutes of the Wesleyan Chapel Trustees, one of whom was 'Coby' Cobb, shew no opposition to this development and betray nothing of the partisan feelings which must have raged in North Lopham, unless it be in the use of the word "our":

"(23rd December 1875) The matter of opening the School Room on a Lease for a Term of Years to a Committee for a Public Elementary School is under consideration subject to the approval of the Chapel Committee.

(3rd January 1876) . . . carried unanimously that the School Room Forms and Desks and play Ground be let to the Committee for the purpose of our Elementary School at a Nominal Rent of Four Pounds per Annum. The Committee to make the necessary alterations.

The Trustees reserve the Right to Use the Room for the Sabbeth School on the Lords day."[450]

The nominal rent was raised to £17-6-0 in the lease of 1878–88, reduced to £12-0-0 in 1888–98, and put up to £24-0-0 for the last year of the Committee's tenancy. Apart from this tribute money, the sight of little Anglicans in compulsory company with little Dissenters must have been an unhappy prospect for the rector. Perhaps it was indirect pressure from the rectory which led to a resolution by the trustees of the chapel in 1887 that "the stone on top of School Room engraved Wesleyan day School be filled in with Cement".[451]* Meanwhile the building was bursting with children and in 1898 the School Board were ordered by government to find new accommodation.[452] Even at that late stage, twenty-seven years after the old rector's supposed chicanery, and with a new rector (presented by the old one) in the chair, a motion to adapt and take over the Albert Rooms for a new school was defeated in a poll of 606 by 16 votes. The new rector, Alfred Caldecott, remarked on the scandal in his Parish Magazine.

"In these days of agricultural depression we shall see

* This inscription is visible to-day.

therefore in our village no less than three Schoolrooms: two of them standing empty all week-days, and the other a brand-new one,* with the rate collector calling quarterly for heavy extra rates for 20 or 30 years: such, we regret to think, is the mutual confidence and regard of English people for one another at the close of Century XIX.

On Sunday, April 24th, Second Sunday after Easter, Temperance Sermons were preached at both Churches by request of the Bishop."[453]

Sermons on the same subject must have been preached many times by the old rector, and no doubt by the ministers at both the Wesleyan and Primitive Methodist chapels. The weavers took exception to Bateman's denunciations. He not only referred to liquor in the looms; he was said to have named names from the pulpit. The weavers had their own ways of expressing condemnation. Round the corner from "the Parson's Idol" on Coby Cobb's† loom there is said to have been pasted a newspaper picture of a famous hangman.[454] One dark night, when they knew their victim would be late to bed, Bateman bumped his head against his own effigy, hanging inside the Rectory Gate.[455]

Since this history has to record such demonstrations of feeling against Bateman it is only just to add that one of the village memorialists remembered him as "a very Kind Man". It seems possible moreover that he had that saving English grace, a sense of humour. *The Diss Express and Norfolk & Suffolk Journal* of May 27th, 1892, reported that

"As a small thank offering for many mercies during thirty years' incumbency, the Rev. J. F. Bateman, R. D., has presented Ellacombe's chiming apparatus to South Lopham Church." (North Lopham Church had been give one some twenty years before.) ". .. On Sunday last the parishioners were made pleased at hearing the tones of their six beautiful

* Presumably he meant that the old Wesleyan Day School and the Albert Rooms would remain empty all the week and that an expensive "brand-new" school would have to be built as a result of the poll.

† Coleby George Cobb died on February 28th, 1893, at the age of 79. P. S. BEALES in describing some of the newspaper cuttings on this ancestral loom was careful to say that the "portrait of a famous hangman" was "not necessarily put there by" C. G. Cobb.

bells again, after their long silence *i.e.* since 14th December, 1887, when the tenor bell broke down while being rung in peal by the curate, Rev. R. W. Pitt. The bell was providentially caught in its fall by two cross beams, or must have killed him on the spot."

The programme of hymn-tunes was no doubt prescribed by Bateman, the benefactor, and the *Diss Express* noted that

"After service on Sunday, Mr. Pitt chimed a well-known tune on the bells (without thinking probably of the fitness of the words suggested) 'Oft in danger, oft in woe, onward Christian, onward go' . . ."

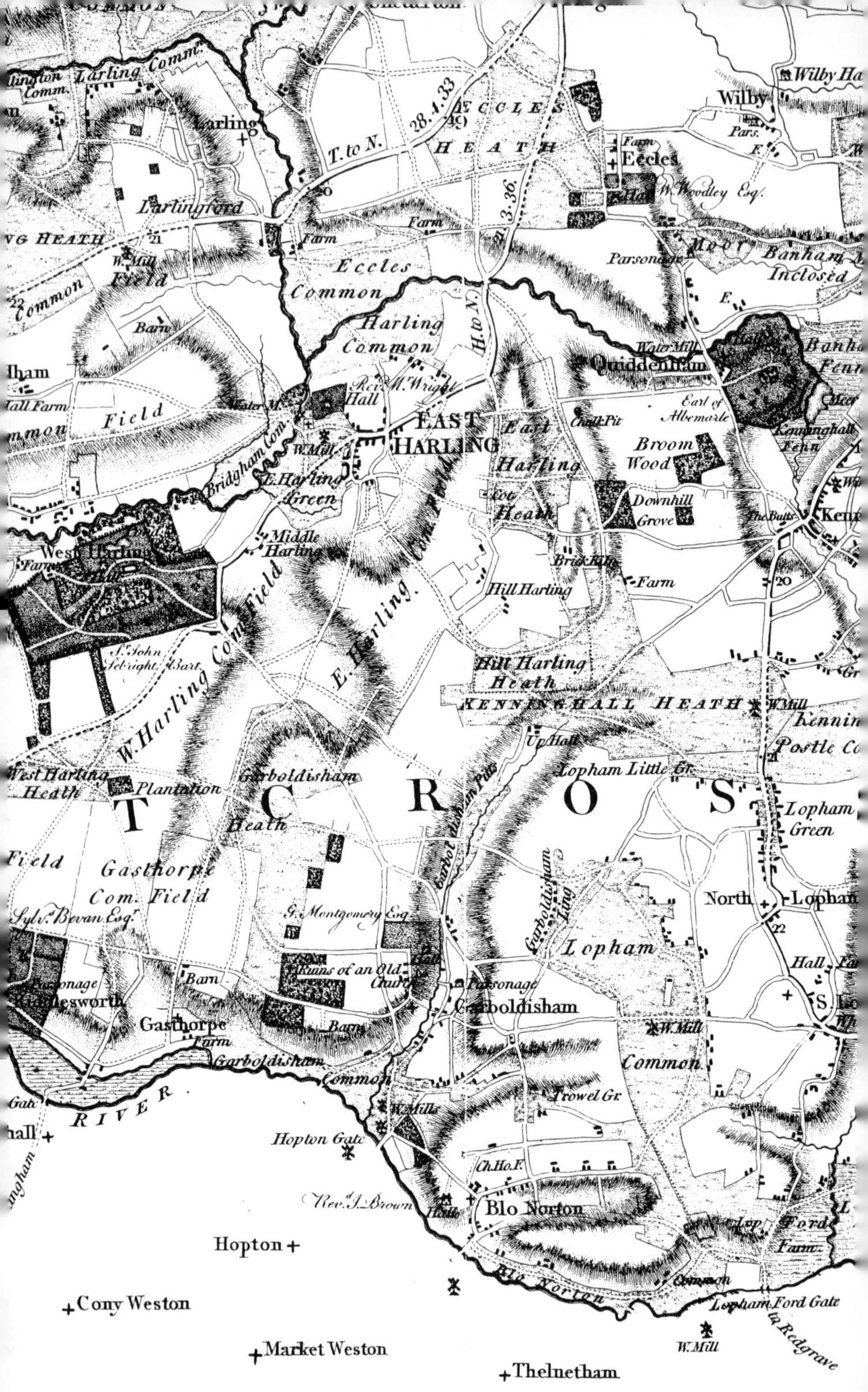
Larling Comm.
Larling
Larlingford
Common
Field
Barn
Field
Water M.
W. Mill
Bridgham Com.
T. to N.
28.4.33
Eccles
Heath
Farm
Farm
Eccles
Common
Harling
Common
H. to N.
31.3.36
Rev. Mr. Wright
Hall
East Harling
E. Harling Green
Middle Harling
West Harling
Hall
St. John Sebright Bart.
W. Harling Com. Field
E. Harling Com. Field
Wilby
Wilby Hall
Pars.
Eccles
Farm
Hall
W. Woodley Esq.
Parsonage
Moor
Banham
Inclosed
Water Mill
Quiddenham
Earl of Albemarle
Chalk Pit
Broom Wood
East Harling
Lot Heath
Downhill Grove
Kenninghall Fenn
The Butts
Brick Kiln
Farm
Hill Harling
Hill Harling Heath
Kenninghall Heath
W. Mill
Postle Co
Up Hall
Lopham Little Gr.
Lopham Green
West Harling Heath
Plantation
Garboldisham Heath
T C R O S S
Field
Gasthorpe Com. Field
Sylv. Bevan Esq.
G. Montgomery Esq.
Ruins of an Old Church
Hall
Parsonage
Garboldisham
Garboldisham Pits
Garboldisham Ling
Lopham
North Lopham
Hall
Parsonage
Barn
Gasthorpe
Farm
Barn
Garboldisham Common
W. Mill
Common
Trowel Gr.
W. Mills
River
Hopton Gate
Rev. J. Brown
Hall
Ch. Ho. F.
Blo Norton
Ford Farm
Blo Norton Common
Common
Lopham Ford Gate
W. Mill
to Redgrave
Hopton
Cony Weston
Market Weston
Thelnetham

Miss Head
NEW BUCKENHAM
Roman Camp
NEW BUCKENHAM COMMON
New Buildings F.
The Ashes
Farm
Tibbenham
Old Hall
WARREN
Furze Common
Street
Haugh F.
The Thicket
Banham
Heath
Wind M.
Banham
Tibbenham Green
Tibbenham
Pristow Green
New Barn
Barns
New Farm
lately Inclos'd
Brick Kiln
The Old Oak
Winfarthing Lodge F.
Birch Wood
Winfarthing Pound
Barn
Farm
Parsonage
Winfarthing
Heywood Hall
Kenninghall Place
Chapmans Entry
FERSFIELD COMMON
Fersfield Lodge
Boyland Hall
Boyland Common
Farm
D
Shelfanger
HEYWOOD
Barn
Burston Hall Fa.
Burston
Shelfanger Hall
Fersfield
Hall Farm
W. Mill
Brissingham Common
Brick Kiln
Darrow Wood
Fersfield Green
Wilney Green
Briss.m Wood
Farm
Roydon Green
Parsonage Green
Brissingham
Hall
Brewers Green
Roydon
Walcot Gr.
Walcot Green
DISS
BRISSINGHAM FENN
WAVENEY RIVER
Roydon Fenn
Wind Mill
Cock St.
Diss Com.
Bridge
from Thelnetham
Wortham
edgrave
Holt Esq.
Palgrave
Stuston

PART TWO:

References

172. H. B. WALTERS: op. cit., p. 218.
173. BLOMEFIELD, op. cit., p. 154.
174. NRO PD 120/22.
175. WALTERS, op. cit.
176. J. G. NICHOLS ed. *Queen Jane and Queen Mary*, CAMDEN SOCIETY, vol. XLVIII, 1850, p. 106.
177. NRO NCC Wills 46, 47 SPYLTYMBER.
178. Do. 34–35 GERMEN
179. Do. 46 CAWSTON.
180. Do. 297 HUSTINGES.
181. Do. 137 JERVES.
182. Do. 354 VESYE.
183. Do. 182 COWLLES.
184. Do. 319 WOODCOCKE.
185. Do. 75 FLACK.
186. Do. 142–44 PUNTYNG.
187. Do. 209 COLMAN.
188. Do. 43 GOLDINGHAM.
189. John VENN: *Biographical History of Gonville & Caius College*, Cambridge 1897, vol. i., p. 43.
190. J. W. FORTESCUE: *A History of the British Army*, London 1910, vol. i., p. 12.
191. MASON, op. cit., p. 110.
192. NRO NCC Wills 77 ROWLAND.
193. BL Add. Roll 66805.
194. See 5 above.
195. NRO NCC Wills 6 ADAMS.
196. NRO Norfolk Archdeaconry Wills (NAW) 115 BOCKEING.
197. Do. 65 BOCKEING.
198. NRO NCC Wills 117 FORCE/Original Wills (O.W.) 50.
199. NRO NCC Wills (Henry DALTON) 75 FLACK.
200. Thos. TUSSER: *Five Hundred Points of Good Husbandry &c*, ed. by Wm. MAVOR, London 1812, p. 153.

201. OED, sub art. "Carl hemp".
202. NRO NCC Wills 252 CORANT.
203. Do. (Incorrectly indexed as "HOLBARDE") 232 MARTEN.
204. TUSSER, op. cit., p. 168.
205. Ibid., p. 172.
206. Ibid., pp. 20, 21.
207. See 169 above.
208. PRO.
209. V. de Sola PINTO: *John SKELTON/A Selection from his Poems* London (1950), pp. 76, 77.
210. NRO NCC Wills 98 PARKER.
211. PRO State Papers (Domestic) Elizabeth 81.
212. Katharine F. DOUGHTY: *The Betts of Wortham in Suffolk, 1480–1905* London 1912.
213. Opinion given to the late Mrs. R. O. PICKERING ("Elizabeth HARLAND") by the Strangers' Hall Museum, Norwich.
214. NRO NCC INV 24/24; NCC Wills 57 COCKES.
215. COX & HALL, op. cit., vol. 4, pp. 336–7.
216. BLOMEFIELD, op. cit., vol. 1., pp. 151–160.
217. NRO NCC Wills 252 TUCK.
218. Do. 3 BATTELLE.
219. Do. 1663 O.W. 92.
220. Do. 1689 O.W. 31.
221. Do. 113 PIDDOCKE.
222. Do. 67 ALLEXANDER.
223. "Indenture Quadripartite" of April 20th 1761, penes auct.
224. NRO NCC Wills 563 TENNANT.
225. Do. 1689 O.W. 31.
226. NRO PURSEHOUSE NOTES R.152 A (transcript).
227. BL Egerton 2713. fo. 169.
228. See 211.
229. Neville WILLIAMS: *Thomas Howard, Fourth Duke of Norfolk*, London (1964), p. 216.
230. Ibid., p. 122.
231. NRO: South Lopham Parish Registers.
232. North Lopham Parish Registers.
233. BLOMEFIELD, op. cit., pp. 153 & 162.
234. Loc. cit.
235. Loc. cit.
236. North Lopham parish registers.
237. BLOMEFIELD, op. cit., p. 163 n.
238. MASON, op. cit., p. 575.
239. See 203.
240. NRO, NCC Wills. 6 ADAMS. See 166.
241. NRO. Archdeaconry Visitations. ANF/1/2.
242. Ibid.
243. Ibid.
244. Ibid.

245. NRO NCC Wills 248 EADE.
246. 2 HENRY IV. 2.1. 143–4.
247. NRO NCC Wills 156 BOWRNE.
248. B. COZENS-HARDY: *Presents to the Sheriff of Norfolk 1600–1603* NORFOLK ARCHAEOLOGY, vol. xxxvi (1938).
249. NRO. 12852.
249[A]. Cal. Pat. 1272–81, p. 472.
250. MASON, op. cit., p. 251.
251. SOUTH LOPHAM INCLOSURE AWARD (SLIA), p. 9.
252. SLIA MAP, County Hall, Norwich.
253. NRO: Lopham Court Book 1755–1765, fo. 16.
254. Ibid.
255. OED sub art. PANTER *sb*. 2.
256. EKWALL, op. cit.
257. NRO. PD 120/66.
258. MASON, op. cit., p. 271
259. BL. Add. Roll 66816.
260. (Arthur CAMPLING): *Miscellanea Genealogica et Heraldica* vol. viii, Series V., p. 318.
261. North Lopham Parish Registers.
262. NRO PURSEHOUSE NOTES. R.152A (transcript).
263. Ibid.
264. Ibid.
265. BLOMEFIELD, op. cit., p. 157.
266. Ibid., p. 75.
267. (F. W. STEER ed.) *The Life of St. Philip Howard*, London & Chichester (1971), pp. 6–7.
268. CAMPLING, op. cit., p. 317.
269. See 260.
270. NRO NCC Wills 143 APLEYARD.
271. See 192 above.
272. BLOMEFIELD, op. cit., p. 66.
273. BLOMEFIELD, pp. 330, 356; CAMPLING, op. cit., p. 317.
274. CAMPLING, op. cit., p. 318.
275. (Laurence WOMACK): *Pulpit-Conceptions, Popular-Deceptions*, London 1662. Sig. B.
276. DICTIONARY OF NATIONAL BIOGRAPHY (DNB), sub art. WOMACK.
277. (Laurence WOMACK): *A Short Way to a Lasting Settlement*, London 1683, p. 30.
278. DNB, loc. cit.
279. CAMPLING, op. cit., p. 319.
280. BLOMEFIELD, op. cit., p. 157.
281. TUSSER, op. cit., p. 322.
282. BLOMEFIELD, loc. cit.
283. DNB, sub art. John SALISBURY.
284. Ibid.
285. NRO MS 14890 37 B1.

286. See 193.
287. BL. Add. Roll 66805, 66816.
288. Ibid. Add. Roll 66805.
289. Do.
290. Do.
291. Do.
292. Do.
293. Do.
294. Do.
295. Do.
296. P. M. REANEY and R. M. WILSON: *A Dictionary of British Surnames*. London (1977) p. 45.
297. BL Add. Roll 66805.
298. OED, sub. art., "Cowl, sb^2.1."
299. BL Add. Roll 66805.
300. Ibid.
301. Ibid.
302. Ibid.
303. REANEY & WILSON, op. cit., p. 21.
304. Ibid., p. 256.
305. OED, sub. art. "Oriel".
306. Loc. cit.
307. BL. Add. Roll 66805.
308. A. LEIGH HUNT: *The Capital of the Ancient Kingdom of East Anglia*, London (n.d.), p. 202.
309. BLOMEFIELD, op. cit., vol. ii, p. 698.
310. Loc cit.
311. HUNT, op. cit., p. 337.
312. T. S. NORGATE: *Introduction* to CHAMBERS'S *General History of Norfolk*, Norwich and London 1829, p. iv.
313. Loc. cit.
314. (Arthur YOUNG): *General View of the Agriculture of the County of Norfolk*, London 1804, p. 448.
315. NORGATE, op. cit., p. vi.
316. YOUNG, op. cit., p. 219.
317. Ibid., pp. 224–225.
318. Ibid., p. 236.
319. NORGATE, op. cit., p. vi.
320. YOUNG, op. cit., pp. 214–215.
321. Ibid., pp. 328–330.
322. A. J. WARDEN: *The Linen Trade*, London 1864 (reprinted 1967), p. 370.
323. YOUNG, op. cit., p. 332.
324. See 223 above.
325. NORFOLK & NORWICH GENEALOGICAL SOCIETY: *Norfolk Pedigrees* Part Two, 1976, p. 164.
326. ANNUAL REGISTER, vol. xvii, 1774, p. 102.
327. Ibid., vol. xvi, 1773, p. 225.

328. YOUNG, op. cit., p. 326.
329. MASON, op. cit., p. 477.
330. DNB, sub art. HOWARD, Charles (1746–1815) 11th duke of Norfolk.
331. MASON, op. cit., p. 474.
332. Ibid., p. 473.
333. See 241 above.
334. MASON, op. cit., p. 58.
335. Cyril JOLLY: *The Spreading Flame* (n.p., n.d.) p. 62.
336. Ibid., p. 18.
337. The METHODIST RECORDER August/September (?) 1910. Cutting held by NRO in FC 17/169 No. 10.
338. LOPHAM COURT BOOK NO. 13 (LCB 13), p. 12r, penes the lord of Lopham Manor.
339. Loc. cit.
340. METHODIST RECORDER, loc. cit.
341. JOLLY, op. cit., p. 69.
342. METHODIST RECORDER, loc. cit.
343. MASON, op. cit., p. 585.
344. Ibid., p. 553.
345. North Lopham Parish Register.
346. METHODIST RECORDER, loc. cit.
347. North and South Lopham Parish Registers.
348. METHODIST RECORDER, loc. cit.
349. Anonymous note of 1951 in North Lopham Wesleyan records.
350. North Lopham Churchwardens' Book, N.L. Parish Chest.
351. White's Directory of Norfolk, 1836.
352. H. G. B. FOLLAND: Sparham Deanery Magazine, February 1973, and the same in conversation with the late Mrs. R. O. PICKERING ("Elizabeth HARLAND").
353. LOPHAM MINUTE BOOK 12.iv.1828–4.v.1855: entry of 12.iv.1828, penes the lord of Lopham Manor.
354 Arthur YOUNG: *The Farmer's Tour through the East of England*, London, 1771, vol. ii, p. 25.
355. Loc. cit.
356. (YOUNG): General View &c., p. 132.
357. BLOMEFIELD, op. cit., p. 155.
358. Ex inf. Captain M. A. N. Mansbridge.
359. See 5 above.
360. Do.
361. SLIA, p. 8.
362. LCB 13 (1792), p. 11r.
363. NRO MS 14912. 37 B1. Charter of 9.v.1349.
364. LCB 13 (1792), loc. cit.
365. NRO NCC Wills (John BARKER) 290–1 ACASTON.
366. LCB 13 (1778), p. 4r.
367. NRO NCC Wills (Bartholomew WADE) 6 ADAMS.
368. SLIA, p. 8.
369. Ibid., p. 9.

370. Ibid., p. 10.
371. See 5 above.
372. Do.
373. LCB 13 (1794).
374. BL Add. Rolls 66811 (1597).
375. Do. 66810.
376. Do. 66811.
377. LCB 13 (1778), p. 4r.
378. Loc. cit.
379. Ibid.
380. NRO PD 120/66.
381. LCB 13 (1778?), p. 75r.
382. Loc. cit.
383. NRO PD 120/66.
384. BL Add. Rolls 66811.
385. LCB 13 (1778).
386. SLIA, p. 1.
387. BL Add. Rolls 66811 (1593/4).
388. OED, sub art. STILE *sb'*.1.
389. Op. cit., sub art. STOCK *sb'*.1.
390. BL Add. Rolls 66811 (1596).
391. LCB 13 (1793).
392. Ibid., (1778).
393. Loc. cit.
394. Lord ERNLE: *English Farming Past and Present*, 6th edition, 1961, p. 299.
395. A. J. PEACOCK: *Bread or Blood/The Agrarian Riots in East Anglia, 1816*, London 1965.
396. Arthur WARNE: *Church and Society in Eighteenth Century Devon*, Newton Abbot (1969) pp. 15–16.
397. OED sub art. FALL *sb'*. 29, quoting W. H. MARSHALL: *The Rural Economy of Norfolk*, 1795.
398. "LOPHAM", a copyhold rental book 1773–1840. Entry of 1816. Penes the lord of Lopham Manor.
399. BLOMEFIELD, op. cit., p. 154.
400. NRO NCC Wills 146 MULTON.
401. BLOMEFIELD, op. cit., p. 154.
402. North Lopham Churchwardens' Book.
403. MSS of Mrs. James GOODERHAM, penes Miss E. M. Gooderham
404. BLOMEFIELD, op. cit., p. 155.
405. North Lopham Churchwardens' Book.
406. Eric PURSEHOUSE Waveney Valley Studies (n.d.), p. 239.
407. BLOMEFIELD, op. cit., p. 155.
408. SCHEME (for Lopham Charity), n.d. (1853?).
409. BLOMEFIELD, loc. cit.
410. SCHEME.
411. MS "Deed of Gift of site for Schools &c in South Lopham", 1862. Penes South Lopham School.

412. W. A. DUTT: Wild Life in East Anglia, London, 1906, p. 294.
413. Ibid., p. 297.
414. Reports from the Assistant Hand-Loom Weavers' Commissioners, Part II. Report by J. MITCHELL, Esq., LLD on the East of England. London 1840, pp. 320 (338) & sqq.
415. Ibid., p. 353 (371).
416. F. J. HIGGINBOTTOM: *The Story of the Lophams*, quoting Albert TYLER, EDP 14.iv.36.
417. MITCHELL, op. cit., p. 354 (372).
418. Loc. cit.
419. Ibid.
420. MITCHELL, op. cit., p. 350 (368).
421. NRO PURSEHOUSE NOTES (R. 152[A]).
422. NRO NCC Wills. Elizabeth, widow of John BUCKENHAM of South Lopham, 24.v.1636. 253 SPENDLOVE.
422[A]. Henry MAUDSLAY and W. P. IVATTS: *Notes and Extracts . . . respecting the family of Bukenham or Bokenham of Norfolk and Suffolk* . . . London (privately printed) 1884, p. 65.
423. Recorded by the late Mrs. R. O. PICKERING ("Elizabeth HARLAND").
424. "LOPHAM" and "Court Book No 13", pp. 152 & sqq. Penes the lord of Lopham Manor.
425. CROWE's Book.
426. HIGGINBOTTOM, op. cit.
427. Teste Percy S. BEALES in a letter of 10.ix.1960 to Eric PURSEHOUSE. NRO PURSEHOUSE NOTES R.152[A].
428. KELLY'S DIRECTORY OF NORFOLK & SUFFOLK, 1900, p. 218.
429. A local story reported to the late Mrs. R. O. PICKERING ("Elizabeth HARLAND").
430. Recorded by the late Mrs. R. O. PICKERING ("Elizabeth HARLAND").
431. NRO. PURSEHOUSE NOTES R 152[12].
432. Recorded by the late Mrs. R. O. PICKERING ("Elizabeth HARLAND").
433. Undated newspaper cutting, presumably from EDP, penes Prospect House.
434. NRO PURSEHOUSE NOTES, loc. cit.
435. PRO. Particulars of Nancy COBB, widow, in 1851 Census.
436. North and South Lopham Parish Registers.
436[A]. Cal. Pat. 1216–1225, p. 590.
437. BLOMEFIELD, op. cit., p. 157.
438. P. S. BEALES in the NORWICH MERCURY of 25.v.29.
439. Loc. cit.
440. GARBOLDISHAM, BLO' NORTON, QUIDENHAM, SNETERTON, AND LOPHAM PARISH MAGAZINE, January 1898.
441. DISS EXPRESS & NORFOLK & SUFFOLK JOURNAL of April 29th, 1879.

442. Loc. cit.
443. Ex inf. Mr. S. Gooderham of Dairy Farm, North Lopham.
444. North Lopham Wesleyan Day School Log Book, penes Mrs. H. Reeder.
445. North Lopham Wesleyan Day School Log Book.
446. Deed penes auct.
447. NRO PURSEHOUSE NOTES, loc. cit.
448. P. S. BEALES, NORWICH MERCURY, loc. cit.
449. Letter of 10.ix.60 from P. S. BEALES to Eric PURSEHOUSE NRO PURSEHOUSE NOTES, loc. cit.
450. N. Lopham Wesleyan Chapel records.
451. Ibid.
452. North Lopham School Log. See Chapter Twenty.
453. GARBOLDISHAM ... AND LOPHAM PARISH MAGAZINE, June 1898.
454. P. S. BEALES in NORWICH MERCURY, loc. cit.
455. Letter from BEALES to PURSEHOUSE NRO PURSEHOUSE NOTES, loc. cit. Local gossip.

PART THREE

Twentieth Century Lopham

CHAPTER TWENTY

Educations

In North Lopham the twentieth century might be said to have begun on September 11th , 1899, when the school re-opened in the altered Albert Rooms. A glance over the shoulder at the last years in the Wesleyan schoolhouse may serve to underline the changing times. William Mann, the master, a first-class certificated teacher of some sixteen years' service, initiated the last volume of the old school record with perhaps an ironical entry:

"This Log began duties December 2nd 1896."

King Log in the fable made a great impression on his arrival but remained supine and uncomplaining throughout his reign. This would not be a fair description of William Mann. On February 12th 1897 he wrote:

"The attendance improved until the 'Harriers' came into the parish on Thursday, when a decided drop occurred, especially at the afternoon session . . ."

Next month:

"A procession of Caravans, or a string of them, carrying Wild Beasts, with elephants walking and Camels, &c. passed through the Village this morning. Many of the elder boys are following it on its way to Harling, and have not returned . . ."

The state of the old school premises may be judged from his record of an inspection day on May 10th, 1898:

"Just as H(er) M(ajesty's) I(nspector) left the school, the children were let out for recreation, and while at play, two girls who were jumping on the flagstones that cover the cesspools of their water closet, caused the stone to break and let them in, they scrambled out, and being frightened, one of them ran dripping into school causing such an abominable stench, that I went to the chairman" (of the School Board), "and told him I could not continue in school nor let the children do so in consequence of it, and sent the children home."

Regular school attendance by children for "efficient elementary education" in the 3 Rs had been made compulsory by Act of Parliament in 1876, and defaulting parents could be prosecuted. But it was a difficult law to enforce in parts of England like Lopham, where it had long been the custom for young children to work in the fields. Sowing beans, "dropping" (planting potatoes), "singling" beet, weeding, keeping turkeys, and picking up acorns for the pigs, are among the various reasons recorded for long absences from school. In 1884 and 1890 South Lopham mothers were prosecuted and fined at Harling Police Court for sending their children irregularly to school. At North Lopham the School Board themselves were unwilling to enforce attendance, and Mann was told in 1899 that one of the members had "been to several houses advising parents not to send the children, that the Average may be kept down"—and so to beat the system. When H. P. Henderson, H.M.I., read this he asked Mann to supply him with the names and ages of absentees and the names of their employers. "He also inquired if the Board had taken any, and, if so, what steps to secure a better Room for the meetings and work of the School . . ." Next day Mann records:

"I have been threatened by one of the members of the Board, that if I comply with the demands of H.M.I., as above, I shall have to put up with the consequences." It is only fair to add that in whatever circumstances Mann may have retired the following year, he himself became one of the first School Managers appointed under the Act of 1902, and that on July 7th 1913,* he was recorded by the master of the day to be "telling parents they may keep their children from school whenever they have a reason to do".

Meanwhile at South Lopham parochial school, where J. F.

* He died in 1917 at the age of 91.

Bateman had installed a "Black Book" for bad language in 1865, successive masters and mistresses continued to monitor the children's morals, but with indifferent results. In 1866 a small boy confessed to stealing a turkey's egg, taking it home to his grandmother "& telling her where he got it from. He also said he took T. Crowe's dinner some time ago. I tied him to a chair & kept him without his dinner. Informed the Rector of this." Next day Bateman addressed the school on the sin of stealing and the master, John Taylor, after caning the boy, suspended him as a thief. Throwing stones, "mobbing" passers-by, "writing on the walls", and spitting at each other were among other sins committed by both boys and girls during the 70s and 80s. The brief but lively reign of Richard James Jump, between January, 1877 and August, 1880, at least provided alternative activities. Thomas Crowe records:

"Mr Jump and he Could Jump ho I remember It well I believe he could Jump 12 yards ¾s not only that he could Jump high as Well I believe he could Jump 15 or 16 yard high More or Less. We was always Jumping at Playtime—he whent away jumping I know not where".

But jumping, even to such Olympic heights, proved no remedy for sin, and the next master, Edward H. Crow, "having heard that the children were apt to be untruthful . . . took the advantage" on his first day "of warning them against *lying, cheating* and *disobedience* which seemed to make an impression on them".

But not for long. Mrs S. Crow, his disciplinarian wife, who was unsuccessfully summonsed by a mother for beating her daughter in 1881, moralised on the problem in 1883. After "severe" punishment to a boy for behaviour on the way home, she remarked:

"It is a usual thing to swear at children who go that way with him also to run after them with thorns and prick them. If he is capable of thinking of such things he must have some sense of what right is. He has several times been spoken to for being impudent to people in the village. He certainly knows better for *in school* there is not a better behaved boy . . ."

Perhaps South Lopham school entered the twentieth century when Marcus Kerr Bardwell and his hard-working wife, Elizabeth, took charge on November 12th, 1883. For thirty-five and a half years until April 30th, 1919, the Bardwell family occupied the master's house and studied and taught in the school. There were ten children: two of the daughters became teachers and two of the sons were killed in action during the first world war. Marcus Bardwell campaigned long and with moderate success against absentees and stone-throwers. He instituted School Entertainments and took what opportunity came his way to tell the children something about the world outside the Lophams and Norfolk, whether it was by persuading "Mr. G. Wild of London" to play his "Gramaphone" to them after lessons on August 8th, 1900; by allowing the first class to read from some numbers of *Tit-Bits* in January, 1902; by exhibiting and explaining to the children a Model of the "Tower Bridge" which he had put together; or simply by taking advantage of the "novelties" which firms such as Beecham's, Holloway's, Owbridge's, Lewis's, Cassell's, Lever's and Colman's were ready to send to village schools as advertisements. With the help of Toogood's of Southampton he was able not only to promote a gardening class but to mount a competition with real prizes. He won no golden opinions from H.M.I.s but perhaps his best achievement was in driving them by his vivid and continual complaints to keep the school buildings in habitable shape.

His campaign against the stoves began in 1906:

"For several days this week we have been nearly suffocated by the smoke from *both* the stoves. It is both difficult and unhealthy to work in an atmosphere of smoke . . ."

The H.M.I. agreed and advised the School Managers that improvements should be made. A stove was patched but the nuisance of smoke continued intermittently throughout 1907, whilst Bardwell vociferated woe. H.M.I. was cautious in approving the open grates and limited ventilators installed at the end of the year. Bardwell went into action without delay, protesting not only against "dense volumes of smoke from both grates" but of soot on all the school equipment, of sickness caused by smoke among the girls, and, by the beginning of 1909, of extreme cold, whether there were fires in the grates or whether they had to be extinguished because of the smoke. To open his log-book at this period is enough to make the reader cough. During the summer and autumn of 1909 the school was closed for twelve weeks because of holidays, epidemics and building alterations. In December Bardwell began again to gird at smoke and soot but he now had the upper hand and alterations were made to the chimney the following day. H.M.I. reported warily in May, 1910, that "the heating arrangements have been considerably improved", and it was not until January, 1918, in swan-song, that Bardwell made his last moan:

"The children unable to write in books as all the ink was frozen. The smoke from the fire places in *both* rooms was a great nuisance all day."

At North Lopham William Mann's successor proved unequal to his task:

"Mr. Dale came Nov. 6 1900 & left after 3 months, delighted to flit: said children had no 'brain power'."

This note was entered in February, 1901, by the sturdy Thomas Bawden, whose comment after his first fortnight was simply

"This is a rough school."

Nevertheless he stayed on to wrestle with his pupils, battle with the Board, and win most of his contests before he retired in August, 1915.

Bateman's first presentation to the Lopham living after his own retirement, Alfred Caldecott,* lasted only three years before he moved to a living in Essex to be nearer his teaching job in London University. At the end of 1898, however, Bateman presented Charles James Eastwood who was to remain rector of the Lophams until 1940, only three years less than Laurence Womocke. Eastwood, evidently well briefed by his patron on the history of the Albert Rooms, announced with some complacency that

". . . the Board School has commenced its use of this building, which has been greatly improved by the alterations and additions. It must be a source of great satisfaction to know that the School Board . . . has saved the ratepayers the great expense of building a new School."[456]

But there was little satisfaction for Thomas Bawden, who recorded as he took charge that

* Who had been his curate.

"The 'Board' failing to secure a house, I have left my wife and my all behind, and Miss Brock continues" (as my assistant).

During the twenty-eight years' boycott of the Royal Albert National School it had only been used for Sunday Schools, evening classes and occasional meetings, and it is hardly surprising that the trustees should have let the "master's residence" in order to maintain an income. Bawden found the "School house", as he called it, occupied by a shepherd, and others, as he remarked in his log entry for July 27th, 1901:

"Ordinary routine, but the noise of pigs & babies in the next house are no help to the school."

He could not persuade Eastwood and the Board to remove these tenants until October, 1901, and then had to spend £142 on alterations, a sum which he was supposed to recover in twenty-five years by the terms of his lease. In 1907–8 there were alterations of the school building, some of which have been shewn perhaps in Chapter Thirteen, but it was not until 1911 that he won his battle for the enlargement of the school, after H.M.I. had agreed that an attendance of well over 100 children constituted "overcrowding". The Inspector reported in December, 1909, that

". . . Seven children in the lowest class knelt on the floor and wrote their copies on forms during the writing lessons—injuring both their bodies and their writing . . ."

We do not know whether the children had been told beforehand to adopt this uncomfortable pose simply because Bawden knew that the inspectors were coming. He was certainly not unkind to his charges. There was very little corporal punishment recorded in his time, and plenty of co-operation, as in the first School Entertainment of December, 1901—"a novelty in Lopham . . . such a pleasing and pleasant surprise that a Second Evening was demanded. The children acquitted themselves admirably". Then there was the voluntary draining of the boggy playground by "The Master with a few boys after school hours". There were all sorts of returns: outings for "the most regular boys and girls" to Yarmouth, Norwich and Cromer; twelve hundred marbles which "Master has given the children to play with in the playground"; the "6 miles ramble" on a May day "teaching the boys how to make

Mr. Thomas Bawden, his daughter Effie, Ellen Brock (later Mrs. Stevens) & the girls of N. Lopham School, *c.* 1906.

sketches &c while the girls gathered flowers"; and the Christmas presents:

"Dismisssed children for their usual 2 weeks Xmas holidays. They were each presented with an orange, picture books, several toys &c &c. Each left with full hands . . ." (1905).

Bawden's grammar and spelling were not faultless, and his discipline did not win the inspectors' admiration; his relations with the rector were poor—"Beloved Eastwood, Saintly Eastwood", as he called him, when he suspected him of obstructing the recruitment of his school-teacher daughter, Effie Bawden, once his wife, Johanna, had become too ill to work. But it is difficult not to believe in him when he writes:

"August 12th 1915.

Having reached the beloved age-limit, I resign and relinquish all the duties and worries of the much beloved profession of Schoolmaster."

Leonard B. Smith, who succeeded him, saw through the war without comment except on a "Useful 'U Boat Menace' Map", and resigned on July 11th, 1919. He had started a gardening class despite what he called the "coarse weather", and educated both himself and one of his pupils on the dangers of imitating nature too closely:

". . . a pair of stoats were seen in the playground & four lads were sent to try to destroy them, in case of accident to any children. One of these boys . . . owned a ferret . . . Another boy . . . held this & was evidently teasing it by darting his tongue in & out near the ferret's nose. The animal snapped and bit the end of his tongue . . ."

These are people still living in Lopham who can remember these school masters and mistresses of the past. One very senior citizen of North Lopham was at school under William and Sarah Ann Mann. She reached the Seventh Standard at the early age of twelve, and since she had shewn her aptitude at sewing she was able to leave school in 1900 to become a dressmaker's apprentice. Her service lasted two years and three months more "cutting out and fitting people". She recalls the elaborate fashions of those times:

"All dresses were made to fit & bodices boned up and a lot of them all buttoned up and lined throughout, and long skirts with frills."

Her junior by a few years, who no longer lives in Lopham, remembers how

"the sound of the shuttle being thrown to and fro was the music we trotted to school with."

She also remembers

"Mr. and Mrs. Billy Mann . . . she had a nasty habit of tapping on our skulls with a thimble and poor old Billy used to sole the boys with his cane."

Another, who is back in North Lopham after travels far afield, was a pupil of the Bawdens and also remembers how you could hear the looms from the schoolroom: "Clickety-clack, clickety-clack." Among her happiest recollections are the Wesleyan Sunday School treats, which carried away so many children that Bawden would close the school for the day. On the summer outing the party travelled in two wagon-loads, drawn by Ambrose Stevens's traction engine. Since you were dressed in all your best you had your anxieties:

"Sometimes the smoke one way, and sometimes the other—you had to watch!"

This rural train would roll first to Garboldisham, then

round to Uphall, where the children were unloaded into a meadow, "with lovely willow trees all growing over it",* for games and the well spread tea. At one stage in the festivities:

"Sweets and nuts were flung to us all in the meadow. We got to grab and hunt for 'em".

Not long ago an elderly Old Boy paid a visit to South Lopham School and talked of his youth:

"Things were different when I was here. Even if you had no coat and no decent shoes in the middle of the winter and the snow was thick—*no* children were allowed in school at dinner time. You ate your packed lunch outside while the teacher warmed his backside by the fire and he stayed there when the children went in!"[457]

Whatever confrontations there might be among the grown-ups, the children were brought up in an ordered respect for their elders. One pupil of Marcus Bardwell's at South Lopham remembers the awe of a Sunday afternoon when she and some other little girls met with

"Reverend Badger of Bressingham. I think we used to think he was God."

* Mr. Cooke of "Up Hall" had given the Wesleyan children the hospitality of this field as long ago as August 12th, 1869.

CHAPTER TWENTY-ONE

The Losing of the Looms

The greatest days of Lopham linen were described in Chapter Eighteen, but the years of decline stretched well into the twentieth century, and there is still a skein to unravel round the weavers and their ways. Some of the causes of decline have already appeared: the difficult skills and heavy labour of the hand-looms and the hard drinking which went with them. Since the weavers were unwilling to take apprentices outside their own families, while their sons, as early as the 1850s, proved unwilling to join them, there was an inescapable end in sight. The weavers themselves were unenterprising and Percy Beales suspected that one of the reasons why David Strachan stayed in Lopham was that few or none would follow him on the Jacquard loom.[458]

A directory of 1864 records 60 looms in use at North Lopham, with eight linen manufacturers in the same village and four at South Lopham. The Post Office Directory of 1875 shews the number of manufacturers reduced to six and three respectively; 1883 five and two; 1900, three and one; and 1912 two only in North Lopham. It was the gradual disappearance of the weavers and the loss of their looms which brought the manufacturers down. At the height of the Buckenhams' prosperity in the 1880s there were not enough looms at work to keep up with the order-book and customers were sometimes kept waiting for eighteen months or more. This was illustrated by a sharp fall in the number of parcels sent away by the Buckenhams between 1883 and 1884: a drop from 243 to 172. The number seems never to have recovered

"Meadow Cottage", formerly the North Lopham Weavers' Arms, *c.* 1910.

beyond 186 in 1886, and by 1893 it was down to 43.[459]

A "watershed" of the same period was the closing-down of the Weavers' Arms (now "Meadow House") and the Barking Dickey* (now "Ferndale Holding"), once among the most popular of North Lopham's houses of call.† This sobering sign of the times points also to the fall in population. The number of inhabitants of all Lopham had fallen by almost a third between 1860 and 1890, from 1500 to 1074. In the hope of checking this decline by providing a means of "getting produce away more cheaply", there were many Lopham signatures to a petition of 1898 for a scheme promoted by a "resident of Bungay" for a "new Railway from Harleston to Thetford, passing near Diss". This scheme proposed a Redgrave Station at the Crossway, just south of Lopham Gate.[460] Perhaps the name of the station ought to have been "Lophamford".‡

* Which might be translated: "The Coughing Donkey".

† Another inn, "The Garden House", now Poplar Farm, had closed before 1865. It had been popular among the drovers who used "Top Drag Way".

‡ See Chapter Six.

Another scheme of about the same date was launched under the cheerful title of the "Mid-Anglian Light Railway". Its original plan included a line beginning at Stanton and passing through Barningham, Market Weston, Hopton, Garboldisham, Blo' Norton, South Lopham, North Lopham, Kenninghall, Banham, New and Old Buckenham to Attleborough, where it was to join the Norwich-Ely line. The project was warmly supported by the North Lopham Parish Council in November 1899. Difficulties soon appeared and in a new plan of May, 1900, it was proposed, in addition to the line just described, to connect Stanton with South Lopham also through Walsham-le-Willows, Wattisfield, Rickinghall Inferior and Redgrave. South Lopham was to become a junction from which yet another line would run via Wortham, Bressingham and Roydon to join the Norwich-London line at Diss.[461]

With the noise of this network, however "light", thundering in imagination through parks, preserves, coverts and champion cattle pastures, the nobility and gentry with land in North and South Lopham, Garboldisham, Kenninghall, Quidenham, Banham, Old and New Buckenham, and Attleborough rose in protest, led by the Right Honourable Earl Egerton of Tatton, (father-in-law of the eighth Earl of Albemarle), and His Highness Prince Frederick Duleep Singh. Their Kenninghall solicitors were instructed to warn the Secretary of the Light Railway Commission of their opposition and their particular objections. Some of these read rather oddly, considering the current situation at Lopham:

". . . there is no demand on the part of the Residents in the neighbourhood for such Railway and . . . it would be of very little benefit to any one . . .

. . . during construction the Railway would be particularly detrimental to all persons occupying land in the neighbourhood and it would largely increase the difficulty of obtaining sufficient Labour which is already much too scarce . . .

All advantages . . . from the proposed Railway might be obtained by the use of Motors to convey the small amount of passengers and produce from one place to another off the existing lines . . ."

The last argument was prophetic enough but as a rich

man's remedy it cannot have been very palatable in its time. Nevertheless the landowners won at the "Inquiry", held at Bury S. Edmund's on August 3rd, 1900, "when Promoters in consequence of opposition abandoned Railway from Lopham to Attleboro".[462]

It is unlikely that anyone believed a railway would save the Lopham linen industry by this time. But if the number of weavers' hands and throats grew steadily less they were all the more fixed in their ways. After the rector had been hanged in effigy* there was a police enquiry, but the culprits were never found. It is said that the local constable feared a beating if he looked too closely round the looms. As it was, he suffered the same humiliation as the rector:

"One morning as the Sun did rise
We threw our Beams across the skies
And there exposed a droll affair
The Village Slop† high in the Air.

Ah such a treat this was for all
The Village people great & small
With one accord all went to see
The Peeler hanging on the tree.

The Paralysed, the Halt, the Blind,
All People left their beds & stilts behind,
The ragged orphan, officer & gent,
The hale & strong, the weak & bent,

The orthodox, the flippant youth,
The little kids and Living Truth
All Lopham trod the Common track
To view the works of Steeple Jack . . .

Then Bateman muttered with a frown
How can we get the body down?
It is a shame that he should stay
Up there upon the Sabbath Day.

Then while the Sun was getting low
And now the wind began to blow

* See Chapter Nineteen.

† Policeman. From the "Back Slang": S(i)lop = Polis.

Which did the merriment enhance
For Bobby he began to Dance.

He danced a reel and then a jig
And then he scampered like a pig,
A Hornpipe he did imitate,
At last the Slop began to skate.

He threw his arms & legs about
Which made the people laugh and shout
Until it seemed that all was rent
With shouts of villagers' merriment.

Oh such a crowd was never seen
before upon North Lopham Green,
For had they not there hanging high
The arms of Law towards the sky?

God's people now began to Blame
The folks all said it was a shame
A worn out Baker there to mock
by making him a laughing stock.

And now it seemed the day would pass
Before they Brought the Slop to grass,
When Annie said at Yonder Shop
She took 2 Bob off Mr Slop
To pay to someone in the town
If they would cut his Image down . . ."[463]

It is said that a favourite spot for these imitation lynchings was upon a tree across the street from the King's Head, "the old Dale tree", and that one day the joke there became black indeed. The weavers had suspended from the Dale tree* the effigy of one Joe Glover of North Lopham, notorious for cruelty to both his wife and daughter. Glover, they say, had a look at what they had done, then went and hanged himself in earnest on a tree up King's Head Lane. There is still a place up King's Head Lane called Coffin Pit. The mock hangings must have been especially ambiguous to the young. A former resident of North Lopham remembers about 1897:

* "Dale" can mean deal, and the "old Dale tree" was probably a Scots Fir.

"... one morning on my way to school, I saw what I thought was a figure hanging from a tall tree (the old Dale tree we called it. It was quite a landmark to Lopham; it was situated right opposite the King's Head, on Banham's meadow. There are Council Houses on it now). I couldn't have been more than 6 years & I turned to another little girl & said 'What's that?' & this is the reply I got, 'It's old Emma G——, *they hung her last night*'. I asked Mum about it, but she was very evasive about it & said it's only a bag of straw but I've got an idea it was rough justice, some poor old dear had kicked over the Traces."

But not all the weavers' jesting was so grim. Since the Middle Ages there has been a tradional grudge against village constables for their persecution of poachers. The art and pastime of poaching in the Lophams was by no means only the weavers' preserve, but it was they who decided to invite the constable to a feast at the Bull in a spirit, perhaps, of forgiveness. The principal dish was rabbit pie but the constable, whatever his suspicions, shewed his tact by concentrating his praise on the accompanying cabbage. It was not until next morning, when he looked at what had been his own cabbage patch, that he realised the poachers' trophy had displayed both flora and fauna.

In the decline of the Buckenhams their rivals the Bealeses became the leading producers of Lopham linen. The Beales family, it seems, were mainly of North Lopham, and had been well established there at least by the eighteenth century. A "William Beeles, singleman of Hockham" arrived in S. Andrew's, North Lopham, on April 18th, 1598, to marry Elizabeth Jeames, a widow.[464] In November, 1831 John Beales of Old Buckenham, "Linen Weaver", appeared in person at the Court Baron of Lopham and was there admitted to a copyhold inheritance of "2 Cottages and Garden without Contents" from Mary Beales,[465] but perhaps he was a wanderer returning to the Beales homeland. A butcher's business in North Lopham seems to have descended from a Stephen Beales of the 1780s to Samuel Beales who died in 1903.* According to the Census of 1851 the Bealeses provided their

* The same business which Mr. V. C. Frost maintains inherited from his father.

North Lopham: Beales's butcher's shop, now Frost's, in 1899 (probably founded before 1780). Jim in front of his father, Willie Carman, Miss Cook, Eddie Beales, Albert Crook, Herbert Hutson and Sam Beales.

village with no less than three butchers, one of whom was also a beerseller, probably at the Black Horse; a tailor and draper; a wheelwright; and a widow linen manufacturess, the relict of Jeremiah, who employed four men. One of these men was probably her grandson, Walter, then aged fifteen and working as a linen weaver. Thirty years later the firm and the family still flourished: Percy Beales, their descendant, remembered in 1960 how

"One side of the village used to be nearly all Beales, of all the trades besides Linen M(anu)f(acturer)s, inn-keepers, wheelwrights, Butchers."[466]

Percy Beales recorded that his grandmother was a Buckenham, but

"There was never any collaboration between the Buckenhams & the Beales's; the latter were smaller rivals of the former & never achieved 'By Royal Warrant'. The Beales weaving sheds turned out the simpler type of linen, mainly sheeting & towelling, & did nothing of the complicated order of the Jacquard-woven 'Traveller's Club' Tablecloth . . ."[467]

Nevertheless it was the Beales family who flew the last flags of fine Lopham linen. On one of their summer excursions, in June, 1910, the Norfolk and Norwich Archaeological Society paid a visit to "Mr. Beales' handloom manufactory of linen cloth", which was described as "practically the oldest industry in Norfolk". This was in the weaving shed behind Stephen Beales's house in North Lopham Street.* Significantly, when Percy Beales, his nephew, was introduced to Queen Mary at Sandringham in the 1930s, she asked him if he was any relation of Stephen Beales. As the daughter of the Duchess of Teck she must have learned to appreciate Lopham linen in her youth,† and when the firm of T. W. & J. Buckenham ceased to produce enough material of high quality she had presumably transferred some of her custom to the Beales looms. It is known that fine Lopham linen continued to be sold in Norwich shops and at some of the bigger London stores in the early years of King George V's reign, becoming ever scarcer and more expensive. There is a story that one seeker after Lopham sheets in those days was told at Harrod's: "But, Madam, they would be ten to twelve pounds a pair!"[468]

As the village memorialist records, Stephen Beales "Died Suddenely this Morning June 20th 1915/He Stephen was at the Butcher's Shop yesterday Saturday June 19th 1915". His name is kept alive by the North Lopham church bells, restored and rehung by his widow in his memory, but his business died with him. Two of his weavers, "Pipman" Keeble‡ and "Tip" Ludbrook took two of his looms to Lancashire, presumably with some encouragement to teach their craft, but what became of their equipment history does not yet relate. It is said that there were restrictions on the manufacture of fine linen during the first world war. This seems to have blocked the Pipman-Tip enterprise, and it must have

* Now known as "The Cottage."

† See Chapter Eighteen.

‡ He was christened Walter, but before that ceremony his father, asked about the new baby, said he was "a fair pipman", a Norfolk agricultural term for the last of the farrow, and a name which stuck.

"Tip" Ludbrook, William Womack of the King's Head, North Lopham & Tom Carman *c.* 1890.

reduced what weaving there remained in Lopham to a small compass.

Elizabeth Susannah and Louisa Ellen Bale inherited land south and west of The Limes, North Lopham under their sister Georgiana Buckenham's will in 1905. The house itself and the weaving shed went to her cousin by marriage, Thomas Buckenham of South Lopham, but the Bale sisters bought it from him in 1906 for £170. Elizabeth Susannah died on June 12th, 1912, but Louisa Ellen, better known as Ellen, continued the Buckenham business after a fashion right up to the time of her own death on March 16th, 1925. Her looms seem to have produced little more than huckaback towelling but some stocks of fine linen remained from the past, and she kept up a shadow of Georgiana's queenly style. She spent most of her life in London but liked to visit The Limes at "strawberry time". She is remembered receiving her guests there, "seated in a gilt bishop's chair, a dignified Victorian figure in a cap with purple bands . . ." Her tea-parties were always provided with brown eggs and honey, "the latter in a huge glass globe two feet high and a foot across, which Albert Tyler, as skilled a bee-keeper as he was a weaver, would each year persuade his bees to fill".[469]

Albert Tyler, "a tall, thinnish man, with red hair", who is remembered by people still living in both the Lophams, was the last weaver in a family which had worked the looms at least since 1851. There had been James Tyler "Who Died at North Lopham March 10th 1909 age 75 years", wrote Thomas Crowe: "He loved telling a tale and a glass and his baca—he did". Then there were Dubbs Tyler and his sons Harry and Albert, who all worked for The Limes. Harry was a

Albert Tyler & his daughter, Mary, winding bobbins at The Limes, North Lopham, *c*. 1910.

memorialist like his friend Thomas Crowe, and lent him books, where Thomas

". . . found out many little itms which I should never have found out If It were not for my Great Friend Harry . . ."

Another famous veteran of the linen industry, with friends North and South, was not so much a weaver as the last of the pedlars. This was Jack Shaw, a stocky, lively man, "always singing and whistling", who lived to be ninety. He had worked at first for Buckenham's but as looms and linen grew less drove round his horse and cart for Stephen Beales as well. He had a 'covered-in arrangement: in the summer-time you could take the top off and make it into a wagonette". Another senior citizen remembers him as the great traveller in foreign parts:

"He delivered at different places on the way (up to London) and collected at stations the parcels that were sent by train as he could only carry his load; and he would stay at different places for the night and then carry on next day. He used to have some tales to tell the villagers when he came back. He got several of the village young men and women jobs in London as he was a regular visitor there and met several people. Our country girls and lads did very well up there: several stayed and married. John Shaw was a very happy man and very sociable to all concerned; made many friends all around his travels." According to another contemporary, "I have heard my mother say he practically had to make his will before he started his journey".

Ellen Bale had been generous to her friends: once she gave a wedding-present of a tablecloth, made in the famous and appropriate "Lopham spider web" pattern, a set of huckaback towels and a bolt of unbleached damask linen left over from an order for dustcovers at Windsor Castle. She gave Albert Tyler the title-deeds of the cottage where he lived, near the Street. There were hopes that she would remember other old weavers in her will, but when she made one on August 13th, 1924,[470] she seems to have left most of her possessions in trust for a niece in Australia. After her death on March 16th, 1925, there followed two great sales: first of her North Lopham properties on November 20th, 1925, at the Crown in Diss; and then of all her goods and chattels at The Limes on November 23rd–25th.

The properties included the blacksmith's shop at the junction of Tann's Lane and North Lopham Street, at that time worked by Gordon Ludbrook; five acres off the Street, known as Chapel Fields; the double dwelling-house "with Antique Circular Chimneys made of patterned brick", now known as "Fortune's Well"; and a two acre field off Fyson's Lane, still bearing "valuable oak and other timber".

The Limes itself did not reach its reserve price at the auction and was sold privately for £900 on April 19th, 1926, to Percy Stephen Beales, then described as a Teacher of Music, of Lechmere, Prestbury, Gloucestershire.[471] In many ways he was the right man to take possession. He was the nephew of Stephen Beales and the grandson of William Beales, wheelwright of North Lopham, and his wife Lois, born a Buckenham; he had a craftsman's hands, a head full of ideals and imagination, and a heart devoted to the Lophams. When Percy and his wife, Rita, arrived at The Limes Albert Tyler was still working his loom and had much to tell about Lopham linen-weaving, North and South. The Bealeses decided to begin at the beginning, short of growing and dressing their hemp:

"I must not omit to say that the *growing* of Hemp at Lopham had long been given up when I used to go there with my parents as a child & stay with my uncle Stephen for holidays .. My wife & I taught ourselves to spin at Lopham by getting a fleece from a farmer & buying 2 spinning wheels from Norway (& taught ourselves Weaving & Vegetable Dyeing in the same way . . . with help from old books). Later we helped with the experiments that King George Vth made with his trials of Flax-Breeding at Sandringham. I spun the 'trials out' of any new flax fiber he grew & became the finest flax-spinner in the country—but that is years ago . . ."[472]

So spinning wheels and a loom went to work in The Limes old weaving shed but their hum and clatter did no more than stir the ghosts:

"When my wife & I bought 'The Limes' we had hoped to be able to revive the Linen Industry somewhat, using the old buildings &c. But we found it quite impossible of course; with the old weavers' recollections, & their family's, they had no desire whatever to have anything to do with such an idea."[473]

Mrs. Rita Beales spinning flaxen yarn in The Limes weaving shed, *c*. 1927. By courtesy of Mrs Rita Beales.

The only place where they seem to have achieved a revival of weaving interest was in North Lopham school. Charles Finch Delogue Castell, who became Head Teacher on March 4th, 1929, was another idealist and soon developed a friendship with Percy Beales. By May of the following year the Board of Education had observed Castell's "invigorating effect on the school . . . and his proposals with regard to Handwork (for which he has very good qualifications) . . ." On May 22nd, 1933, their inspector reported that

"The school possesses ten looms for weaving—the traditional occupation of the village—and the older girls are producing some admirable work . . ."

Four years later:

"The senior girls reach a high standard in Weaving, while the Bookcraft of the boys is of satisfactory quality."[474]

It is significant that by 1932 Percy Beales was representing North Lopham school on the Village Hall Committee, of which he was already the chairman; and that one of his many enterprises was a private press.

Did he ever try to persuade his friend Charles that the boys should learn weaving as well? Perhaps not, for even in 1929 his articles in the *Eastern Daily Press* "About the old weavers" were taking on a valedictory note:

(On May 25th, 1929) ". . . there still stands the very last of the old Lopham looms, exactly where it was worked for at least a century and a-half. Remnants of old looms are still to be seen here and there in the neighbourhood of the old weaving shops now serving as gateposts or fencing, for they were of solid and sturdy construction. Though not so interesting a 'specimen' as the fine example in the Norwich Bridewell, the loom still standing dusty and desolate is probably much older, and is not without its story . . . The loom is of the primitive type for plain, full-width sheeting. To swing the heavy batten of it all day long and every day, save the Sabboth" (sic) "for years and years, was no weakling's job."

This was Coleby Cobb's loom which is now in Thetford Museum. The verses on "The Parson's Idol" which Percy Beales transcribed from it, and which are quoted in Chapter Nineteen, have disappeared but in 1978 there remained a newspaper cutting about the execution of one Jackson for the "Strangeways Murder", with a portrait, perhaps of the executioner. There were also a picture, apparently of Christ and the Samaritan Woman, and portraits of Joseph Arch, the pioneer of agricultural trades unions; John Kensit, the anti-ritualist agitator and Secretary of the Protestant Society; and the Reverend Thomas Penrose. Other newspaper cuttings displayed propaganda for the Liberal Party; a satirical piece called the "New Voter's Catechism"; and a variety of simple, sometimes ribald humour. One story of marriage with a door-key when the wedding-ring had been mislaid was linked to the announcement:

> "WOMACK—LUDBROKE. Sept. 30th (1887?) at North Lopham by the Rev: J. F. Bateman, rector, Oswald, youngest son of the late Mr. John Womack of the Chestnut Tree Farm, to Elizabeth, second daughter of Mr. Thomas Ludbroke of the same place."

According to Percy Beales,

"Upon all the old looms were to be found numerous clippings regarding stock and property sales in the locality, racing events, records of exhibitions, and prize winnings, not to mention spicy tit-bits of scandal, regardless of locality."

There seems to be none of these exhibits left on the Jacquard loom presented to the Bridewell Museum in Norwich by Ellen Bale. It would be interesting to know whether any survive on the other looms in the museums named below.

The first Lopham loom to become a museum piece seems to have belonged to Stephen Beales, and to have been presented to the Ipswich craft museum by his brother, Robert, after Stephen's death in 1915. Ten years later, when the Buckenham linen manufactory had also closed, an advertisement of November 4th, 1925, in the *Eastern Daily Press* drew "particular attention" to the "OLD ENGLISH LOOMS suitable for Museums", and the large stock of Famous North Lopham linen . . ." to be sold at The Limes on November 23rd–25th. The linen is said to have fetched £1500 altogether, but fortunately a number of good pieces remain as family treasures in Lopham. One loom, apparently of the seventeenth century, is said to have gone to the Ipswich Museum for £9. Two sheeting looms and one damask loom were bought by Prince Duleep Singh for prices between £1 and £5-10-0, and one of these is said to have passed on to the old Greenland Fishery Museum at King's Lynn. Another may have gone to the South Kensington Museums. The "most interesting of all", according to Percy Beales, went to the museum at Halifax whose curators describe it as "basically an 18th century type of loom" with "20 sets of headles selected and lifted by 'witch' engine, worked by a single treadle". (Illustration on p. 112)

That was the end of "the ceaseless thud and swish of beater and fly-shuttle, and the rattle of bobbin-winding", which in the eighteen nineties "could still be heard from one end of the village to the other . . . 'I hear it in my dreams', said an old weaver to me".[475]

CHAPTER TWENTY-TWO

The Good Old Days

There is no catching up with history and the times always move faster than the men and women who live in them. To be left behind is lonely and inglorious but your company and self-esteem will soon improve if you turn round, look back, and meet all those people running in the wrong direction. That is why to every generation there were better times than now. The Good Old Days are difficult to date by the calendar but they are real enough in remembrance: an imaginative selection of your own and other people's experiences in bits of existence which you prefer to the present.

This chapter draws upon affectionate memories of the Lophams sixty-five to ninety years ago, a period in which there are distressful records enough of farming poverty and of the local industrial decline described in the last chapter. The decline in the population of the Lophams slowed down however, and from 1890 to 1914 S. Andrew and S. Nicholas continued to muster about a thousand inhabitants between them. Between them also they were perhaps as self-sufficient a community as they had ever been—unless we look back to the seventeenth century when they had their own apothecary-doctor, buried in North Lopham church in 1692 as "Francis Bogas, Gent".[476] For a long time the Lophams had looked mainly to Kenninghall for a doctor, but in 1890–1914 there was no health service and villagers looked to any doctor only when needs must. Pills and potions, if you believed in them, were among the many things you could get or make for yourself, like bread and clothing. The physicians

North Lopham Black Horse (now Black Horse Cottage), *c*. 1906. Sid Hutson, Herbert Hutson (landlord), Florrie his wife, and Fred Hutson.

were sometimes beholden. Martha Smith, landlady of the Bull, North Lopham, from 1883 till 1914, used to prepare "chaps of pork in old beer in sweet pickle which she sold a lot of to doctors and chemists".

Her granddaughter has given a succinct account of the amenities of North Lopham in the 1890s:

"There were 5 Public Houses/Bell Inn Mr. Howard/Black Horse Mr. King/Kings Head Mr. Womack/Bull Inn George Smith/Cherry Tree Inn/Also Curate & also Wesleyan Minister/Farmers who kept Cows & Pigs/Sheep & Plenty of Poultry all sorts/there was no need to go out of the Village for anything."

There was no need to go out of South Lopham either unless it was to the larger village of the North. South Lopham had only three inns at that time: White Horse, William Pitchers; Crown, Charles Hawes; and Chequers, Henry Goddard, but it also had the rector. In addition to their churches, chapels and schools, both villages had post offices and both had millers, bakers, butchers, blacksmiths, wheelwrights, carpenters, builders, cobblers and general shops. North Lopham

North Lopham "top shop", *c.* 1910, with unidentified boy, Len Blowers, Mrs. Shoal, Eva Grant, Albert Bussey, Herbert Grant (proprietor) and Ray Grant.

sometimes had more amenities, such as a vet, a solicitor, a stonemason, a plumber, a draper and a harness maker. It was there that

"Peter Ruddock Tailor made all sorts of clothes, had cloth in the Shop", while Arthur Keeble and Josiah Coe, shoemakers of Barracks Yard, made "heavy boots for farm work and Boots & Shoes for all sorts: School wear & Sunday, children, Ladies, Gents". A "large Drapery Shop sold everything from pins, cottons to Dress Materials Also Millerny to suit all dressmakers in the Village: Mrs Betty Barham, Miss Mary Cox, Mrs. Clarke".

Dressmaking was only one of the home industries: enough sixteenth century traditions survived to leave a significant part of the linen industry in the hands of the womenfolk. The late Mrs. Eleanor Baker, who was born a Ludbrook in 1872, could remember in 1961 how her mother "in the Hemp

Barracks Yard, North Lopham, *c*. 1919. Mrs. Eliza Holden and family, Mrs. E. Bowen, Mrs. Jennie Emms and unidentified boy.

Days" had still worked a spinning wheel. Those days were over before the period of this chapter began, but she remembered other skilled work, some of which continued into the early twentieth century. The rolls of newly woven linen went first to Bressingham for the attentions of "Bleacher Thurlow"; when they came back in all their whiteness they were marked off into lengths of sheeting, then "made" by hand. This meant that they were hand-stitched, seamed and ironed by Mrs. Ludbrook and other weavers' wives and daughters. There was another skill for women's fingers: the marking of the sheets in red cotton cross-stitch. As Mrs. Baker remembered the job, it was three halfpence for every dozen letters, and forty-eight pairs of sheets at a time. But perhaps there was glory in it, for sometimes you were stitching for the Queen: "VRI", followed by "Balmoral", "Buckingham Palace", or some other royal address, and a crown.

Home food production was also abundant. The common rights of gleaning were still exploited, but with a strange mixture of mediaeval practice and modern mechanical assistance. In one family, for example, up to eight combs of wheat were gleaned in the ear at shacktime, and kept ready for Ambrose Stevens's steam thrashing machine which travelled from house to house. Then they would carry the grain to one of the three mills which were still available, and when the flour came home "it was shot straight on to the floor". In this house, when they needed to bake, the women sifted the flour through a fine sieve and made loaves for a faggot oven. Harking back to the times when the Lophams were "most wood", the men would cut great bundles of faggots from the fences and burn them down to hot ashes in the ovens where the loaves were cooked.

Modern commerce and technology were biding their time. In North Lopham there was

"Mr. Banham Bread Baker & anyone in the Village took Meat or cakes to them; they would bake them for 1 penny meat & cake but you could take a tray of Bread for them to bake for 3 pence . . ."

An ominous corkage charge on gleaners' bread? But memories of the flavour of hand-gathered corn, floor-garnered flour and home-kneaded dough have survived decades of "dead bread" and "old comical-chemical stuff" from the food factories.

A self-sufficient community is apt to be self-regarding, and the Lophams are fortunate in a record of what they saw in themselves during the long, quiet years before the earthquake of the first world war. It would have added much to Chapter Nine if a comparable record had survived from mediaeval Lopham, for Crowe's Book, as we call it, preserves fragments of ordinary life from an almost forgotten society, and reflects the common opinion of that society rather than the individual views of a diarist.

The Crowe family in Lopham seem to have originated in Malteyward* Crowe who came there from Wetheringsets, Suffolk about 1840. By 1851 he was farming thirty-five acres in South Lopham, employing one man and two boys, one of them his eldest son, Robert Coates Crowe, then aged eleven. There had been Coateses in the Lophams since the eighteenth century at least and the fact that Malteyward and this wife,

* The Maltywards of Suffolk seem to have been at Rougham and Hawkedon, Suffolk in the seventeenth century.

Mary, gave the middle name of Coates to their first born daughter as well as their first born son may suggest a family relationship. The mother, however, may have been a Brown by birth, and came from Crowfield, Suffolk. Their youngest child in 1851, Thomas Peck Crowe, may have been the first owner of "Crowe's Book" which has the date "1879" pencilled inside the front cover. But he died in 1881, and it was his son, Thomas Crowe, who collected and entered most of the contents. In 1879–1884 Thomas Crowe was at South Lopham school. In 1895 he joined The Prince of Wales's Own Norfolk Artillery, and after six years military service returned to live at North Lopham. His mother seems to have been one of the Sares of South Lopham and he was related to various other local families such as the Womacks and the Lands.

The purpose of Crowe's Book is described in a rambling preface as the recording of "all sorts of news" likely to interest the parishioners of North and South Lopham:

"If any one wish to look through this book they can do so with the Greatest of pleasure. they will I am sure find some very Interesting pieces in, Such a(s) Ship Disasters, and Executions, and Colliery Disasters, both small and Great, and Epitaphs taken from Books and Grave Stones and Wills of Great men and small men and deaths of all pepople", (sic) "youn(g) Men, Old Men, Maidens and Children, Gents Poor Men, Good Men Bad Men I expect as they were not all good men Who died, Neither were they all good or all bad or at least we hope not . . ."

The Deaths have been collected "from various pairshes round about". It has taken "a lot of pain and worry and trouble to Collect all the names that I have taken Down, but never mind so long as I like doing so . . . I think my self that any can spend many a happy and Comfortable hour in looking this book through or at least I have been told so by some folks . . ."

In other words Thomas Crowe and his collaborators were memorialists. His concentration upon disasters and deaths shews no more than a sound appreciation of the news people liked to read—and still do, to judge from modern newspapers. Thomas and Bob Crowe, Harry Tyler and the other contributors to the book were by no means morbid men: their own "epitaphs" on friends, neighbours and relations are best described as lively. It is these, not those "taken from Books and Grave Stones", which are valuable in this history since they reproduce the gossip of 1880–1914 and the standards which went with it.

Sometimes there is a short story in a sentence:

"they always said he had a lot of Money but he had not enough to pay his death";

"Pairsh Clerk for 67 year following his Grandfather Foot Steeps but He was a Wonder he let the Clergy Men down the fire Place one Sunday but he could not help it he was 89 then he forgot to put the Irons up down he Whent";

(Caleb, whose wife died ten months before him:) "He Caleb promised his house-keeper that he would marry her after his Wife had been dead 12 monts but you can see the Result";

"Poor Liney there was not many of his friends Loved him till he was dead then It was too late";

"David was a Regular Church Man and His Wife also he was going to Church one Sunday with out his Pattens* Oh his Wife called out David you have forgotten your Pattens";

"Farmer—He carted his Corn one Sunday And Every body helpt him";

"Who hung himself on a turnip Grinder poor Man . . . but she soon married agen";

"Found Drowned at S L. Oh how the poor Man did Shout but no one help him";

"Good Old Little Billy—A Regular Churchman and had his regular Alowance from C. Brown† & Mr. Bateman";

"He was a very Miserable Man with his money he said he would like to have a little with him but his Sons said No."

Passing judgement upon other people is the essence of gossip, since the judge is bound to feel superior to the judged and therefore better for the exercise. Such "judges", however, are less concerned with rules of law than with the assessment of their "jury's" opinion, in other words "what

* i.e. clogs, to keep out of the mud.

† i.e. Charles Brown, farmer of Lodge Farm and churchwarden of North Lopham.

the neighbours will say". The refrain of "So They Said" in Crowe's Book is repeated often enough to demonstrate the writers' intentions not to express private views but to answer for public opinion in North and South Lopham both. There are even attempts to assess the reliability of particular pieces of hearsay:

"He Grumbled for 77 yrs With out a break So I have been told/I have heard him Every time I see him So I don't think Its far out but Its all one Now Poor Old Man."

He had died at the age of eighty-two. Was there a general belief that nobody starts grumbling before they are five years old? For of a woman who died at eighty-four the Book records:

"She was like her Husband, alway Piping always grumbling they said that she grumbled for 79 years without a break."

Moaning ranked high among social misdemeanours. It is possible to grade these and the corresponding virtues from a comparative study of the "epitaphs". The worst offence was ill-treatment between husbands and wives:

"they said that Her Husband never allowed her enough money to by Bread with Poor Woman";

"he loved his Pipe but his wife would not allow him any Beer";

"Bob Starved her to Death";

"She had three Husbands and she haited the lot she had a way (to) get read of them";

"He loved his pints more than his Wife";

"Sophia used to thrash her husband dreadfull whe(n) he was drunk".

The fifth commandment was high on the Lopham list:

"He was . . . a very bad man to his Mother and Father";

"He was a Robber he Robbed his poor Old Mother".

But there were exemplary families as well:

"A very Kind and good Husband he loved his Church, he was an un smoker also an un drinker";

"Robert was one of the Best and kindness Husband that ever was born and the kindness master that ever was born and a good father to his Child";

"The last words she said Isaac have you said your prayers nice words";

"He Robert was a good husband always get the Meals Ready Cleare away and washed up sweet dry";

"I have a few wor(ds) to speak of David, Poor Old Man. A very nice quiet Comfortable Old Chap (to) All, he used to tell me he would like to do more work but of Course his Working day Were over. But he was a good Husband, to His Wife but she is Well seen after now by the Expence of the Esq of the Village—I remember him telling me once how pleased he Was When Mr. J. Womack Came that Way from North Lopham, and he spoke to Old David, and David told me that he J. Womack gave him 2 pence and he was so pleased with It and I told David I hope that he would be rewarded for It and David said the Same//I forgot to say that David used to Chop Sticks for his Wife also get in all Coals, and Sweep up the yard Also Clean up the House, and make a fire for his Wife Cleane all Windows knives forks Boots and shoes and always took up a Cup of Tea for his Wife's Breakfast So I think that he was a good Husband. Off Course he did not take much Harm Him and his Wife had the Old age Pension total 10s And he Had 2/6 a week from the Esq of the village also his Wife 2/6 a Week and Rent free and Coals found, and other things found So he did not take any Harme/I forgot to say that he used to fetch all Water get all Firing In/Ready (to) run of Earnets" (errands) "for his Wife/David was a good Husband he never was angry in all his life never."

"The fourth head of the wicked beast of hell is unwillingness . . . This unwillingness which is sloth maketh that man hath a bad beginning, a more evil amending and a worse ending."[477] Whatever bewilderment of doctrines the Lophams may have suffered over the centuries, this fragment of a thirteenth century sermon on the seven deadly sins would still have found a ready hearing in Victorian and Edwardian Lopham. Faith in the virtue of labour well done is matched in Crowe's Book with the belief that willingness to work brings its own reward, even when this may be hard to descry:

"A Wunderfull Man for hard Work";

"(She) Worked up till the last Minite";

"(A father and son.) They were both very fond of plowing the fields I don't know which could do it best";

"(Another father) Oh what a man he was for Sowing

Seed"; (and son) "of Course I knew him/He loved sowing Seeds";

"(A Shoemaker) He would work all day and then in the Dead of the night go on with his work, poor Man";

"(An innkeeper) What a Man he was to Work but he poor Man never gained any thing";

"Poor George . . . said he had not time to be Ill but poor Man Died the Next Day So I was told by a very truthfully Woman Who was never Known to speak an untruth Now She is Dead . . .";

"(Another) George was a rather pecquiler" (peculiar) "at times but one of the Best he work well."

In contrast to these:

"Oh What a Walker he was/never worked only ½ the year".

The unsociable sins, besides grumbling, were bad temper, gloom, greed, meanness, dishonesty and conceit:

"Oh What a Bad Tempered Man he Was";

"Now he was a funney Old Man If things whent Wrong";

"She was a Miserbale Woman that ever Lived";

"not a very Happy Man always on the Grab and always Grumbling till he died";

"What a Robber she was and a Grabber to she Loved her pint";

"What a Man he Was for Grabbing and Grousing and Grumbling";

"he had many a pint what belonged to otheres";

"What an old Swank he was he Loved telling tales";

"(A well-to-do farmer:) He loved every one to take Notice of him/there your ar(e)".

Some kinds of snobbery were mocked:

"Commoly Called Lady L— The Lady was a great Bower to the R(ev.) J. F. Bateman",

but a prudent respect for the 'squire was understood:

"Poor Old Man he had to go with two Sticks, but I am pleased to say that he had some very good friends, as they behaved to him very Well; And he dearley loved his tabaca, for he was nearley always smoaking when ever I see him but he would soon take his pipe out if the Esq came by/He was a Wonder for getting Money."

As for the Quality, their ways were hard to understand. There was a Norfolk baronet who was killed by a mountain-lion in Canada:

"Its a great pity that he did not keep at Home—He was not oblige(d) to go away only I suppose he likes it."

Then there was an aged Major General who slipped from his chair and died of a broken thigh.

"I hope he was not Drunk as them Maj(ors) love drink".

There were some on whom no moral judgement is passed but who won their fame as characters:

"He loved to Set by the blacksmith fire and Roast";

"he Dick loved to be out when there was a tempest";

"He Loved his Donkey";

"He would not let us Boys Get in front of him when he was carreing the flag";*

"He loved getting out on the Spree So they Said".

Among the social virtues conviviality was prized as much as kindness and good nature, so long as it kept within bounds. It was admitted that drink sometimes produced bad manners and worse habits:

"he was a man for shouting and drinking";

"He was a Lover of a Pint Mug";

"Arthur Drank so much So It Shartned His Days";

(Of a weaver who died in the Kenninghall Union:) "All his own fault."

However, even a drinker could have redeeming features:

"He drank more than what done him Good but there";

"He was a Wonder More Espelly When he was with his Fiddle Espelly Whe(n) he had emp(ti)ed His Mug for some time";

"Oh What a Man he Was for his Glass";

"She loved a drop of Beer and Especly her Pipe Poor Old Girl".

But there was more to tavern meetings than the toping: there were the tellers of good stories, the conversationalists and the singers:

"a familurer Old figur both at N and South Lop: . . . She was a gay old Spark that Everybody Knew well Oh the tales

* Perhaps the club flag in the Whitsuntide procession described below.

she could tell were Wonderfull but not alway the truth of Cours no one always speaks the truth";

"He loved to tell you a tale in his young days";

"A Wonderful old Man for his talking/always Exacertaged his tales when talking":

"Oh what a man he was for talking about Roesbery* Oh Dear";

"He would Set and talk the Whole Night If you like;"

"He loved Musick very much and singing and his pipe."

The mixture of such ingredients in a merry meeting about 1890 was described in a ballad by the Lopham Laureate:

"This Song is Called the La de dar.
Late at an inn one afternoon,
The Landlord's name I'll mention soon,
The D(octo)r came there from the Spar,
His band struck up a la-de-dar,

The trumpets blast was loud and long,
and soon a hurly burly throng,
Came (r)ushing in with all there might
Regardless of the time of night

There names I'll tell one was a loper
You know him well old alley sloper
And Arthur Shaw I do believe
Was there, and also Righteous Reeve

Diamond Frost and Sam so plucky,
Aldis Cole and Banham Ducky,
Honor Shaw and Emma Glover
And John Clark her daughter's lover

Saville Bowell and young Shaw Jack,
Robert Beales and William Womack,
And Mr Norton to they say,
Concludes the lot that had to pay,

I'll name them all not favoure any,
There's Glover Joe his Daughter Jenny,

* i.e. Archibald Philip Primrose, fifth Earl of Rosebery, Prime Minister 1894–95. This appears to be the only reference to politics in the whole of Crowe's Book.

Three young Bakers green and silly,
Roger Trudgill likewise Billy,

William Bussey, Albert Thurlow,
Ludbrook Charles and Rodger Shaw
Three Pearses helped the room to fill
Their names are Liney George and Will

Two Miss Holdens Jack their Brother,
Jack Raynar too he was another,
I think this was the lot but Stay,
Four from South Lopham came to play,

Miss Womack waited at the Bar,
and then there was her darling Ma,
All listened to the band, pom, pom,
They laughed and sang and drank hot Tom

So blithe and gay they saw no fear,
But Aldis came and said look here,
This noise is quite enough to Craze us.
The Landlord said you go home," (to Blazes?)
"How vain and foul the Slop must be,
To pull a quiet lot like we,

But how I came to make such a Jar,
By leaving out the Great Alfar,*
I'm sorry the name it was omitted,
But I'm no Sch(o)lar so must be pitied."[478]

Some of these revellers have nicknames but not Righteous Reeve, the thatcher, called after his father, who was entered under the same name and occupation in the 1851 Census of North Lopham, as a native of Diss. "The Doctor from the Spa" and his "band" were presumably itinerant musicians, perhaps from Thetford where there was a spa in the 1820s. Crowe's Book records that

"(When P.C.) Aldis caught this lot at the Kings Head North Lopham he pulled" (i.e. gave a police summons to) "the Lot but he had a few favourets he did not pull/Mr. & Mrs. Womack keep the Kings Head at that time/they had to appear at Harling you might be sure."

* Identified as Alfred Emms.

The ballad, apparently by the author of the verses quoted in Chapter Twenty-One, confirms that village policemen were not as highly respected as they may be today. If P.C. Aldis was considered officious however, he may have earned this reputation when he arrested Noah Elner of South Lopham on Sunday, November 16th, 1890. Noah was eighteen and lived with his stepfather, Henry Self, a roadman. On weekdays he worked as a miller but about forty minutes past seven that Sunday morning he was visited by Edward Cox, the thirteen year old son of a farmer of the same name, who was after a rabbit in his father's field and knew that Noah had a double-barrelled gun. Together with Edward's little brother they went hunting, Noah carrying the gun.

". . . the triggers were down and the left hand barrel had a cap but a piece of a lucifer match was put on to make it go off . . ." They had been in the field and Noah was turning round to come back through the hedge when "the movement must have jarred the match" and Edward Cox, who was close behind him, was shot through the head and died at once. Noah, in much distress, ran first to his stepfather and then to Edward's father to break the news. It spread fast and as soon it reached Aldis he arrested Elner. In what kind of custody he put him does not appear, but on Monday morning he brought him before

"Cecil F. Montgomerie Esq. and Major Keppel at the Occasional Court House, Kenninghall."

Noah was remanded until the inquest which was held at the Crown Inn, South Lopham, the same day by

"H. E. Garrod Esq. Coroner for the Liberty of the Duke of Norfolk." The shadow of the mediaeval "Liberty" of the Mowbrays had not yet disappeared. The lordship of the manor of Lopham had been sold by their Howard heirs in 1872 to the same local lawyer, Henry Edwin Garrod of the Grove, Diss, but the duke still exercised the fifteenth century privilege of nominating the Coroner for the Liberty.

The jury returned a verdict of accidental death. Remembering perhaps the unexplained death of ten years before, when Towy Raynor of North Lopham "Was shot or he shot himself at Garboldisham" at the age of twenty-seven, they added a sensible rider that the gun should be destroyed. The coroner agreed but said he had no power to order its destruction.

"(He) called attention to the fact that the lads being out shooting rabbits on Sunday was against the law."

Perhaps it was in consequence of this remark that Aldis's unlucky prisoner was not discharged from custody until the following Wednesday.[479]

History does not relate the particular breach of the queen's peace for which P.C. Aldis brought the King's Head innkeeper, his wife and customers before the magistrates at East Harling, nor do we know what punishment they got. The "la-de-dar" in North Lopham Street cannot have been as painful as the juke-box cacophonies which inns elsewhere are allowed to noise abroad to-day, but the assessment of nuisances is relative, depending on times, tastes and tolerances. In the Lophams the first mechanical music to be heard was possibly not the "Gramaphone" of "Mr. G. Wild of London" in whatever refined ditties Messrs. Bardwell and Eastwood permitted at South Lopham school. It may have been the gramophone belonging to that master of machines, Ambrose Stevens of North Lopham, "thrashing machine proprietor; contractor for hauling and sawing by steam power; distance no object . . .", whose solitary record was soon known by heart in both villages:

> "Father won't you speak to Sister Mary
> Every day she's getting more contrary,
> She had money for the Bread—
> Bought Beer instead,
> So Father do please speak to Sister Mary!"

Entertainments from the outside world were few and far between. Apart from visits by the Doctor from the Spa there were occasional lecturers, for example Mr. John de Fraine "in South Lopham National School Room on Tuesday 21st March 1899" on the subject of "Funny Folks". "There was a fair attendance", wrote the rector, "and the oration was listened to with evident pleasure".[480] It all depends on what you find funny, and it may be doubted whether Mr. de Fraine had an intimate understanding of Lopham's sense of humour in the good old days. To put a ferret in your wife's bed; to balance a bag of swedes on a steep Norfolk stair, shut the door at the bottom carefully behind you, then tell your wife to fetch something from the bedroom; or on Halloween to tar a neighbour's single-seater petty just before the regular nightly visit was due: these were jokes which needed no oratory. It seems likely that there were larger attendances and louder applause whenever Messrs. Crotchet and Dartnell, the travelling puppet masters, came to the Lophams and set up their theatre at the King's Head or in the great barn* at the White Horse. Some of their performances were for adults only, by the standards of the time: "East Lynne" and "Maria Martin or Murder in the Red Barn"; but from the memories which persist in both North and South it seems likely that children were able to wriggle in. There was a puppet pantomime in 1907 which presumably had a "U" certificate in parental eyes, and there was an "exhibition" for which you paid one penny to see all the wonders, including snakeskins . . .

There was "Chapman and Family" who came once a year with their travelling fair; then "Chrightons show came on Bakers Meadow in front of the Bull—Swings, shooting gallery, stalls, Horse roundabout, cocoanut Shies . . ." But North Lopham's Whitsun revels were mainly home-grown, and sound as though they carried echoes from the Middle Ages:

"I think our 'Whitsuntide' was dropped after the first war, we had high Jinks on the Kings Head green. I think it had something to do with either the Oddfellows club or the Foresters . . . I don't know if we had any music apart from a big drum, but I think there must have been, because I remember people dancing. We started at the Kings Head, *first stop*. Womacks farm across the meadow, then down Tann's lane, stopped at the Mill which was owned by another Womack (William), then on to the Lodge—Farmer named Brown (Charles)—then from there to the Park farm—'Tom' Womack. I don't know if the men collected money but they had drink brought to them & by the time we arrived back after a stop at the Cherry Tree & the Bull, a matter of at least 4 or five miles the banner was at an angle of 45 degrees & the sound of the drum was very erratic but lost nothing in volume.

* On the site of the present car park.

Tann's Mill, North Lopham, *c*. 1922.

North Lopham Cherry Tree Inn in 1902, with Dursley Pedersen-style cyclist inside.

Then the men went into the Kings Head club room & had their dinner, supplied by Mrs. Womack, then after the kids had swallowed a hasty tea at their homes, with Mum practically waiting on the doorstep with it, now *our* fun started. There was a huge Swing boat, on the Hill, nearly as big as a lifeboat, with the young bloods vying with each other to see who could go the highest. I know I thought my brother Albert was going over the top. There was a cockle stall & Jack Raynor with his peppermint rock & Hazle nuts & oranges, & a cocanut shy. I suppose we had a penny or two to spend, but we were happy just chasing each other round. 'What a *thing* it is to be young!' Now at ninety, I have got all the time in the world to think, forgetting what happened yesterday or even what day it is, but remembering so vividly what happened 80 or more years ago."

Other occasions were provided by the two North Lopham chapels: the Wesleyans and the Primitive Methodists or 'Ranters'. "The poor old 'Ranters' Chapel is pulled down—we used to have fun there. It had a gallery all round, boys sat on one side & girls the other. We hear so much of the errors of the young these days, but we were *no better*, except for the violence, (we didn't get that.)" For both old and young.

". . . also in the Summer camp meetings for the Wesleyan Chapel in the Meadow on a Sunday 2–30: Waggon for the Preacher also Harmonium music for Hymns in the afternoon, and in the Chestnut Tree Farm Camp Meeting on a Sunday 2–30 for the Methodist Chapel: Waggon for the Preacher also Music for Hymns always had good congregations."

On a calm summer Sunday afternoon these two camp meetings must have been within earshot of each other but the rival rhapsodies of Wesleyans and Ranters could hardly constitute a La de dar. Besides, whatever P.C. Aldis said, the Lophams loved to sing. Some people had their own signature tunes. There was William Rush with his "Watercress song", chorus:

"She promised that she'd marry me
all on the first of May
And she left me with a bunch of Watercresses";

Ted Baker with his

> "My Father's face, that dear old face,
> its loss is what I ever shall bewail;
> Don't break an orphan's heart
> and with that oh do not part:
> don't hang my Father's picture up for sale!";

Emma Holden and her

> "Sitting by the fireside
> Smoking a long clay,
> That is how I like to pass
> The winter nights away.
> With a glass of grog
> And a plumy log
> To blaze up now and then
> It makes me feel as if I were
> In the Happiest Years of Men!";

"& Laura Collings was the first to sing this song in Lopham:

> "Just break the News to Mother"";

while it was Ky Carman who introduced his sensational variations on the theme of

"But it won't last very very long, no it won't last very very long!"

Then there was a song for flirts, best sung in the pub where they all sat round in a hollow square, their backs against the wall, as they still do in the North Lopham Bell to-day. The writer has received more than one version of this song, with names arranged to suit the belles of different clubrooms perhaps:

> "On Monday I meet Mary Ann,
> on Tuesday Mary Jane,
> on Wednesday I meet Miss McCann,
> on Thursday Kitty Payne;
> on Friday nights it's Sarah Jones,
> on Saturday Miss Small,
> on Sunday night I stayed at home
> for fear I should meet them all."

Arthur Mouncer was a photographer who lodged at the Bull for over twenty years. "He took photos all around the villages—he used to sing as well—this is one

"She sang like a Nightingale
Twanged a Guitar
Danced the Gogosher
Smoked a cigar
Oh what a form
Oh what a face
she danced the fandangle
all over the place".

He was well placed at the Bull where songs were abundant, particularly at the Horkeys, or harvest-feasts, some of which were held there.

The Hocky, Hawkey or Horkey was one of the most ancient festivals of East Anglia, the culmination of harvest customs which dated from pagan times. James Mitchell in his report of 1840 had noted how

"The labourers go about and collect money for the largess, or drink at the harvest supper. The farmer generally invites his friends to be present on the occasion. About midnight the labourers go outside and shout, Largess! largess! largess! after which they come in and collect money from their guests, which they spend next day in drinking at a public-house, and sometimes they get money enough to enable them for as much as two or three days to keep on drinking . . ."[481]

At the Bull, North Lopham, fifty years later, largess was spent also on a dinner of

"Salt Beef & leg Pork cold with all sorts of pickles & sauces and Hot Mashed Potatoes & Hot Plum Pudding with Brandy Sauce after also Mince Pies."

The feasting ended with a sing-song, comprising such favourites as

"Just like the Ivy on the old garden wall", and

"Ring down the Curtain I can't sing tonight".

How long had it been since the Lopham harvesters sang the "Duke of Norfolk", in which one singer, a staff in his hand and a cushion on his head, would begin:

"I am the Duke of Norfolk
Lately come from Suffolk,
Am I not to be attended, now, now, now?"

Whereupon the rest of the company would stand and sing:

"Noble duke, be not offended
For you *shall* be attended
With all the respect that we owe, owe, owe."

To which the duke replied:

"If I am not attended
This company is ended,
And parted I know not how, how, how."

The company responded:

"Noble duke be not offended
For you *shall* be attended
So toss off your liquor, you know how, how, how"—

The duke drank down a presented mug of ale and the company went on:

"And if it is all out
Let us see, see, see."

After the mug had been inspected the duke rejoined:

"And if it *is* all out
We will drink another bout,
So here, my fine friend, here's to thee, thee, thee!"

He drank another mug and the song continued until the harvest horn was blown and the staff and cushion were handed to the next man round the table.[482]

But Pope Gregory the Great's policy of tactful transformations, described in Chapter Four, was still leavening the Lophams and other parts of Norfolk in the eighteen-nineties. It is with no surprise that we read in the *Diss Express and Norfolk and Suffolk Journal* of October 5th, 1894:

"SOUTH LOPHAM. In accordance with the wishes of the parishioners, a harvest home tea and public meeting was held at the White Horse Inn on Wednesday evening"

(October 3rd). "At 6 p.m. a bountiful tea was placed on the tables by Mrs. Howard, to which 60 persons sat down . . ." A religious service and a public meeting were held "after the tables were cleared . . . The local brass band played several hymns from Sankey's selection. Hearty thanks brought a most successful meeting to a close; the people giving proof of their appreciation of the efforts of the Non-conformists of the neighbourhood" (North Lopham?), "who during the summer months have held meetings on the meadow or in the large clubroom, kindly lent by Mr. Howard . . ."

Horkeys were becoming Harvest Festivals.

Now and then there were royal occasions for a feast. At 3 p.m. on Queen Victoria's Jubilee Day, June 21st, 1887, "620 persons sat down to a dinner provided by the Committee, some in a booth at North Lopham Lodge Farm (Mr. C. Brown in the chair), and some at Pantshorne Farm (the Rev. J. F. Bateman in the chair) when 'the Queen's health' was right loyally received. A Tea was given by the Rector to 280 children under 14, and to 30 widows, some in the Albert Room decorated by a beautiful shield and flags sent by Mrs. G. E. Buckenham, and some in Pantshorne Barn. Games and sports were kept up with vigour till a late hour, when the day was happily concluded by a display of Fireworks on Mr. C. Brown's beautiful lawn, and by the discharge of three fine rockets from the top of South Lopham Church." If the sum of the guests be added to the probable number of the hosts, the Committee and their families, it looks as though pretty well the entire mobile population of both Lophams took part in this feast.

There were further junketings at the Diamond Jubilee of 1897. In South Lopham 370 dinners cost £22-18-0; the Band £4-10-0; and Prizes and Decorations £6-6-8, all paid for by subscription. At North Lopham there was "a slight deficit". Both villages tried to establish memorials of that Jubilee Year. North Lopham was given a Jubilee Meadow as a sports ground at the top of Tann's Lane, and rechristened the lane accordingly. There is still a Jubilee Cottage but the meadow has been occupied by bungalows and the new name of the lane survives only on the maps of the Ordnance Survey. In South Lopham, on February 1st, 1898, "three Jubilee Cedars were planted on the little Green . . . by the Rector (for Mrs. Caldecott), Mrs. Crowe and Mr. Bardwell (for Mrs. Buckenham). They will be fenced in, of course, and we trust will grow to be a beauty to the village. How many of us will see them as much as 30 feet high?" By the time of Queen Elizabeth II's Jubilee in 1977 only two, alas, were left, neither of them more than ten feet tall and one of them dying.

Records survive of one more royal revelry before the first world war: the North Lopham Coronation Festivities on Thursday, June 22nd, 1911, when King George V and Queen Mary were crowned. An invitation card for the Celebration Dinner is inscribed: "Please bring Knife, Fork, Glass and Plate", with satisfying implications. The Childrens' Dinner was at 1 p.m., Adults' at 2, and the "Committee, Waiters, Carvers" dined at 3. The subsequent "Programme of Sports" challenges the imagination with a "Slow Bicycle Race", a "Threadneedle Race" and a "Toilet Race", the last over 220 yards for Men and Boys only. Special prizes of Flour and Malt were offered by millers Bush (of Kenninghall?) and Womack of Lopham. The sports were followed by an Open-air concert at 8 p.m., with "A Singing Competition, Men and Women (none taking part in Musical Entertainments to compete); Prizes 2/6 Men; 2/6 Women". The Bonfire was lighted at 10 p.m. and the rest of the programme was unscheduled.

These feastings, however, by church or chapel or village inn must be seen against a darker side of existence. A free meal means more than festivity to an empty belly, and these were times when the Lophams were beset by hunger and poverty to an extent which is unimaginable today. When Rector Caldecott wrote of "agricultural depression" in 1898 (Chapter Nineteen) he referred, for example, to an agricultural labourer's wages. In East Anglia these had fallen from an average of nearly thirteen shillings a week in 1875 to eleven shillings in 1895. By 1903 this average had risen only to thirteen shillings and twopence halfpenny.[483] There has been much nostalgic talk about the price of beer and baccy in the good old days. It is recorded, for example, that before the first world war you could buy a good dinner, a pint of ale and half an ounce of tobacco at the Bull, North Lopham for fivepence halfpenny.[484] If you relate this price to wages of some one hundred and sixty pence a week on which you had to house, feed and clothe perhaps a wife and four children the golden age soon disappears and even a penny pint becomes an extravagance.

A member of one old Lopham family, the Carmans, remembers his childhood in those days. His father was a horseman who worked seven days a week and could add two shillings to his weekly wage if he worked twelve hours a day. There were seventeen children, eight of them attending school together. He remembers picking acorns before and after school to add something to the family income. The worn out clothes of the parents and the older children were cut up to fit the juniors. In the early days when it was cold all the family would go to bed to save firing. For breakfast they had a soup of bread and hot water flavoured with pepper and salt. One night when there was no food in the house someone put four loaves on a chair inside the door and nobody knew where they came from. Parish charity, he says, was better than the Relieving Officer who was "a bit of a tyrant".

When he began work as an agricultural labourer in 1911, aged eleven, he was paid three shillings a week. His wife, whom he married in 1922, earned ninepence a week when she began "living-in" housework in 1913. It should be remembered that your cottage as a farmworker was usually tied to your service and whenever you changed your job all your family would have to move. Farm servants were commonly hired from Michaelmas to Michaelmas, and it is significant that on October 14th, 1904 the master of North Lopham school records:

"Owing to so many house-removals several children have been absent this week."

As another witness of those times remarks:

"Good old days, and you had to touch your hat for it."

Perhaps there were compensations. Far away were the days when the prospects of an evening would depend on a printed programme of sensations to be blazed from a shop-window installed in the living-room. For the most part the villagers relied on their own resources of company, conversation and song whenever they took time off to enjoy themselves. Or you could simply enjoy yourself at work:

"Helping William To get his Beet off to day Monday Nov: 8th 1915 and It was a Most Glorious day What a good thing it was getting them of to day as It was such a beautifull day We could not have had it a better day If we had picked It and I must say that we all enjoyed the day in getting them off. I should liked to have another happy day like It, and I think William enjoyed it as much as I did lets hope I shall be able to help get them off next year. It turned out very wet to day Tuesday Nov: 9 so Its a good Job we got them off When we did".

It seems to have been the same memorialist, Thomas Crowe, who gave a hand with the sheep sometimes and tells of one old man:

"I knew him Well he was a Shepard and he always boasted that there was not any one could beat him, he always said that he never drove his sheep, but he always said that the sheep followed the Shepard. that was his idea. he never used a stick nor a dog for his sheep every body said he was a wonder."

Pride, the first of the deadly sins, is apparent in this story and Thomas may have preferred "a very quiet man" of South Lopham about whom he says:

"I was keeping sheep on the Road once" (i.e. on the grass verges) "and he told me to put them in his Wheat field but I dair not."

Quietness, as reserve and reticence, could be reckoned a virtue even though it limited conviviality:

"a very quiet Man he poor Man Counted of his Pence".

Or it might mean mystery and unplumbed depths:

"He had three Wihves very quiet Man".

Crowe's Book only once acclaims perfection:

"Oh What a fine Man he was/he was a Wonder for his up right in all his Ways", but Thomas was a great reader of parish magazines and perhaps his most heartfelt admiration went to

"A Worthy Old Character well know(n) for his quaint face and kindly actions, as long as he had health and strength. Few will forget his Regular reply to the Greeting, How are you George (?) Middlin In health but sa: hard o' hearin. He had been failing health for some weeks and our kind hearted Parish Doctor tried to persuade him to take a little Medicine but, No he had done wi'out so far and he war'nt agoin to begin now. On the Sunday Morning as the Bells were Chiming for Service he was tottering about in rather a purposeless way When his Niece Offered him a Chair. Ah, he said, Let Me Rest. He sat down, and In a instant his Spirit passed away to that God Whom in his humble fashion he had long Loved and Trusted/I remember him Well".

It would be wrong to end this chapter without remembering the judgement of one Lopham patriarch who enjoyed the good old days but compares them to their disadvantage with the new. He likes to think and talk of the times when you worked from dawn till dusk: the family, the farm servants, and extra hands at harvest. There was no idleness of mind either, and no need for artificial entertainment. But sometimes when he goes out into the fields and watches one man with a piece of machinery perform in two hours work which used to take four men four days to do, he cannot help regretting the waste of effort in his prime.

Between the era of horse traffic and the episode of the internal combustion engine. Hinchley's carpenter's shop, North Lopham, *c.* 1929 (Now part of Trenel House.) Eddie Pearce, Reggie Poulter and Cyril Wilkes.

CHAPTER TWENTY-THREE

The First World War and Afterwards

The first world war took many Britons by surprise, and in the Lophams, as in most villages, where local affairs predominated in the news of the day, this collision of powers beyond their ken must have puzzled most people. Four months after its beginning:

"This has been a bitter cold week Dec: 1 & 2 & 3 & 4 & 5/6 &—1914 and this War seems to last a long While I hope it will soon be over and we shall win be sure of that Thos: Crowe North Lopham Norfolk."

It was nothing new for Lopham men to go to foreign wars. At Calais in 1347, for instance, Edward III had pardoned a certain William of Lopham for "breaking from the king's prison of Lynn . . . in consideration of his good service in the war of France", perhaps at the battle of Crécy some fourteen months before. Nor was Thomas Crowe a stranger to campaigns abroad.[484A] He was an old soldier who had already recorded in his book:

"The Roll of Honour for North and South Lopham for the South African War 1.899—all Men Called up*

NL Robert W. Anderson 20 Bttery R H Artillery
Alfred Bailey 1st Battalion Coldstream Guards
Joseph Last Royal Army Medical Corps
W Joseph Carman Glover Driver R H Artillery

* He means that they were all called up from the Reserves. It is a Roll of those who served, not of those who were killed.

Robert Crowe 3 Bt. Norfolk Reg. Militia
T. Crowe P W O N Artillery Gt Yarmouth"
(SL) "Walter Corble 2nd Norfolk Regiment
Albert Dove 2nd Norfolks
Robert Ellis Wallis 2 B Norfolk Regt.
Spencer G Wallis 3 B Norfolk Militia
William Oakley 3 Kings Royal Rifles
James Mullenger 2 Norfolks"

But except for those who fought in it the Boer War had been far away from the Lophams. One of Mrs. Mann's schoolgirls writes:

". . . We got a day's holiday for the releif of 'Ladysmith', at least ½ a day, for it was midday before we got the news through from Eccles station, by someone who went to fetch the *papers*, also for the releif of 'Mafeking'—no wireless or tele then."

The new war would come much nearer home. First there were the increasing demands of the Forces, the anxieties of families for their absent men, and the loss of lives. Although farmworkers were protected to some extent from conscription there were plenty of Lopham men who went to war. The Roll of Honour in South Lopham church shews ninety-three, nearly half the total male population. This must have put a strain on the remaining labour force as well as a blight upon village society. It is said that there were strong feelings against conscientious objectors. According to one story a man who professed such views was tied to the Dale tree and stoned. Another version has it that he was stripped by the women and fastened to a burning hedge.

The North Lopham War Memorial records the names of fourteen men who lost their lives in this war:

Thomas Baker, Sydney Emms, Wilfred Emms, Albert Holden, Bert Cocksedge, William Cullum, Frank Emms, James Emms, Frederick Brown, William Crowe, Arthur Hogg, Alan Garnham, William Smith, Frederick Hutson.

The South Lopham Memorial has the names of ten:

Arthur Thomas Betts, George Bond, Robert Corble, Arthur Flatman, Godfrey Hawes, George Hawes, Albert Halls, Edward Halls, Percy Prentice, Frederick E. Smith,

but there were three more whose deaths in action are recorded in the South Lopham School Log:

Marcus George Bardwell, Edward Bardwell and Sidney Wallis. The same source gives the "total no. of ex-scholar casualties" as 16 "so far as is known" on October 2nd 1918. This leaves three more names for commemoration, unless they were North Lopham men who had their schooling in South Lopham but went to war from the other village.

Thomas Crowe, the veteran, kept a list of "The Addresses of My Boy Soldiers Who I write to" and entered some of their fates:

"Wounded with the DCM"
"Dudley Infirmery Birmingham—this was his last Place"
"Wounded"
"Not ever heard no mor"
"Wounded"
"Died of Wounds".

He also recorded and no doubt circulated in his news-book the appalling casualty figures of the first years of war.

For the first time for many centuries the Lophams suffered enemy invasion, but only in air-space. Zeppelins came over but dropped nothing worse than an aluminium water or fuel tank in the safe expanse of Nine Acres on High Common. Part of this was seized by a cowman as a windfall for his henhouse roof, but the police searched him out and impounded it. Another part, a brass "double tap", was found by a farmer whose wife would not allow him to keep such perilous goods inside the house. So he buried it as a "curio" to be recovered after the war, but when that time came it could no longer be found. If it remains buried for another hundred years it should present a nice problem for the archaeologist.[485]

Meanwhile civilian life in the thinly populated Lophams continued much as it had been before the war. Food was never as short in the country as it could be in the towns but the wages of farmworkers shewed little improvement. The Women's Land Army did not appear at either Lopham though one or two local women found men's work in the fields. Communications were simple and sparse and the villages remained largely dependent on their own resources, for example their wells. Main water supplies would not reach them until after the next war had begun.

After the Armistice there were such celebrations as the community could afford and one North Lopham man can remember winning half a crown as second prize in the Sack Race. This shews an increase of 25% above the same prize for the same event in the sports at King George V's Coronation and illustrates perhaps the rise in the cost of living. The official end of the war was marked by a week's "Peace Holiday" for the schoolchildren, apparently from November 3rd–8th, 1919. This was fortunate for North Lopham school where there was an interregnum of supply teachers and where seventeen of the boys, very much in the fashion of the day, had been

"'on strike' because there was no fire in school. These were withdrawn & when some of them came to school next morning they were punished. Most of those so punished and those who did not come on Wednesday have not been to school since. Two boys who went 'on strike'", writes this cautious reporter of obscure industrial action, "came back to school on Thursday & Friday respectively, but were not punished because the other boys stated that these were the ringleaders and it is desirable to investigate the matter before suitable punishment is administered."

After careful adjudication, thirteen of the boys were punished on October 29th for "striking". One was thrashed for "refusing to take punishment", and the rest were awarded "strokes" on the hand: three sixes, three fives, three fours, one three and two twos. But the strike seems to have been a success for when "M. Reece" arrived to take up duties as a supply teacher on November 10th, he or she "found the school was" (still) "closed for want of coal".

A new era began for North Lopham school in January, 1920, with the appointment of Lionel Twiddy as Teacher-in-charge. He reformed the curriculum, much to the satisfaction of H.M.Is, with particular attention to "rural science", in other words practical lessons in carpentery and gardening for the boys, with prospects of cooking and even personal hygiene for the girls. The Twiddys in their nine years at North Lopham laid the foundations for the long and successful reign of the Castells, parts of which have been described in Chapter Twenty-One.

North Lopham School top form in 1927. Top row: H. Smith, C. Solly, R. Drury, J. Aldous, W. Holden, B. Bailey. Middle row: G. Worby, S. Smith, E. Brock, S. Goddard, J. West, E. Taylor. Front row: A. A. Crook, B.

By April, 1922, Lionel Twiddy had been elected to the North Lopham Parish Council where he became a leader of post-war advances towards modern times. In 1924 he made the first proposals for telephone links between Lopham and the rest of the world, and in 1925 he negotiated successfully with the Charity Trustees for a contribution to a nursing association for North and South Lopham. The first district nurse was Doris Barnes, who became Mrs. Sidney Brock. She retired in 1957 after a career of thirty-two years, pursuing all her earlier errands of mercy on a bicycle. She had become District Nursing Sister not only for North and South Lopham but also for Fersfield, Kenninghall, Blo' Norton and Garboldisham, helping who knows how many of the present generation into the modern world.

These were not the only forward steps of the 1920s. As long ago as October, 1901, the Guiltcross Rural District Council, then the proprietors of "a public watering pit, known as 'Letchmere' situated in the centre of the Parish of North Lopham", had been asked to abate the nuisance of drainage from private premises "into the public sewer" and so into this pit. Eleven years later ratepayers were still complaining of the nuisance from this drainage but it is not until July, 1920 that a proposal of the Parish Council reveals just how public the sewage was. It was then proposed that

"Pipes be laid and covered in by the side of the Road leading from the Primitive Methodist Chapel in the direction of the Post Office and that the ditch be levelled with Clay in such places where no Pipes are laid and where necessary . . ."

Eventually, but by no means finally, in May, 1925, a meeting was arranged on the malodorous banks of the Letchmere between the County Surveyor, County and District Councillors, and the Parish Council. It was decided that the drainage running into the pond "should be carried away to Tann's Lane" and that Letchmere should be cleaned. The county should pay for the drainage and the parish should pay for their pond. But it is doubtful how much action was taken on this agreement. At the annual parish meeting of March 20th, 1930, Charles Castell, Twiddy's successor as teacher-in-charge and reformer at large in North Lopham, declared

"The general state of the Sanitation of the Parish . . . to be in a deplorable condition. Members of various committees who had met the R.D.C. on this question at various times informed him the reason why no steps had been taken to improve the matter viz: the tremendous cost which would fall on the ratepayers if any systematic scheme of drainage was entered into & did not consider any useful purpose could be served by going any further into the matter."

Another expensive and more pressing question was housing. In 1890 Dr. Augustus Jessopp had written of Norfolk villages:

"Houses?—Faugh! Houses? Why you may see whole rows of hovels in no one of which would any farmer in the parish put his nag for the night without indignant protest—rows of hovels where there are only two rooms, one above and one below. I could point to three of these disgraceful tenements immediately contiguous to one another, in each of which, by a strange coincidence, there were lately a father, mother, and seven children all sleeping in a single room. In one case the mother produced an eighth child in the night, her only helper being her daughter, a girl of fourteen, who did her best while the father ran to fetch the mid-wife!"[486]

At North Lopham in 1851 there had been 832 people in 185 dwellings, and at South Lopham 731 in 155. In 1931 the comparable figures were 567 in 154 and 346 in 107. There had been very few new houses built in either village between 1850 and 1930. The school logs illustrate the unhealthy and overcrowded state of the cottages with their records of children sent home because they were verminous, and of long closures because of epidemics. In 1919 the Thetford Rural District Council sent the parish councils "A Letter re Housing of the Working Classes", asking for information about the needs of each parish. The North Lopham council reckoned that they wanted six new houses and decided also to see whether the owners of decayed houses were willing to repair them. In the following year they objected strongly to the R.D.C.'s proposal for houses on Tann's Meadow (which had evidently lost its Jubilee name) and considered

"the Field near the Blacksmiths Shop the only suitable Site for Building Houses in the Parish."

The Housing Committee of the R.D.C., in spite of

reminders, were not persuaded to talk with the parish council and the ratepayers at a public meeting until April 14th, 1930. They then undertook to recommend eight houses for North Lopham, half of "parlour" and half of "non parlour" type. They rejected two sites in Tann's Lane, one of them presumably the field by the smithy, because of the condition of the lane "and the fact that an open drain from the Farm ran past & was very objectionable". By March, 1931, four houses had been built across the road from the King's Head* at a cost of £400 each, but the Annual Parish Meeting criticised them on the grounds that they were "not in harmony with surrounding property"; had inferior sanitary arrangements and inequitable rents. Nevertheless the outstanding four houses were still wanted, and in October, by dint of appealing to the County Council, the doughty councillors of North Lopham achieved a meeting with the Clerk to the R.D.C. and the County Medical Officer of Health. The M.O.H. "inspected many houses in the Parish" and gave it as his opinion that further houses were needed:

". . . there are families with young children living in unfit houses which might be made fit for elderly people. There is also one bad case of overcrowding where two adults & three children have to live & sleep in one room & a scullery." But the R.D.C. maintained that there were other parishes in greater need, and seven years seem to have gone by before the missing four houses were built in King's Head Lane.

It is reasonable to suppose that the parish council of South Lopham were struggling into the twentieth century at the same time as the northern neighbours, but unfortunately the records of their parish council in this period cannot be found. South Lopham had been pioneers in road improvement for by October, 1888 they had raised £77-0-11 towards their target of eighty pounds for the South Lopham Crown Bridge. The Parish Magazine expressed the hope that a mysterious body, "'the County' or the 'County Council', if then established, will contribute half the cost" of building this bridge over the ford on the parish boundary at the Hundred River. Little did they think in those innocent days how the future A 1066

* Demolishing no doubt "the old Dale tree".

South Lopham Green & White Horse Great Barn, *c*. 1913.

would tear their village in half. The motor-car was still welcomed after the first world war and South Lopham's first petrol pump was planted close by the Crown.*

The peaceful integrity of South Lopham in the nineteen twenties was celebrated by a decision to clear the triangle at the centre of the village and transform or restore it into a green. At the time when this photograph was taken the place had been a dump for the local smithy, whose forge stood a little way up the Garboldisham road. When the new day dawned and the weeded, levelled, and fresh seeded plot broke greenly into the light of day, it transpired that the private improver had sown not grass, alas, but lettuce.

Nevertheless it was private enterprise which led the march into modern times, and despite the tradition of the looms progress was soon linked to mechanisation. As far back as 1883 Robert Womack had operated a steam mill in South Lopham, and in North Lopham, after the turn of the century, came Ambrose Stevens with his thrashing machine and steam tractors, "in his time the largest thrashing tackle dealer in Norfolk".[487] These were preliminaries to an industrial revolution in agriculture which took some fifty years to arrive. Mechanised transport advanced more rapidly, led by the solid-tired lorries of Jesse Green and Arthur Brock, eroding the Lophams' isolation, enlarging their outlook, and eventually changing the whole character of their existence.

Some of this advance was due to one man, Herbert Augustus Crook, who was born in 1886, the son of Charles Edward Crook, the North Lopham blacksmith, and his wife, Laura, formerly a Ludbrook of the same village. Herbert left North Lopham school at the age of twelve to help his father at the smithy, and by saving up the pennies he earned for soldering and other odd jobs he managed to buy an old bicycle with solid tyres. By taking it to pieces, repairing it, and putting it together again he made it rideable and at the same time learned the workings of the machine. He was soon repairing other early bicycles in the two villages and earning himself

* By Stanley Hoskins in 1929. He started his business in 1927 with cycle repairs and the charging of wireless batteries but in this far eastern corner of the Lophams extended it further to second-hand guns and chocolates, then to the motor-car.

Jesse Green & one of Lopham's first lorries. Alfred Bailey at the steering wheel. Wharton Womack at the bonnet was the builder of the cabin and the "buck", i.e. the carrier.

Sidney Brock, Charles Crook, Blacksmith, and Gordon Ludbrook at Tann's Lane Smithy, N. Lopham, 1913.

enough money to buy himself a better model. With a friend, Percy Womack, he rode in races organised by neighbouring villages and won a number of prizes. Soon he was graduating to motor cycles.

In 1908 Herbert married Edna Maria Goddard, the grand-daughter of Martha Smith of the Bull, and established his own cycle business at the inn. He bought cycle parts and built machines which sold so well that he was able to realise a bigger ambition. This was to go up to London in 1910 and buy a car, a second-hand Darracq. He went with a friend, Sidney Whiting, the blacksmith of Garboldisham. Neither of them had driven a car before but on the peaceful roads of those days they taught themselves how to drive on the hundred long miles home. The Darracq became the first hire car of the Lophams, famous for weddings, funerals and travelling in style. In 1914, an established success, Herbert became the landlord of the Bull.

He went into the army in 1916 and was sent to Egypt in the following year. He was still there in 1919 when his wife, who had kept the Bull going till she was

"fed up . . . got the address of his officer and wrote a letter and told him my situation alone with 3 children and got his release."

The combined energies of the Crook family soon revived the cycle business, together with the taxi service, car repairs, and a flourishing Bull. There had been a time when Herbert used to ride a motor-cycle to East Harling "with 2 Petrol cans round his neck for Petrol at 9d a gallon", but by 1926 he had made contracts with Shell and BP for the installation of petrol pumps. Three years later there was the pump by South Lopham Crown, but even so, there cannot have been much motor traffic through the villages. On March 9th, 1931 the Annual Parish Meeting of North Lopham represented to the Thetford Rural District Council

"the disgraceful state of the highway passing through the village from Kenninghall to South Lopham. This main road, which has never been metalled with granite is in a dangerous state for fast traffic & needs rebuilding without delay."

Meanwhile the social life of North and South was taking a turn towards concord. A "Lopham United" football team made its first appearances after the war,* and the two villages also combined to field a cricket side. But although they played well together a witness of those days says that off the field the relations between North and South were "a bit of elastic". It was the womenfolk who achieved the first enduring degree of union in 1926 with the establishment of a Women's Institute. Mrs. C. J. Eastwood, their founder and first president, had started "Mothers' Meetings, to be held in each parish" as long ago as November, 1899, and no doubt she had her husband the rector's support in the new venture. But the cordial and inter-parochial relations which developed within this novel society soon moved beyond rectory control, and one year after its foundation the Lophams' Women's Institute entered on a course which led to direct and public confrontation with the rector.

In 1927, according to Percy Beales, "the local Women's Institute" (meaning the North Lopham membership?) "proposed a fete towards building a village hall for the two parishes, though at that time no definite scheme had been formed either by the Institute itself or any responsible public body. The help of the men folk of the village" (North Lopham?) "was obtained, and the fete had been carried through by privately called meetings with no legal authority of any kind. Realising the dangers of such an unsatisfactory state of affairs, the fete money was paid into a Diss bank credited to 'The Lopham Hall Fund', upon the understanding that a proper and legal representative committee of the two villages should be appointed to shoulder the responsibilities."[488]

At the same time, it seems, a committee which was less than proper and legal had organised the fête and pursued its aims under the leadership of Percy and his friend Lionel Twiddy. Twiddy retired from the Vice-Chairmanship of the Parish Council and from the head-teachership of North Lopham School in October and December, 1928, on appointment to another post, and amid general applause for his services. When there was a question three months later about records of the fête organisation he was able to say that

* Inspired by Lionel Twiddy and encouraged by Leonard West, who lent the players his Bell Meadow in North Lopham.

"everything was taken out of his hands, so that he could not produce the names of the old committee."[489]

It was Percy Beales who made the first public démarche. On January 31st, 1929, the North Lopham Parish Council met to discuss a letter they had received from him "relating to the funds of the proposed Village Hall," and decided that since the same letter had been addressed to the South Lopham P.C. "no useful action could be taken" until the two councils met together. South Lopham, however, declined the invitation to a joint meeting and informed the North Lopham Clerk that they had appointed "two Trustees of Village Hall Fund". North retaliated by calling for a public meeting to be held at their school (the historic Albert Rooms) on March 1st.

According to the *Eastern Daily Press*, "several weeks' lively controversy" followed Percy's letters to the two councils. Some of the fur that flew was Lionel Twiddy's. He declared at the March 1st meeting that he had

"a letter that would refute suggestions contained in a letter that had appeared in the Press. He was sorry to say that over the affair he had received rough treatment."[490]

Whatever these suggestions were, and whoever made them, the public meeting—"representative of the business and social life of both villages"—went against Rector Eastwood. He had been elected to the chair but allowed some prejudice to appear from it against the proposal for a joint village hall:

"Alluding to the controversy that had arisen the chairman said that it was argued that although the money" (£77-14-0) "had been raised for a village hall a hall for the two villages would be useless. It was said that if the hall was put up in North Lopham it would not be used by the people of South Lopham. (A voice—Why not?) Because of the distance. Then it was said that if you had it in South Lopham the people of North Lopham would not go down to it and that if you had it in the middle of the two parishes it would be awkward. Some had therefore suggested that the money should be divided between the two parishes. He was making no suggestions, but simply stating that these things had been spoken. The money in the bank, he believed, was in the name of Mr. Twiddy and Mr. P. Beales, and one thing the meeting should do was to appoint trustees. It had been suggested the Parish Councils should appoint trustees, but they could not assume the responsibility, and only from that" (sic—? this) "meeting could come the appointment of trustees . . . The meeting was open for the ventilation of opinion. If they decided to split up the money, they would have to appoint somebody to divide it.

Mr. Bilham Woods" (of Lodge Farm, North Lopham) "asked for what purpose the money was raised.

The Chairman.—The Women's Institute raised the money to get a village hall.

Mr. Woods—Well, that's how the money should be spent. (Applause)

The Chairman—Don't think I insinuated anything else.

Mr. Woods—It's no use dividing the money.

Mr. A. S. Vincent" (of South Lopham) "—The object of the fete was to raise money for one good hut, not two small huts. The idea was to provide a place for the young people of the two parishes to meet and fraternise more. (Applause.)

It was then agreed that the fund should be utilised for one hall . . .

The following were appointed trustees: Mr. L. J. West" (North Lopham), "Mrs. Gooderham," (North Lopham) "Mr. L. Witton," (South Lopham) "Mr. A. S. Vincent" (South Lopham) "and Mr. B. Woods." (North Lopham).

"Mr. Vincent then urged the meeting to get on with arrangements for holding another fete. This was agreed to and the rector vacated the chair in favour of Mr. Timothy Stevens" (Vice Chairman of the North Lopham Parish Council) "who consented to serve as chairman of the fete."[491]

It was an historic moment. When had North and South Lopham last joined in public agreement on a common cause? Against pagan Danish invaders in the ninth century? It was for no unchristian purpose that they united against their rector, but he never forgave them. He had been a hard-working parson, remembered in his time to have held four services a Sunday, two for each parish; to have kept up the "Sheet and Blanket Clubs" for the poor; and to have attempted social meetings for the young men at the Albert Rooms and the South Lopham Mission Room respectively. But he attached importance to the separation of the two parishes and he was not popular in either, perhaps as one on whom the mantle of Bateman was seen to fall. Eastwood was so much angered by the opening of the joint parish hall in July, 1931, that he sold the "Mission Room",* which Bateman had built in 1883, and used the proceeds to convert the rectory's sixteenth century tithe barn into a "South Lopham Village Hall", solemnly opened by the Bishop of Norwich in November of the same year. In spite of its use for "the pictures" and for floor-shows of a remarkably "free and easy" kind, it did not prove a success.

But if the Church frowned on any union between parishes which had been officially separate since the Middle Ages, the ancient feudal lords of the never-divided manor smiled on an auspicious occasion. Bernard Marmaduke Fitzalan-Howard, who had succeeded his father as sixteenth duke of Norfolk in 1917, was approached by leading inhabitants, some of them tenants of his Lopham lands, and decided to present a playing field as well as a site for the joint village hall to the new community.

The duke's generosity was celebrated in style and he was invited to attend the opening ceremonies on Saturday, August 2nd, 1930. But Percy Beales was before him with a local presentation, roping in the Church as it were in the rector's teeth:

"*Memorial gates*: Large double gates and kissing gates made of native oak, which had been given to the village in memory of the late Zadia Beales by members of her family. They were designed by Mr. Percy S. Beales and made in the workshops of Mr. Wharton Womack at North Lopham with wrought iron work by old craftsmen from Wretham. The gates were dedicated on Friday evening by Canon R. W. Longley, R.D. (Rector of Banham), assisted by the Rev. C. J. Eastwood (Rector). A hymn composed by Mr. P. S. Beales, 'The Hymn of the Gate' was sung."[492] The gates have long disappeared but the dedication plate is said to survive.

Next day Colonel Edward Mornement, C.B.E. (Military), of East Harling, no doubt a connection of James Mornement, the Churchwarden of North Lopham, who had been the

* Now Magdelan House, South Lopham.

twelfth duke's tenant at Park Farm in 1822,* began the proceedings by offering the twenty-two year old sixteenth duke "a cordial and kindly Norfolk welcome". He "thought it was a matter of some twenty years since the parish had the honour of being visited by a member of his Grace's family". The chairman was followed by the Lord Lieutenant, Mr. Russell Colman, who had evidently briefed himself on Lopham history, and thought perhaps that his office required him to introduce a disciplinary note. "Having wished the Lophams success in the competitions for which they might enter in the field of sport, the Lord Lieutenant said he had heard that in the past there had been a certain amount of rivalry or jealousy between the parishes. He was also given to understand that that was now buried. He hoped it was, for he wanted to see the two parishes work harmoniously together, and so achieve results they should achieve from the greater multitude of numbers. (Applause.)"

Percy Beales, "describing himself as a 'plain Lopham man', also thanked the Duke . . . The gift laid the foundation of a new Lopham. It was no ordinary village in the sense that in the glorious past the village was noted for its craftsmen, especially in hand loom weaving . . ." (He said that) "by fetes and other means they had raised £200 towards the village hall. Expenditure in connection with the playing field amounted to £25, and promises for this sum had been received . . . The village hall was a most difficult scheme. They wanted the best village hall in Norfolk. They had £200, and wanted £1,000. Mr. Beales then presented the Duke with a photograph album of calf, bearing the Duke's arms, which had been made entirely by hand" (and by him?) "in the village."

In reply the duke first apologised for being late. Dorothy Sayers might have had him in mind when she wrote about Lord Peter Wimsey's misadventures on the way to Denver in her "Nine Tailors" of 1934. "To tell the honest truth," said the duke, "there are so many roads in Norfolk that I took the wrong lane and got lost." It was his first visit to the county from which he took his title. In his thanks for his present he said that

* See Chapter Seventeen.

"The first pictures he would place in the book would be photographs of the people of Lopham present that day. (Applause.)"

In the sports and games which followed we may wonder if he stayed long enough to photograph the Pillow Fight. It was won by a Garboldisham boy and a Diss lad took the second prize, but it would be unreasonable to suppose that the Lord Lieutenant forbade the "greater multitude" of the Lophams to take part in such an inflammatory exercise. There seems to have been no veto on their handling of projectiles, for it is recorded that

"Mrs. F. Stone (Quidenham) judged a men's jam tart competition, in which Mr. G. Coleman (South Lopham) was the winner . . ."[493]

It was a great day for Percy Beales and the Lopham unionists in both villages, but they did not get everything their own way. In addition to the appointment of trustees, the public meeting of March 1st, 1929, had led to the establishment of a "Village Hall and Playing Field Committee" under the chairmanship of Percy Beales. The meetings of this committee seem to have been held for the most part in public, and perhaps the chairman and his friends were carried away by the initial appearances of public support. At a public meeting held apparently in September, 1930, the unionists succeeded in proposing and electing a "Lopham Village Council" to take over the functions of the committee and presumably with designs upon the two parish councils. On October 3rd the North Lopham Parish Council discussed a letter from the secretary of the Village Hall and Playing Field Committee asking them to nominate a representative "on the proposed Village Community Council", and on the motion of Timothy Stevens, a friend of Beales and Castell, the Clerk was directed to represent them. Presumably a similar invitation went to the South Lopham Parish Council, but we do not know the result.

The ladies of Lopham, the originators of united action for the two villages, may have had different ideas from the unionists'. Mrs. Mary Gooderham, the first woman trustee of the Lopham Village Hall funds, had been appointed secretary at the trustees' first meeting on April 5th, 1929. She and her husband, James, were Suffolk people who had moved from

Thorndon in that county first to Diss Heywood, then in 1907 into Dairy (formerly Noddle) Farm, North Lopham, where Mrs. Gooderham soon became celebrated for her good housekeeping, particularly for her prize-winning bread. With Mrs. Bilham Woods of North Lopham, another Suffolk immigrant, to whom she attributed the first proposals for the village hall, she took a leading part in the Women's Institute from the time of its foundation in 1926. At a meeting of the Hall Trustees, held at Dairy Farm on November 3rd, 1930, and attended by their hostess as secretary, Mr. H. P. Styles of South Lopham was elected chairman. Then "After considerable discussion the Trustees agreed that the Council recently set up, does not appear generally acceptable to the Public". The views of the Public were canvassed three weeks later at a meeting of the Village Hall and Playing Field Committee held in South Lopham School. The chairman "explained the objects which had led up to the setting up of a Village Council at the last public meeting. A lengthly" (sic) "discussion took place" after which Mrs. Gooderham proposed and Mrs. Woods seconded that:– "All the business of the previous public meeting, and the aims for which the Lophams Village Council was elected be hereby rescinded. This was carried unanimously." Perhaps to demonstrate the counter-revolution, the old committee was divided into two: one for the village hall and one for the playing field, each to be representative of both villages. Percy Beales was accorded a unanimous vote of thanks "for his splendid services, numerous & handsome gifts, and assistance, to the Village Hall & Playing Field Scheme in the past".[494] At the first meeting of the new Village Hall Committee, incorporating the trustees, he was unanimously elected chairman on the proposal of Mrs. Woods, seconded by Mrs. Gooderham, and until illness prevented him he continued to serve in that post for four successful years. He seems to have borne no grudge against Mrs. Gooderham and, years later, expressed his admiration for her as a Quaker. Perhaps she had persuaded him that too hasty and thoroughgoing a union of the Lophams would not be conducive to brotherly love.

How much excitement had been generated between the unionists and their opponents may be guessed from the results of the council elections at the North Lopham annual parish meeting on March 9th, 1931. James Reeder, a leading Methodist farmer, who had been Chairman since April, 1928, Percy Stephen Beales and James Gooderham were all equal at the bottom of the poll and were not elected. It may be noted, however, that Charles Castell, who was elected equal second in the same poll and who was a particular friend of Percy Beales, proposed only two years later, on March 28th, 1933, "that a letter be sent to Norfolk County Council that with reference to the coming redistribution of Rural District Areas this Parish Council request the C.C. to explore the possibilities of amalgamating the parishes of N. & S. Lopham." The motion was carried but nothing more seems to have been heard of it within the limits of this history.

Meanwhile the common aims of the village hall and the playing field prospered. A first section of the hall was opened in July, 1931, by the Dowager Lady Suffield, and annual fêtes were held to raise funds for its completion. The extension was achieved in 1934 and both sections were built by William Wharton Womack of North Lopham. The playing field gave a stimulus to both cricket and football, ensuring the re-establishment of Lopham United after the second world war, an enterprise in which Mr. W. F. E. Speer of the North Lopham Bell and Mr. T. Williamson of the same village played leading parts. As recently as 1965 this team was said to have the best football pitch in Norfolk.

These were not the only competitive games in the Lophams between the wars. One of the most popular was quoits, introduced by Herbert Crook at the Bull, where he and his son laid down quoits beds, circles of clay round the pins. Once the sport had taken hold he bought and restored an old charabanc so that the Bull team could play home and away matches as far afield as Forncett, Wacton, Wramplingham, Hingham, Aslacton, Botesdale, Gissing and Kenninghall. Darts, draughts and dominoes were also played but the Lophams never took to bowls.

In their schooldays, apart from cricket and football, the children played rounders, netball, stool-ball (an ancestor of cricket), leapfrog, marbles and hopscotch. Alternatives were

Staghorns, Pig's Whistle,* Egg Hat,† and Drops.‡ In their season tops were spun and hoops were run, while the weapons of child's war were pea shooters, catapults and pop-guns. As in Shakespeare's day, the last were made of hollowed elder-shoots loaded with acorn bullets—or with unpoetical newspaper chewed into wads.

Organised games were beginning at school, and Miss Mary Gill who became head teacher at South Lopham in October, 1920, seems to have taken immediate action on the H.M.I.'s report of February 18th, 1921:

". . . The children enter with zest into their games but the playground space is limited: it would be a great advantage if arrangements could be made for the use of the adjacent playing-field . . ."

This was Church Meadow, in which the first Lopham United used to play. Mary Gill noted under the same date that she had got "permission from Mr. Nottidge, one of the Managers, to use the Church Meadow one hour every week for school games".

Unfortunately her relations with the principal Manager and Correspondent, Charles James Eastwood, the rector, were much less cordial. It is difficult to judge how the trouble began and to guess what dark looks preceded the bleak words of the school log. A red ink entry of March 16th, 1922, records that the head teacher was given "verbal notification" by the Correspondent on that day "of the appointment of Miss Solly as Supplementary Teacher, to commence duties on Monday, March 20th". Miss Solly's commencement also appears in red ink, perhaps displaying the anger of a head teacher who had not been consulted on appointments to her staff. Three weeks later Miss Solly was transferred to Standards II and III while Miss Cockrill replaced her in charge of Standard I and the Infants. This was the head teacher's decision and on May 4th she "Received Form 9E, & completed it on the same date". This was presumably the pro forma used in complaints and explanations, for the two rubric entries of May 9th and 22nd record the handing of Form 9E to the

* An elaboration of leapfrog.

† Not as exciting as it may sound. It was bowling balls into school caps.

‡ Flicking cigarette cards.

Correspondent, the receiving it back from him, and its posting "to the Office". Five months later Miss Solly "finished duty", apparently on good terms with her head, and "Miss Sadler commenced duty as an uncertificated Teacher".

For ten months Form 9E and who shall say how much surrounding correspondence and conversation smouldered away until on March 16th, 1923, the anniversary of the "verbal notification", came the explosion:

"School closed all day by order of Education Committee, an Enquiry being held to investigate charges made by the Correspondent against the Head Teacher. Archdeacon Buckland, Miss Cozens-Hardy & Mr. Goldsmith members of the Education Committee being present. Also Mr. Davis the Secretary, the Rev. Eastwood; & the Managers. The Rev. Eastwood brought forward Miss Cockrill & Miss Sadler, assistant Teachers, also Mr. & Mrs. Hawks as witnesses. Miss Gill was supported by Mr. A. A. Thomas, Solicitor for the National Union of Teachers, &c also Miss Solly who came as a witness."

Mr. and Mrs. Hawks were the parents of Leslie Hawks, a pupil who had been the subject of entries for late attendance since Mary Gill took charge.

Whatever happened during the Enquiry its findings were not announced perhaps on the same day. It was not until April 11th that the accused "Completed Forms 9b E & 9a E and obtained the signatures of Mr. J. Kerry, Mr. S. Bowhill & Mr. R. W. Sare, managers, & despatched them to the office on Friday 13th April". Meanwhile both protagonists had been trying their strength. On March 21st the Correspondent had visited the school for twenty-five minutes and "Questioned Head Teacher as to whether she had followed the Time Table for that morning". The Head Teacher had contented herself with critical notes on the conduct of Leslie Hawks and his cousin Richard H. Durden, and on the efficiency of Misses Cockrill and Sadler.

After the return of "9bE & 9aE", presumably acknowledgements of her acquittal, Mary Gill was heartened enough between April 1923 and February 1924 to make seven animadversions upon Leslie Hawks, including the reflection that "The outside influence has inteferred" (sic) "with his work", and to send him home twice. She also replaced "Miss Saddler" with Miss Mary Catherine Orgill. All this was plainly too much for the rector and on February 1st, 1924, he put forth all his strength:

". . . The Rev. Eastwood came into the School at about 3–35 p.m. waited till the lesson finished, then he took the prayers, dismissed the children, told the assistant teachers not to fill in the registers" (Insertion by Miss Gill: "this statement was made to me by Miss Cockrill") "and then left the school taking with him the teachers. He did not address the Head Teacher."

The log is disappointingly reticent after this crisis. Another invasion of the schoolroom on February 20th, this time by Mr. and Mrs. Hawks, was repelled, and by October Leslie had moved to Redgrave school. H.M.I. reported on November 25th that

"Several changes in the staff and other difficulties have seriously impeded the progress of the work of this school during the past three years . . . until the staff is more settled and a better tone and steadier discipline prevail it is not possible for the school to reach a really creditable level of efficiency."

Perhaps it was conveyed to the rector that his visitations had been too frequent. In July, 1925, he blundered in his ecclesiastical capacity by failing to warn the head teacher of a coming diocesan inspection and the inspector was unable to examine the school in Religious Instruction. It may be that the diocesan authorities came to agree with H.M.I.'s reservations, for by November, 1926, James Reeder junior had replaced Eastwood as Correspondent for the South Lopham School Managers. The rector continued to check the school registers in a managerial capacity at irregular intervals between 1928 and 1933 but there is no record of his interference with the teachers or pupils during this time.

The effect of all this friction on the head of a church school and on her relations with her pupils and their parents can only be guessed. In 1927 H.M.I. reported "Marked improvement . . . in the tone and discipline of the School", and on May 8th, 1930, he wrote:

"The Head Mistress interests herself in the general welfare

of the children and readily gains their confidence. Her influence is evident in all the classes."

After more than nine years' struggle with the most powerful though not the most popular man in the parish Mary Gill might have begun to feel that she was winning her own. But the rector had been more than thirty years in office; he was an unforgiving character; and his influence on public—and parents'—opinion may still have been stronger than her own. We do not know what her social situation may have been but when she was invited in November 1930 to represent her school on the newly established Village Hall Committee the reply was that "Miss Gill does not wish to serve on any committee".[495]

Perhaps she was losing her grip. In June, 1932, she was notified by the County Education Office that "owing to a decrease in the numbers of pupils in attendance, there would be a reduction of staff". H.M.I. reported cautiously on March 27th, 1933, that

"... The children are inclined to be reticent, but they have received a sound training in the elementary subjects and in habits of neatness and order ..."

Four months later the log records:

"Police Constable Hines visited the school to question certain of the children with regard to the theft of Head Teacher's gold watch, which was taken from her desk on July 7th during the afternoon session." We are not told if the watch was ever found but it looks as though the owner's nerve was broken. On December 22nd, 1933, she wrote:

"I, Mary Gill, finish my duties as Head Teacher in South Lopham School."

Perhaps the watch had only been hidden. The Lophams of those days had a rough way in their practical jokes. There was the custom of "humstrumming", for example, a joke of great antiquity played upon newly-married couples. A village couple would usually spend their wedding-night at the home of the bride's or bridegroom's parents, and after the pubs were shut, about ten at night, some of the topers would collect old buckets, sticks, and pieces of corrugated iron to serenade them at the parents' door. The racket would continue until the door was opened and the revellers were given refreshments such as home-made wine and cake. After a ritual exchange of banter suitable to the occasion, the couple were then left in peace. On one occasion a performer who had beaten his piece of metal into silence asked his mates for a replacement and was handed a "spare" bucket in the dark. Next morning when he went to milk his cow he found to his chagrin that the "spare" had been his best milking pail, which was now a useless lump. "Humstrumming", well-known in Germany as "Polterabend", was practised in the Lophams as late as the mid 1950s.

The refuge of a honeymoon at an undisclosed or distant place was far beyond the means of village folk in the years between the wars. The wages of an ordinary farmworker in the early thirties were twenty-eight shillings for a forty-eight hour week. These were the men who did the jobs with hand tools where there was no machinery; and there were plenty of them. Horsemen earned thirty-five shillings for a fifty-five hour week. The extra hours were worked first to have the horses fed and ready for the labourers when they arrived at six in the morning, and secondly to feed them on Sundays. For the cowmen, working seventy hours in a seven day week, the wages were forty-five shillings. In spite of their hours, cowmen were held to be luckier than others since they could eat their meals indoors. Ordinary farmworkers would have to find shelter where they could, whether from the cold and wet, or from the hot sun and the flies. Often they would be standing in a ditch or huddling under a hedge to eat their dinners of bread and cheese, washed down with tea. The tea-bottle would be cold in summer, but in winter you could wrap an old sock round it to try and keep the heat in.

In 1937 the basic wage was raised to thirty-three shillings, but the working week remained the same and it was not until 1939 that farm workers were awarded three days holiday a year. Rents of tied cottages between the wars ranged from half a crown to four shillings and sixpence a week. You could lose your job and your cottage if you exhibited the wrong kind of politics but in general the relations between farmers and farmworkers were easy. Agricultural labour was large in numbers but little organised and lacked the experience of worker-employer confrontations in urban industry. Relatively few farmworkers had served in the armed forces during the war, and many had never travelled far from their native villages. The result in the Lophams, according to one well-informed witness, was that

"They were a happy and contented people and almost all their conversation was work." The standards of the "good old days" had survived the first world war.

One advance towards the coming revolution in the agricultural industry was the arrival of an electricity supply. Such tasks as chaff-cutting, slicing beet for cattle and corn-grinding had hitherto demanded men and horses, though some power was provided by paraffin engines. Electricity would not only drive the farm machines; if would lead to the factory production of artificial foodstuffs, replacing the fodder planted, grown and processed by man-power on each self-sufficient farm.

The power-lines did not reach the Lophams until 1934 but the demand for a link with the National Grid had been raised by the North Lopham Parish Council in January 1933. It was led by Councillor Charles Castell who seems, characteristically, to have recommended joint action with neighbouring parishes, but the letters sent to the electricity authorities in February stressed North Lopham's needs in isolation, with predictable results.

The telephone had already arrived but had been installed in the post office at North Lopham—and possibly at South Lopham—with an extraordinary disregard of village life and village gossip. In September, 1931, the parish council addressed a letter to the Head Postmaster at Diss, explaining some facts of life:

"The telephone placed in North Lopham Post Office is of no use to the residents as no arrangements for privacy have been made. The residents of the village therefore have either to go to a neighbouring village, or adopt other means of communication, with a consequent loss of revenue to the Post Office. The P.C. therefore request that suitable arrangements for privacy be made."

Post Office Telephones fought back unsuccessfully with a demand for a guarantee, then in February, 1932 conceded a cabinet inside the post office. The council, led as so often by

Castell, returned to the charge in September of the following year to point out that a kiosk outside the office could be used when the shop was shut. This point was also won eventually, but in 1938 the Telephone Manager, asked for means to use the telephone at night, replied that the question whether a light should be installed in the existing kiosk or a new kiosk erected "was still under consideration".

One respect in which North Lopham seems to have been less than enterprising was the need for a mains water supply. In November, 1935, the Wayland R.D.C. circulated a questionnaire together with proposals for a district water supply. Whether it was concern over the prospect of water rates, faith in one of Lopham's Supplementary Wonders, the "inexhaustible" well of the Womacks, or a general distaste for the element as a beverage, the parish meeting rejected the offer. In answer to Question One: Has there been a definite water shortage? 34 said No and 10 Yes. A motion that "This parish meeting declines to participate in the Water scheme as put forward by R.D.C." was carried by twenty-nine votes to nine.

But the District Council were not daunted. In June, 1939 they made a contract with F. W. Shanks Limited of Hunstanton to provide a water supply for the majority of the villages in the Rural District, including both Lophams, based on a source just outside Old Buckenham. The laying of mains northwards to Attleborough and southwards to the Buckenhams went on rapidly, but the beginning of the second world war in September raised a critical question whether the works should be suspended "for the duration", leaving only Attleborough and the Buckenhams supplied. After a visit by a Ministry of Health Inspector it was decided in the interests of food production for the war effort that work should proceed, although at a slower rate. In June and July, 1940, there was an additional delay when all the mechanical excavation equipment was borrowed to make trenches across the fields round Bodney aerodrome as an obstacle to the landing of German gliders during the expected invasion. The fortunes of war allowed the excavators to return to the job and the Lophams got their mains water supply in early 1941.[496]

There are minutes or is it centuries of difference between fetching the water from the well and turning it on from the tap. A farewell look at the Lophams, before this and more drastic changes began, shews a pretty quiet place, with simple pains and pleasures. Enough has been said of men's work: the women had plenty to do caring for their families; cooking, washing and cleaning; making new clothes and mending old; helping both ends to meet. Some would go to the monthly meetings of the Mothers' Union or the Women's Institute, and a few would aspire to higher responsibilities such as the Parochial Church Council or the Village Hall Committee. By the mid-thirties some would be seen on bicycles on summer Sunday evenings, when whole families would enjoy a "ride round", sometimes calling at a pub on the way home.

For the children and youngsters a game of football "Up Hunn's"—an enclosure off the Green at North Lopham—or on Church Meadow at South; fishing down the "Drift", a particular farm road; playing games; and watching the men play football, were the main pastimes. If you had the money, you could hire a bicycle at sixpence for the evening and go to the pictures at South Lopham or the cinema at Diss. In the late thirties bike rides to Norwich to support Norwich City or to visit the Norfolk Show were the red-letter days.

Flowers and vegetables were matters of family pride. There was great rivalry for the earliest potatoes, the longest runner bean, the best grafted rose or apple of your own contriving, and the biggest gooseberry. Other competitive occasions for grown-ups were the monthly Whist Drive and Dance, first at the Albert Rooms and then at the Village Hall, where every now and then there would be a children's party instead.

There were seven pubs: four in North and three in South. Some men would go to one or another of them every or almost every evening. There was beer at fourpence a pint, with a game of cards or dominoes for a winter night, played before a fire in the light of an oil lamp. When the weather was right some would be playing football every Saturday afternoon and quoits every Saturday evening. Quoits were a regular feature at the South Lopham Chequers as well as the North Lopham Bull, always followed by a sing-song and the circulation of the "gallon can". Song still held social sway in the Lophams and instead of "Time, Gentlemen, please!" the

North Lopham Bull rethatching in 1962.

landlord of the Bull would give his famous rendering of "The Village Pump":

"There's a pretty little village far away
Where they grow new potatoes corn and hay;
There's a trickly little rill that works a little mill,
And the Mill keeps turning all the day.
There are lots of little houses in a lump,
There is one that's called the Magpie and the
    Stump;
But you make no mistake: the thing that takes the
    cake,
The pride of all the village is the pump.

Chorus: It's the pump, the village pump,
  The P-U-M-P-PUMP.
  It's the pump, the village pump,
  The village pump, pump, pump, pump, pump.

Now we had a new policeman t'other week,
A sloppy sort of fellow so to speak,

They say he's not all there
But Oh dear I do declare
He's just what you might call a living freak.
Some people say as how he's off his chump,
'Cos one night he come across a biggish lump:
He said Move on, you're tight, but when he turned
his light
He found that he'd been talking to the pump.

Chorus: It's the pump &c.

Now our Squire who likes a bit of fun,
When his gal was twenty-one
He gave them all a treat,
There were nuts and things to eat
And the girls they had an Orange and a Bun;
There was candy for the boys and girls to crump,
And games at which you hop and skip and jump,
But to celebrate the Day in a proper sort of way
He shoved a brand new handle on the pump.

Chorus: It's the pump, the village pump,
The P-U-M-P-PUMP.
It's the pump, the village pump,
The village pump, pump, pump, pump, pump."

CHAPTER TWENTY-FOUR

The Second World War And Twentieth-Century Lopham

"(Sunday). At 11–15 a.m. the Prime Minister, Mr. Neville Chamberlain, broadcast a statement to the nation, intimating that our country was now in a state of war with Germany."

So wrote Mrs. B. A. Smith, head teacher of South Lopham school, opening the school and the log-book on a Sunday in the depths of the Harvest Holiday. It was news which she and most of her fellow-citizens in town or country received simultaneously on September 3rd, 1939. Wireless had now become cheap and popular, and there were few households in either Lopham who were not within earshot of a receiver. But listening in had been voluntary. It took a war to shew that wireless and its sequel television had ended village life as a retreat from the world. News would never stop. Communications became as compulsory and inescapable as the war itself.

The first world war had cost Lopham lives, some suffering, and a little peace. But much of its events and consequences had passed over the villagers' heads and the last chapter has shewn that there was little change in their standards, their ways of life and their pre-war outlook, despite the large material changes of the twenty following years. The two Lophams had become more tolerant of each other through the Women's Institute, the village hall and the playing field, but the only respect in which they were really united was probably a reserve towards outsiders: people who had the misfortune not to have been born or bred in North or South; and towards outside events of which it could be fortunately said, They did not happen here.

The second world war would destroy this isolation. In terms of historical development the Lophams would be so violently shaken both backwards and forwards that they would never be the same again. Backwards to a warfare of the Dark Ages in which unarmed civilians would be deliberately attacked as much as or more than the military forces. Because it never came, the expected poison gas attack from the air tends now to be forgotten or disregarded. Yet fear of such a barbarity was officially encouraged from the first day of the war, and the gas masks of Lopham schoolchildren were still being inspected and reported for their "defects" to the Senior Air Raid Warden as late as April, 1944. What nightmares were suffered from the sight of these bogey-faces upon children's bodies is better forgotten, but it told the Lophams that their remote part of Norfolk was as much in the front line as anywhere else in the island.

Soon they were more so and further back in history. In 1940, when the British Army and allied troops were driven from the Continent, the Lophams reverted a thousand years and more to become a defensive point in the area of expected invasion. On May 14th of that year Eden called for Local Defence Volunteers between the ages of seventeen and sixty-five. A quarter of a million volunteered within a week, a Lopham squad among them, armed with dummy guns. By September 2,500 self-propelled barges had been sighted in the ports of France and the Low Countries, and Lopham Gate was fortified with the booby-trap described in Chapter One.

Memories of the L.D.V. or the Home Guard, as Churchill renamed it, are of a military discipline and state of alert a good deal more rigorous than "Dad's Army", but of sociable interludes such as the nocturnal custom of baking potatoes on an old drumhead to while away the hours of night patrol. The Lopham Home Guard were never called into action against an invader, but the villages were attacked from the air. On February 27th, 1941, Mrs. B. A. Smith recorded that

"At about 12–40 p.m. today a German Raider machine-gunned the school and schoolhouse, but, fortunately, as the weather was so bad, all the children who have lunch in school were in either the cloak room or the classroom and no one was hurt and no damage done."

The same raider sent a bullet through the open door of the White Horse but no-one was hurt nor even dropped a glass of beer. Across the road, by the post office, thatch proved an inadequate defence against machine-gun fire, and George Smith, when he came home from work, found that a bullet had penetrated his roof and his blankets, ending up on the bottom sheet.

On another occasion an escaping raider discarded a five hundred pound bomb which fell near an old, empty house at the junction of the High Common road with the A 1066. The bomb went off and a little plaster fell but the oaken girdered frame was unbroken.

Meanwhile Lopham men went as readily to the fighting line as they had in the first world war, but eight women went as well, four from North and four from South. The North Lopham War Memorial records the names of five men who lost their lives:

Bertie Emms, Bertie Payne, George Pratt, Lionel Syzling, Charles Worby.

The South Lopham Memorial names two:

J. J. Corbett, L. J. Corbett.

There were war deaths in the Lophams too, though not of Lopham people. The United States Army Air Force, which came fully into the allied air offensive in 1943, were well-known in the two villages as visitors from the Snetterton airfield before January 29th, 1945. On that day eighteen of them fell from the skies and lay dead in the snow of North Lopham. The villages had grown accustomed to the sound of the Flying Fortresses which climbed into formation over North before they rumbled across the sea to bomb the Germans. This time two of the machines collided and twelve bombs fell on the parish. In one of the aircraft the bombs had been armed but all six exploded in the open fields. The other six fell along North Lopham Street, all unexploded. One fell outside a house and slid underneath it. The inhabitants were an elderly married couple, the husband being "in a poor way". When they were asked to leave for shelter with neighbours until the bomb could be removed, he refused at first to go. He said he had never done any harm to Hitler and he didn't see why Hitler should want to do any harm to him.

Other by-products of Hitler's war were less immediately dramatic but much more lasting in their effects. To begin with, the week after the war began, the country population of the Lophams had a compulsory injection of townsfolk, at a ratio of about one to six in South and one to nine in North. Each of the village schools was required to receive some sixty children: from the Orchard School, Hackney, in South, and from South Hackney Parochial L.C.C. School in North. With them came teachers and some parents, and all had to be billeted. A "lively time" is remembered in South Lopham where the villagers were startled to hear the London children address their headmaster by his Christian name. He and his staff were happily quartered on the White Horse; how life was lived in the mixed households amid the encounter of strange tongues and inharmonious habits is another question. Englishmen and Englishwomen from such different parts of England were never likely to agree on the way that Englishmen and Englishwomen should behave, but what of the children?

Initially there were attempts at segregation, prescribed apparently by the Norfolk education authorities. Charles Castell recorded on October 23rd, 1939, that "Consequent upon a decision to divide local and evacuated children as far as possible", the North Lopham scholars were to be instructed by their own teachers in three classrooms, while the Londoners, under London instruction and discipline, were piled into one. "This group works almost entirely as a separate entity, under the direction of Mr. E. W. Relf." Next week in South Lopham the County Inspector "arranged for all evacuated children over seven to be taught in Rectory Hall" (i.e. Eastwood's "South Lopham Village Hall".*)

It did not work. The overcrowding at school may have combined with other factors such as the "bore war"—the six months and more after September 3rd in which there were no

* Re-named "Eastwood Hall" by his successor.

air raids and England seemed to some to be almost detached from hostilities—to increase the drift of the evacuees back to Hackney. But whatever the academic and parental arguments may have been, segregation was bound to be ineffective. How could children be expected to remain "separate entities" out of school and at play? On April 29th, 1940, Castell recorded that

"This morning the evacuated children (31 from South Hackney Parochial School, 1 from Ealing and 1 from Willesden) were merged with this school." South Lopham held out until November 14th, 1941, "when the Evacuee School and South Lopham Village School were amalgamated" and the school re-organised. At this date there were 87 on the School Roll: 63 local children and 24 evacuees. The senior children were to be taught by an L.C.C. teacher named Williams in "Rectory Hall", while the rest would be taught in the South Lopham school building. One South Lopham mother told her daughter to come home if the seniors were all sent to the Rectory hall, and on November 19th Mrs. Smith recorded that

"I insisted on her going to the Rectory Hall, but she has not been at school since Monday at noon."

Evidently there were local misgivings about the manners and perhaps the morals brought into Lopham by children of the Big City. Considering the steady decline in the numbers of the evacuees—by April, 1942, there were only eighteen left at South Lopham—there may have been comparable distrust or dislike among the Londoners. Castell recorded an experiment at North Lopham School in the Harvest Holiday of 1942 which had curious results:

"During the holiday the school was open for fifty sessions as a recreation centre under the N.E.C. scheme for the care of children during school holidays. The maximum number of children attending at one session was 17 and the minimum 6. The average attendance for the whole period was 8. None of the evacuees attending this school availed themselves of the facilities offered."

What were they up to? No good, helping the harvest, avoiding an institution where they found themselves an unpopular minority, or simply shunning school in holidays?

Whatever the answers and whatever the real relations between the town and country children, it is interesting to speculate what unofficial education the Cockneys gave to their Norfolk playfellows and the Lopham folk to the Londoners. They were all mingling at impressionable ages and, as regards the Lophams, it is hard to believe that their traditional reserve towards outsiders was not shaken by the experience. As for the Londoners, perhaps they learnt something about self-sufficiency in a simple life.

It may be therefore that the first invasion of the Lophams in the second world war, the descent of the metropolitan refugees, pushed forward their historical development. But it was the second invasion, of 1943, which produced the more immediate advance to modern times. The Americans were friends rather than foreigners, long exhibited to Britain by films, newspapers and radio as expected English-speaking allies, and they first appeared in Norfolk with all the glamour of the United States Cavalry galloping to the relief of a beleaguered British stockade. In the eyes of some Lopham lads and lasses they may have represented the glitter of those celluloid heroes they had seen in Diss or at the South Lopham pictures, and who now walked from the screen and their dreams into their company at the inn or the village hall, talking, at least, in the romantic accents of their cinema patterns. It is hard to disentangle yourself from the world of propaganda, especially in wartime, but there were some early disappointments: unpronounceable names, unintelligible English and unacceptable habits. The visitors, for their part, found the British sadly un-American, and tended at first to make their bases into their own stockades, from which they raided the hinterland for recreation, girls and beer. They were not very good at the beer, which seems to have been stronger or more insidious than their own, and this made some of their recreations distasteful to the natives. They were more successful with the girls, towards whom they observed gallantries of a fashion almost forgotten among English suitors. This success could cause bad blood, or even draw blood, as on one occasion at a Lopham Village Hall dance.

As time went on and the two nations began to realise that neither of them was going to win the war single-handed, relations between the American military and the British civilians among whom they lived grew easier. These Americans were no isolationists. They were friendly, generous and full of talk; almost as ready to seek information as they were to impart it. Shyness and reticence were uncommon features among them: if they came across a strange person, principle or property they would declare their surprise, ask for an explanation, and deliver their judgement. This provoked or encouraged the taciturn English both to talk and think. It is held by at least one witness that the democracy exhibited by the U.S.A.A.F. in their conversation and behaviour had as marked an effect on the Lophams as their economic standards.

There was magic still, of a material kind, in what came out of the U.S.A.A.F. Commissaries. Lopham people found themselves confronted and often presented with luxuries beyond even peacetime expectations. The thin times of war rationing threw these creature comforts into high relief, but it was not merely that they were treats which made them exciting. These rich foods and drinks, these cigars and American cigarettes, these nylons, ball-point pens, self-winding watches and other customary indulgences of an affluent society were totally new to most of the Lopham beneficiaries, and revealed to them an existence they could never hope to lead by pre-war standards. Many people lived to learn that they preferred Scotch to Bourbon, Player's to Camels, and home-grown meat to American ham-in-molasses. But the strange flavours and the glimpse of riches left them restless and discontented with the pale prospects of post-war Lopham. Perhaps the war shook them further forward here than British history would ever justify.

One post-war prospect of a baleful kind was largely hidden from war-time Lopham by petrol-rationing. The needs of the war, especially for more and bigger airfields, had developed the roads of East Anglia into highways capable of carrying the heavy logistics of defence and attack. There are people living in South Lopham to-day who can remember when the village smith used to trundle cart-wheels across "the street" to the platform where they were fitted with their iron tires. Even during the war a police constable who patrolled the same road, now the A 1066, can remember bicycling under orders without lights through hours of darkness in which no kind of vehicle would pass. The traffic which has since developed night and day through both Lophams, without control on speed or size, has abolished their quiet, shaken their peace of mind, and destroyed the village freedom to saunter and to gossip down the street.

The parish councils of North and South could not be expected to foresee this huge increase of motor traffic, nor would they have wanted to restrain the development of roads to win the war. But there was a related question where their support of the war effort led to a loss of freedom which, on a longer view perhaps, they could have limited to the "duration of hostilities". As early as 1904 the North Lopham council may be seen maintaining a common right of the kind once protected by fines in the manorial courts. This was the upholding of free passage along those footpaths which had survived or outlived the Inclosure Awards as public rights of way. From time to time farmers would plough these up or try to prevent their use by obstruction, whereupon notice would be served on them by a letter from the council requiring them to repair and restore the passage. One footpath, which started from Bell Corner in North Lopham and passed through the Church Farm meadows in a rough parallel to the South Lopham road, became of increasing use to the parish after 1930 as a short cut to the playing field and the village hall. As late as June, 1940, a "Barbed Wire Obstruction" was removed from this path by order of the council, but in March, 1941, it was reported that new obstacles had been placed on it "at 3 points". Representations were made to the new owner of Church Farm about this and another obstructed fieldpath but it seems that both subjects were removed from the agenda after a letter from the Rural District Council had been accepted by the parish council in June, 1941.

Presumably the R.D.C. had put the case for the suspension of both rights of way in the paramount interests of food production. Next to the men and women who had joined the forces, this was the Lophams' principal contribution to the war effort, and so long as the emergency lasted the parish council would do nothing to restrain the cause of agriculture.

This was a war in which not only the Women's Land Army but even prisoners-of-war were brought to work on Lopham fields.

Between April, 1945, and April,1947, the North Lopham council seems itself to have gone into suspension because of an invalid election of councillors in 1946. Two years later the rehabilitated council decided to write to the "Highway Sub-Committee" of the Wayland R.D.C. about "the dangerous nature of the road from Yeates shop to the Playing Fields". Subsequent correspondence led to "a lengthy discussion" and the R.D.C. were told that they had not answered the parish council's questions. It is not recorded whether in correspondence or discussion the revival of the safe short cut from Bell Corner had been raised. It is said that nowadays very few people dare to walk to the village hall because of the traffic on the South Lopham road, and that a proposal for a children's playground on the playing field was rejected "because the back footpath is now closed".

The long-lost days of village street sociabilities were exemplified in the life of Daniel Gooch, "the Lopham philosopher":

"Like his father before him, he had with horse and trap, and latterly with a barrow, been a hawker of fish and fruit. With hard worn clothes, soft trilby pulled well down and tied with string, Dan, with his shaggy, sandy moustache and weather beaten face adorned with wisps and ringlets where the modern Don Juan wears his 'side-boards', was a familiar figure on the roads, and he seldom went out without carrying a message or parcel for someone in one village to another.

Though he had no schooling, to chat with him was the only way to learn that here was a man of wisdom acquired by hard experience, and to understand why he was regarded as the local philosopher. Dan taught himself to read and it became his main hobby. His pockets were invariably full of newspaper cuttings, those dealing with the odd and curious side of nature and human life.

He had his own views on education. Friendly with the children, he would ask those about to leave school what they had been learning. If they said arithmetic he would point to his barrow and say, 'My beet are two for 1½d: how many must

I sell for 1s 11d?' He said the answer he always got was 'I could do it if I had paper and pencil.'

If the children had been taking geography he would ask them the capitals of different countries and said many of them would look at him blank and be unable to tell him. He would sum up the position by saying that from what he saw of the youngsters nowadays he didn't miss much by not going to school.

As for the war, Dan would tell his friends that all the talk about a new order and a new world did not impress him and only fools talked about a world at peace as there had always been wars and always would be. Dan's allotment was the envy of the parish. It was impossible to find a weed in it. Recently he said to a reporter, 'You will never have peace while people are without healthy work'. He advocated healthy work and walking for a contented mind.

For forty years Dan assisted at Messrs. Gaze's cattle market at Diss on Fridays. Lover of animals that he was, he condemned all acts of cruelty and was the most practical supporter that the R.S.P.C.A. ever had."[497] Dan's travels took him two or three times a week to Garboldisham and it was on his way there in a storm on January 30th, 1943 that he was killed, not by a car, but by a falling branch.

There are some alive in the Lophams who remember Daniel Gooch and more who have survived not only the vicissitudes described in this chapter but post-war developments in which more than half their neighbours have become newcomers. Of such Lopham folk it may be said that "a little plaster has fallen but the oaken girdered frame is unbroken".

PART THREE

References

456. GARBOLDISHAM ... AND LOPHAM PARISH MAGAZINE, November 1899.
457. Ex. inf. Mrs. C. R. Twidle, South Lopham School.
458. NRO PURSEHOUSE NOTES (R 152[A]) Letter from BEALES to PURSEHOUSE of 25.vii.1960.
459. NRO PURSEHOUSE NOTES.
460. GARBOLDISHAM ... AND LOPHAM PARISH MAGAZINE, August, 1898.
461. MSS penes Mr. C. W. Farrow of Sprowston.
462. Ibid.
463. Local sources.
464. North Lopham Parish Register.
465. Lopham Minute Book 4.xi.1831.
466. NRO PURSEHOUSE NOTES (R 152[A]). Letter from BEALES to PURSEHOUSE of 25.vii.60.
467. Ibid., letter from BEALES to PURSEHOUSE of 10.ix.1960.
468. Recorded by the late Mrs. R. O. PICKERING ("Elizabeth Harland").
469. Ibid.
470. Deed of 19.iv.1926 penes Mrs. Lockey of North Lopham.
471. Ibid.
472. NRO PURSEHOUSE NOTES (R 152[A]). Letter from B. to P. of 25.vii.1960.
473. Ibid., letter of 10.ix.1960.
474. North Lopham School Log.
475. DISS JOURNAL of May 25th, 1929.
476. BLOMEFIELD, op. cit., p. 154.
477. Dan MICHEL: *Ayenbite of Inwyt* (1340) translated from LORENS: *Le somme des Vices et de Vertues* (1279), ed. by Richard MORRIS, London 1866, p. 31 (Modernised by the writer).
478. CROWE's BOOK.
479. The extracts were transcribed by Thomas Crowe from a DISS EXPRESS OF 1890.

480. GARBOLDISHAM ... AND LOPHAM PARISH MAGAZINE, April, 1899.
481. MITCHELL, op. cit. p. 334 (352) & sqq.
482. EAST ANGLIAN NOTES & QUERIES, III, 264.
483. ENCYCLOPAEDIA BRITANNICA, 11th edition, Cambridge 1910, vol. I, p. 413c.
484. Unidentified local newspaper of 7.ii.1958.
484[a] Cal. Pat. 1345–58, p. 562.
485. Ex inf. Mr. W. Hogg of High Common, North Lopham.
486. AUGUSTUS JESSOPP: *Arcady for Better for Worse*, 5th edn., London 1890, p. 113.
487. SOUTH NORFOLK NEWS of May 30th, 1975.
488. EDP of 4.(?).iii.29.
489. Loc. cit.
490. Ibid.
491. Ibid., and another unidentified newspaper of similar date.
492. EASTERN DAILY PRESS of 4.viii.30 and contemporary newspapers.
493. Ibid.
494. MS minute-books of Lopham Village Hall Committee.
495. Ibid.
496. Ex. inf. Mr. H. W. Temple Cole of Bury St. Edmunds.
497. NORWICH MERCURY of 11.ii.1943.

Appendix

The following notes have been prepared by residents of North and South Lopham to give an account of the villages between the end of the second world war and the Queen's Silver Jubilee in 1977, and to present the institutions of both parishes as they were in early 1979.

VIEWS ON VILLAGE LIFE IN NORTH & SOUTH LOPHAM, FROM THE SECOND WORLD WAR PERIOD TO THE PRESENT DAY

BY MR. R. W. BAKER

Ever since time began, progress has been made all the time, however slow. But for three or four years after the war, village life remained very stable, perhaps too stable, after the exciting war years. I am thinking of the main industry, agriculture, which is the basis of life anyway: *everything* and *everyone must eat*. The Government of the day only realise this when an enemy is sinking food ships at sea: they even made agriculture a Reserved Occupation. After that time lag, things altered very fast in agriculture. I must mention agriculture first, because as I have said, it is the backbone of village life. At this time seven out of ten workers in the village were working directly on farm work, light industry supporting it, e.g. agriculture machine factories, vets, M. M. Board, mills for cattle feed and handling the farms corn crops. The

Blacksmith was an important member of the team because horses were still the main power on farms and they had to be shod. N. Lopham had its Blacksmith's shop as well as S. Lopham, The smiths made, as well as mended, all kinds of wheels, iron and wood, also machines, which were small then, no more than what three horses could pull.

But as progress was made, horses became the first victims of the now familiar word redundancy. Tractors of all sizes took over, enabling much larger machines to be used. Work could be done in a quarter of the time, which in turn meant a lot less farm workers were needed. Villages could no longer employ all the men they did, men had to go further afield to small towns for work. About the same time as this change from horse power to tractors, big changes were made in the live stock.

Each village N. and S. Lopham had one large farm and several smaller ones, several carried cows. One in N. Lopham actually supplied milk which was delivered around the village by bucket and measure. Almost all the farms had pigs and chickens and some a few bullocks: these all provided cash for the farmer *all* the year. The big crops, Wheat, Barley and Sugar Beet gave a seasonal income of cash, as now. But modern means and ways were soon to make farmers change their way of life, culling the chicken, pigs and fat stock, including cows; at the present time, only two herds of cows remain in the two villages. Most farms are only arable, very few carry livestock of any kind, only larger units can compete in this modern age, carrying *one* kind of animal e.g. cows, pigs or chickens; small farms arable only.

The social life of the village after the war for about ten to twelve years was fairly full. Dances at the Lophams village Hall were held quite often. Young people had not got the transport to go further afield: cycling to Diss or other smaller towns in winter with a girlfriend was not very pleasant. The not so young were also glad to get out of the house, as their only other entertainment was the radio and gramophone. Public Houses were still popular, seven premises were still licenced up to the middle fifties. In 1954 there were only three televisions in N. Lopham. Whist Drives were also popular. The W.I. during the period under review (thirty three years

1946–1979) has remained almost unchanged either in numbers or in functions.

Outside functions were also held; some were held every year, such as the village fete, a very special day. It was quite a large sporting event: cycling, tug of war and lots of races of all distances. Music was for years provided by the Thorndon Reform School band, about thirty strong. A travelling fun fair was also booked to call during the 10–12 years after the war, a whole outfit, not a few side shows. The day used to finish up with a grand dance.

The Lopham Football club has been very popular and had many honours over the years and is still very much alive today. The cricket club survived until the mid fifties before it ended.

All these functions seemed to need a fair amount of policing; there were in this period three fulltime policemen in the two villages; now we haven't got one to call our own.

The Churches and Chapels also had a healthy following; there were three Sunday schools in the two villages but there are none now. There was a service at least once a day in both churches at this time. We had as you might say our own Rector, not like today where we have a group practice.

The Lopham Village hearse, *c.* 1925.

The Clergy is not the only change in that field since the war ended. The villages provided their own Funeral services, from start to finish, by this I mean actually making the coffins by hand, digging graves and providing the Funeral transport. It was like this until a year or two after the war, a Hearse and carriage actually stood at N. Lopham. There were three Undertakers in the two villages; today there are none. Now everything is provided from outside the villages, a kind of mass production conveyor belt type of service, costing three figures instead of one, as in the days I described. But we must remember that wages were very low at this time and inflation was only mentioned when your Football suddenly deflated.

The children of the village spent all their school years at the then Elementary School, unless they were clever enough to win a scholarship to the Grammar School at Diss. Children who had to stay to dinner, had to bring a packed lunch. Then in 1948 school meals were started. The early fifties were to bring more changes to school life. The village Elementary school was renamed Primary School, educating children up to the age of eleven years, then on to Diss Secondary Modern for the rest of their school time, which was fourteen years until this time, but was altered to fifteen. The normal age of school leaving was to rise yet again in the mid seventies to sixteen. Children's numbers were steadily falling in the villages from 1948 until 1979, although adult population increased, a lot of the new arrivals coming from the London area.

The houses in the villages were by and large a pretty low standard at the end of the war; toilets were very primitive: open closet outside or a few buckets, and only four bathrooms with flush toilets in North Lopham in 1948.

From this time new houses and bungalows were being built, which of course had bathrooms and W.C. built in them. Owners of houses took advantage of Government Grants and brought their houses up to date, using septic tanks and a soakaway for drainage. Septic tanks were not a new invention in this period. It was the big hall type houses that had this much improved drainage. (I know at least three that were in use in the early part of the century.)

The roads in the villages have altered very little in all the post war period. The main improvement came in the early fifties: cat's-eyes were installed on our main routes, a great help in our narrow dark country roads.

As time passed, corresponding to the change in the agricultural pattern, (fewer livestock, larger fields, fewer men), the roadside hedges started to come down. The *local* roadman like the *local* policeman, his days were numbered. The roadman's job up to the sixties was to clear the gulleys and mend pot holes, trim hedges and grass verges, clear drains as well as sweep the roads. In winter icy corners on roads had to be gritted and in the event of snow falling, 4 inches was the fall needed for him to turn out the snowplough, pulled by horses from a prearranged farm. These were guided by the horseman of the farm, with the roadman handling the plough, which was usually made of wood, with a metal shod front end.

But as I have already said, all was to change almost overnight. The work is now all done from outside the villages: machine sweeping, road mending, cutting grass verges, gritting roads and snow clearing. One small improvement worthy of a mention: now the school has a patrol light flashing signs each side of the control crossing for the children going to and from school. The volume of traffic, including the articulated lorries, had gone up many, many times, so that a crossing was very important on the highway.

VIEWS OF A LONG-ESTABLISHED LOPHAM FARMER

Farm land round the Lophams is mainly fertile sandy loam, or sandy clay loam, with a clay subsoil.

The area to the East has belonged to the Dukes of Norfolk, presumably since the days that their main palace existed at Kenninghall and their gaol at South Lopham; and only in recent years have they shown signs of parting with some of it. The area to the West has been traditionally small farms, mostly owner occupied; and continues thus.

Farming practice has been based on the Norfolk four course rotation, and methods instituted by Coke of Holkham and Turnip Townshend of Raynham, with only minor variations, have been used. Some livestock; bullocks, pigs and cows are kept; but sheep which used to contribute large numbers to the big sheep and lamb sales at East Harling and Diss are now seldom seen; and it is many more years since flocks of turkeys were shod with tar and sand before the walk to London for the Christmas trade. However the emphasis is on arable production.

Since the second world war changes common to most of East Anglia have occurred. Mechanisation has inevitably resulted in a considerable reduction of numbers of farm workers: large combines capable of harvesting over 300 acres each have replaced men with scythes; sugar beet harvesters can do similar acreage, compared to one man with a hook, to ten acres per season; now one man can milk 140 cows, a task which occupied ten men only a few years ago.

The numbers of farm workers employed in this country have decreased from about 1,000,000 in 1945 to about 125,000 in 1979. During the same period the wages of a farm worker have increased by more than ten times. In 1949 a tractor cost £700; in 1978 it cost £7,000. In 1949 a farm worker's wages were £4.00 a week; in 1978, £50.00.

With new varieties, the discovery of selective herbicides and fungicides, yields per acre (once coombs per acre, now kilograms per hectare) have increased, and have every appearance of continuing to do so.

The enlargement of fields to fit in with modern farming, and new methods of containing stock, has sadly resulted in the removal of some hedges and trees, but where opportunity permits these are being replaced by strategic planting, to retain the beauty of the countryside.

The Lophams have long earned a name for good farming and high yields, a reputation there is every appearance they will retain.

VIEWS OF A POST-WAR RESIDENT ON THE LOPHAMS SINCE 1945—EMPLOYMENT, TRANSPORT, HOUSING, SHOPS

The motor car must have brought greater changes to village life than almost any other single factor. Before World War II, only about twenty people in the two Lophams, including those who ran taxi services, possessed any more advanced form of transport than the bicycle although a few had motor cycles, so villagers' everyday travels were restricted to the limits of the infrequent bus service to Diss and Norwich operated by the Eastern Counties Bus Company. Some people took holidays on the East Coast, Great Yarmouth being the favourite resort, but there were some who never travelled further afield than Norwich in their entire lives.

At the end of the 'forties and during the 'fifties the Lopham folk were employed mainly within the villages although some men cycled to Fersfield aerodrome to work on maintenance of the runways and in the hangars used for storage purposes, until its closure. Within the two villages there were five builders, a blacksmith, a baker, a butcher, two Post Offices, three taxi services, a milkman, three shopkeepers, a pedlar selling buttons, laces etc., many farmers and farm workers.

As the use of the motor car became more widespread, people were able to work further afield, and in particular people who would have worked on the land were obliged to obtain their own transport to reach employment elsewhere as farming practices changed and brought less need for manpower.

The industrial development of Diss and Thetford has drawn many into factory work, whilst Sainsbury's "egg factory" at Kenninghall has provided employment for Lopham women. Several factories send their own buses out to the villages each day to fetch and carry their employees.

As well as drawing Lopham people away from the villages each day, the development in the surrounding towns, combined with the motor car, has meant that numerous people have moved into the Lophams who would once have been unable to enjoy living in rural surroundings whilst working in towns. In 1967, as far as I can ascertain, there were only two men living in the Lophams whose work was not connected with or dependent upon the villages: one made veterinary equipment and the other was Civil Defence Officer for East Norfolk. Twelve years later, we see an entirely different population, including businessmen, solicitors, antique dealers, teachers from the U.S.A.A.F. bases at Mildenhall and

Lakenheath, a merchant navy officer, an airline pilot, a social worker, a sound recording artist, and many others, as well as those who have retired here or who have weekend cottages here. The few remaining farm workers have had to learn new skills (especially mechanical skills) to keep pace with the new developments in agriculture.

Obviously these changes have affected the wealth of the villages, and have been reflected in the state of the buildings and the erection of new dwellings. Cottages once rather neglected, with flaking paintwork and leaking thatch, have been carefully restored, re-roofed with tiles instead of thatch in many cases, and with utilitarian vegetable plots transformed into neat flower gardens. Many small plots of land scattered throughout the villages have been developed with houses and bungalows; in 1949 a row of council houses was built in N. Lopham where one of the old forges used to stand.

Only three public houses now remain (the White Horse in South Lopham and the Bell and the King's Head in North Lopham), as the Bull ceased trading as a pub in November 1963 and became only a petrol station, and the Cherry Tree closed in September 1971.

Many trees, particularly the fine old Horse Chestnut trees which flourished within the Lophams, have been cut down, and outside the villages the once sheltered and leafy lanes are now open to the wind and skies with wide views across the countryside which used to be obscured by high hedges. In South Lopham, the Diss-Thetford road has been widened, the ford bridged and the gradient of the hill reduced, but the narrow bend in the centre of the village remains unchanged and very unsuitable for the enormous lorries travelling to and from the East Coast ports.

Increased mobility has altered people's shopping habits, which has had a drastic effect on the village shops. The large supermarkets in the towns are able to offer their goods at lower prices than the small country shops, who are unable to bulk-buy goods at cheap prices because of the limited storage space. With rapidly rising prices, increased rates and running costs, it is very difficult for their owners to operate them at a profit; as a result, the largest shop in the two villages, North Lopham Stores, has changed hands five times since 1968, and it now deals solely in groceries and newspapers when once it provided all the villagers' needs, including tailored jackets, boots, matting, cartridges and a whole host of goods besides food. At one time before the war it employed eight assistants.

The distribution of milk has undergone a drastic change since the end of the war. Until the nineteen-fifties, the milk from the local farms was taken round the villages in churns and ladled into customers' jugs with a dipper, but after the formation of the Milk Marketing Board the milk from the farms was sent to Norwich for bottling and returned to the villages for delivery to customers in glass bottles. There has been no bakery in the villages since about 1960, when Yeates' shop closed; the forge ceased operating in 1946; and there is now only one, semi-retired builder, still in business, and one taxi service.

VIEWS OF TWO RETURNERS FROM THE SECOND WORLD WAR

I. After the pleasure and relief of servicemen and women returning from all parts of the world (over 50 were in the forces from North Lopham) and the sadness expressed to the families of those who did not return, the job of resettling to a different pace of life, to work, for those who married to find a house to live in, occupied much thought and time. Many items were rationed, fashions had changed, there was a noticeable American influence in dress habits, and there was a demand for cycles to enable people to get to work. The football and cricket clubs were restarted, more electrification and more telephones were installed, and in the boom of the mid and late 1950s more cars were purchased. The days of the "old banger" had arrived. In the 1960s holidays at the seaside, coach tours and the occasional trip to France were common, and in the 70s Spain was a "must".

Between 1946 and 1976 about 60 new dwellings were built in North Lopham and the number of cars increased from 25 to over 150! The old smithy near Tann's Lane was demolished and 10 council houses were built. The 1970s saw major changes in farming techniques; small fields disappeared and hedges and ditches were removed; broiler houses sprung up almost overnight; an egg depot collecting station at Kenninghall was extended and rebuilt, employing many people from nearby villages. The new factories around Diss and Thetford would send first of all lorries, then vans, then buses, to collect employees. With the new intensive farming methods less men were required, so a different form of Exodus had begun.

II. When people returned from the forces, life in the villages seemed quiet, and rural life carried on. Most people had to find new jobs and getting to work was sometimes difficult. Transport was limited; cycling or walking were the only ways.

Farm wages were only 30/- per week which compared with £47 today seems incredible.

Rationing of food was still on and also clothes rationing, and everything was marked "utility". (END of food rationing July 1954.)

Entertainment in the village was limited, sometimes a whist drive was held in the Village Hall and occasional few dances. T.V. was only just thought of.

Electricity was connected in the villages but only a few dwellings were lucky enough to have it. Oil lamps were still used in many homes, and oil stoves were used for cooking.

Holidays were almost out of the question, but people seemed quite happy to work, and to make the most of their own entertainment. There were the local sports: football and cricket.

The men would go to the village pub and play cards on a Saturday evening and would leave their wives and family at home; in those days it certainly was a man's world, and it was the man who ruled the home.

Fashions were getting more americanised with girls wearing "jeans" and some people would say how bold it was; elderly people did not like the fashion at all and the young girls were scorned upon.

The village people raised funds for all who served in the forces and a sum of £7 was given to each serving person at a social evening at the Village Hall.

The Evacuees (children) who had lived with families in the

villages returned to London. Some were well liked and returned in later years to see the people they had shared homes with during wartime.

People in the village rarely went on holiday in 1948, but as time went on some would go to the coast: Yarmouth, Gorleston or Lowestoft. Occasionally a coach for a day trip would be arranged and children would go with their parents.

Also the Royal Norfolk Agricultural Show which was held in or around NORWICH was a great occasion for local and farming people. There would be a great display of all farming machinery. Also horses, cattle, pigs, sheep and many other interesting events, including a wonderful flower show, also many Norfolk crafts. In the early days a bus would take people to the show starting from the village at 8.30 a.m. and returning at 8.30 p.m.—everyone dressed in their best suits and dresses.

The London coach would go through the village each morning, and the Norwich Bus would go three times weekly, Monday, Wednesday and Saturday, and that was the only transport to the Norfolk & Norwich hospital if anyone was in need of treatment.

Then when the health service started a hospital car service was organized and patients were taken to hospital free of charge, and the same service is given today only on a much larger scale. There are about 200 drivers doing this job in Norfolk.

In the early 60s wages improved and more women went out to work to help the family income, and that meant people could go further afield for holidays. Quite a lot went to Spain, Italy, France, Germany, also to America and Canada.

Some of the girls married American service men and went to live in America after the war. Some enjoyed the life, while others came home to England. One village girl came back and her remarks were she would rather stay in little old England. Living out there, she said, everything was so large: cars, houses etc., and even their "ROBINS" were as big as our Thrushes.

VIEW OF A RETURNER FROM DAYS GONE BY

Having known South Lopham many years before settling in the village comparatively recently, it is inevitable that one recalls the village as it was not so many years ago without the heavy noisy transport vehicles which have taken over the village street and other roads and now greatly diminished the former quiet, peaceful atmosphere.

This apart, the village seems not to have changed its character to any great extent and it is a joy to be part of such a friendly rural community.

The attractive Norfolk dialect fortunately still holds sway, but it does seem to be becoming less marked in the younger generation of the indigenous population.

Local buses which come to South Lopham to take up passengers for Diss and Bury St. Edmunds are much valued. There is a friendly, unhurried atmosphere on them and yet the service provided is at all times efficient and reliable. To travel by them is a pleasure, especially to such delightful Market Towns.

Buses: Simonds of Botesdale on Wednesdays to Diss & Bury St. Edmunds

Petch of Hopton—Fridays to Diss

SOME NEWCOMERS' VIEWS

On one of the hottest days in August 1975 we moved in to North Lopham, having travelled the breadth of England from our former home in Worcestershire. Not only were we newcomers to the village but also to East Anglia, and although we were used to a rural way of life our heads were full of the stories we had heard of the insular East Anglians treating "foreigners" as aliens for the first twenty-odd years. In fact it sounded very much like my native Cornwall!

However, we need not have worried. From the moment we arrived everyone was very friendly and we felt that the village made us welcome. We were especially pleased to find that we had good neighbours who lent us a scythe with which to attack the jungle we found where a garden should have been, and helped us to "settle in".

Having children, we became involved with the school immediately of course, and this gave us a point of contact with many people. Before long I had helped to re-form a Pre-School Playgroup and started giving music lessons. We formed a group of singers from the village and are now connected with many village organisations. As we have also increased the population of the village by one since moving here, we hope that we are in some way adding to the life of the village!

Although there are several different organisations in the village, there seems to be a lack of "community spirit", and unwillingness to change or try any new venture, although those schemes which have been pushed through have been successful, the clearance of the Lechmere for example, and the family services at the church.

This is the only criticism we have of North Lopham and perhaps being slow to change is not altogether a bad thing. Certainly there is an abundance of friendship and neighbourliness, and we now feel quite at home here.

VIEWS OF A LOCAL GOVERNMENT REPRESENTATIVE ON LOCAL GOVERNMENT IN THE LOPHAMS

From the beginning of the century the Lophams had been part of the Wayland Rural District administered from the Council Offices at Attleborough. In 1974, when Local Government was re-organised for the first time since 1888, the late Miss A. Brindley of Lynn Cottage, Mr. R. N. Burrow of Box Tree Farm, North Lopham, and Captain M. A. N. Mansbridge of the Court, South Lopham, were members of the Council. On reorganisation Kenninghall joined the Lophams and the West Guiltcross ward, as it is now named, continues to be represented by Captain Mansbridge.

During the period between the Wars 16 council houses were built in North Lopham and 15 in South Lopham, and since 1945 a further 10 and 5 were added respectively, and mains water made available. Both parishes are still without main drainage and likely to be so for the foreseeable future as the cost of such sewerage schemes becomes impossible to fund. However, pre-war houses have been modernised during the past few years, some at the time of writing, indoor bathrooms being provided and kitchens brought up to standard. In some cases pre-war houses which cost £240 to build, now require £5,000 for modernisation alone! A further six new council bungalows are about to be built in North Lopham costing just on £80,000.

The Lophams are now part of Breckland District Council, the fifteenth largest district in area in the country, with 53 members. The Product of a Penny Rate in 1978—less Government Grants—was £485 for the two parishes. The old Wayland Rural District Council had 54 members, and the estimated Penny Rate in 1973/74 produced £430 from the Lophams. The Rateable value then was £46,686 and in 1978 it had risen to £55,528. Though Breckland District Council has made every effort to keep rates down, the district rate has doubled since 1973/74 from 6p to 12.2p. But then in such a period of roaring inflation that is a very creditable performance, and any comparisons are hardly possible.

Following the reorganisation in 1974, political parties have competed with each other within the Council, and where before councillors tried to reach decisions judged best for their ratepayers, such may not always be the case now. However, at present the Lophams are still represented by an "independent" member, as are many other wards which believe politics to be irrelevant at district level.

Both villages were designated as Conservation Areas in 1976. That can only be for good, as the sole aim is to conserve and preserve what is best, and to try to ensure that new buildings are designed in keeping with their surroundings.

NORTH LOPHAM PARISH COUNCIL
(7 members, 1 vacancy)
Mr. W. Vernon (1969) Chairman; Mr. A. Rednall (1974) Clerk; Mrs. C. Brock (1964); Mr. D. Brock (1973); Mr. A. Crook (1951); Mr. F. Daly (1977); Mr. R. Griggs (1970).
Long serving members: Mr. T. Williamson, Clerk (1948–1974); Mr. C. F. Castell 1948–1964 (chairman 8 years); Miss H. Grant 1954–1971; Miss A. Brindley

1954–1973; Mrs. Farrow; Mr. A. Crook 1951–1979 (chairman 8 years).

Events noted by the Parish Council

1971 Sewerage scheme cancelled by Breckland.
New chains installed around War Memorial.
Prompt action by Gordon Bell-Tye and John Bush helped to save the life of Robert Calver (all residents of North Lopham) in an electrical accident at Kenninghall.

1973 Installation of Warning Lights at school crossing, and attendance of a patrol officer.

1974 End of Wayland and beginning of Breckland District Council.

SOUTH LOPHAM PARISH COUNCIL

In common with many other parishes, membership of the Parish Council has remained fairly constant for many years. Few inhabitants take a personal interest in the Council, and members are normally replaced only when they leave the parish for one reason or another. However, those that give their time and interest would seem to carry out their duties reasonably well, otherwise they would no doubt be ousted when the opportunity occurs! This of course happens regularly every three years, but for a long time members have been re-elected unopposed since no one seems keen to take their place.

The Council meets four or five times each year and deals mostly with County matters—concerned mainly with highways—and with the District in connection with Planning Applications and various aspects of council housing. It is in constant touch with these authorities, and when necessary enlists the co-operation of our Member of Parliament, County Councillor, Police and other organisations, and though not always successful, ensures that the views of the parish are at least made known and considered. The ever increasing flow of heavy, fast traffic through the village has been one of its chief concerns for almost twenty years, and but for economic restrictions might well have resulted in an improved situation before now.

The Village Green has finally been registered in the name

of the Parish Council (April, 1979) and the War Memorial and Bus Shelter are owned and insured by it. It will be remembered that the War Memorial was demolished by a lorry in the early 70s and re-erected at a cost of £600, fortunately not borne by the Parish. Financially, members have kept expenditure to a minimum and the Parish Rate has never been more than the old or new penny.

Members of the Council in 1979 are Mr. A. C. Frost, Mr. W. B. Havers, Mr. A. H. Howard (Vice Chairman), Mrs. P. E. Howard (Clerk), Captain M. A. N. Mansbridge (Chairman), Mr. E. A. Pearce, The Rev. J. E. Postill, Mr. P. N. Reeder, Mrs. C. R. Twidle.

CHURCH HISTORY 1940–1979

Since the death of the Rev. C. J. Eastwood in 1940 there have been five Rectors of the living of North with South Lopham: Rev. J. T. Poole, 1940–1949; Rev. G. A. H. Cooksley, 1950–1952, who died tragically of polio*; Rev. K. Liley, 1953–1957; Rev. F. W. Burgess, 1957–1959; Rev. C. E. Beevers, 1960–1968.

After the second world war much work has been done to maintain the beauty and dignity of the two churches. In 1965 the six bells in South Lopham were completely restored and rehung. Since 1960 in South Lopham church the chancel has been re-decorated and part of the South Nave aisle rearranged to form a Memorial Chapel and a Ladies' Choir Vestry. The major work in North Lopham was the renewing of the South Aisle roof on the Nave in the 1960s.

In the 1969 the Living was suspended because of a Pastoral Reorganisation by the Diocese of Norwich and the two parishes became part of the Winfarthing Group of Parishes in the Deanery of Redenhall. There have been since that reorganisation two Team Vicars residing in the Rectory: Rev. C. E. Babcock, 1969–1973; Rev. J. E. Postill, 1974–1979.

* And of whom it was said that in two years he did more to establish good relations between the Lophams than had been achieved in the last two hundred. (Author's note.)

Rector G. A. H. Cooksley unites the Lophams in 1951.

NORTH LOPHAM PAROCHIAL CHURCH COUNCIL

Rev. J. E. Postill, chairman; Mrs. C. Brock, Treasurer; Mrs. K. Ford, secretary; Mr. J. Arnold; Mrs. G. Crook, churchwarden; Mr. A. Fox; Mr. M. Fuller; Mrs. V. Gilbert; Mrs. W. Logsdail; Mrs. C. Muncila; Mrs. C. Solly; Mrs. L. West, organist; Mr. A. Wright, churchwarden.
Long serving members: Miss A. Brindley, secretary; Mrs. T. Stevens, organist; Mr. T. Stevens, churchwarden; Mrs. M. Witton, churchwarden and treasurer.

SOUTH LOPHAM PAROCHIAL CHURCH COUNCIL

Rev. J. E. Postill, Chairman; Mr. I. Murdoch, Vice-chairman; Mr. J. Baskerville, treasurer; Mrs. C. R. Twidle, secretary; Mrs. D. Brundell; Mr. H. Ford; Mr. & Mrs. E. A. Pearce; Mrs. J. Postill; Mr. & Mrs. P. N. Reeder; Mr. & Mrs. K. D. H. Self. Churchwardens: Mr. P. Reeder; Mr. I. M. Murdoch. Organist: Mr. R. R. Reeder.

NORTH LOPHAM COUNTY PRIMARY SCHOOL MANAGERS

Mr. M. L. Fuller, M.Sc, Chairman; Representative from Thetford Area Education Office, Secretary; Mr. A. J. Barnard; Mrs. L. Broadhurst; Mrs. G. F. Brown; Mr. A. Crook; Mr. E. Davey; in attendance, Mr. R. Griggs, Headmaster.

NORTH LOPHAM COUNTY PRIMARY SCHOOL TEACHERS

Head: Mr. R. O. Griggs; Deputy: Mrs. K. M. Roberts; Other teacher: Mrs. M. Dain. 61 children on roll, 1978: canteen supplies meals for North Lopham, South Lopham and Kenninghall.

NOTES ON NORTH LOPHAM SCHOOL BY MRS. M. M. BROCK

I returned to North Lopham School in July 1945 after the birth of my son, having resigned in December 1944.

The staff then consisted of Mr. Charles Castell, Mrs. Ellen Stevens, (the Miss Brock mentioned by Mr. Bawden in the Log Book), and Mr. Sparrow who had not returned to Hackney when other evacuee teachers returned home. Mrs. Castell, who formerly had had no teaching experience, was also helping in school. Mrs. Stevens very reluctantly retired in 1949, having taught the Infant Class for 50 years, being much over retirement age. She was succeeded by Mrs. Nora Reeder, who taught the Infants for the next 16 years.

When Blo' Norton School was closed the children were transferred to North and South Lopham Schools and it was then that the North Lopham Canteen was opened first for meals for children from Blo' Norton and finally for the whole school.

Mr. Alan Chapman was appointed to the staff to cope with the extra numbers in school but was soon replaced by Mr. Roy Jones from Diss, when Mr. Chapman was appointed to a post at Gorleston. Mr. Jones remained on the staff until reorganisation took place and the senior children started at the Diss Secondary Modern Schools. He is now a headmaster in Suffolk.

Mr. Castell retired in 1964 at the age of 65, having been headmaster for 35 years. He had intended to retire at the age of 60, but stayed on after his wife's death in 1960. He was succeeded by Mr. William Limmer, who had been headmaster of a school in the Lebanon. Both he and Mr. Roy Griggs who took his place when the former became head of a large school in Bedford, were much younger men (with families) and had more tolerant views of children's behaviours and misdemeanours.

On Mrs. Reeder's retirement, Mrs. Carol Parker was appointed as Infant teacher, and on her resignation to take a post at Roydon, Mrs. Doris Clarke from Attleborough was appointed.

On my retirement in December 1969, Mrs. Viola Rout from Banham was appointed to take my class.

Of course there were very many changes in curriculum and teaching methods during the 40 years that I was teaching. Children now receive instruction in a wider range of subjects, especially so since the introduction of radio and television in school, but I must record that North Lopham was always considered an "up-to-date" school during Mr. Castell's time and children received a sound basic education.

Since the Second World War and the building of many more houses, great changes have taken place in the village, as they have in most villages. I used to know all the children and people in the village—now I know only the older inhabitants and a few young people with families who have settled here and are taking part in village activities.

In conclusion, I feel I must just mention the fact that had Mrs. Stevens (our infant teacher for 50 years) still been with us, she would have told of her nephew, now Lord Brock, who was knighted for his work in heart surgery. His father, Herbert Brock, was brought up in the village of North Lopham, born at the house now known as "Ferndale" on the Harling Road.

NOTES OF NORTH LOPHAM PRIMARY SCHOOL BY MR. R. D. GRIGGS

I began as Headteacher on 6th January 1969. There were approximately 80 children in school. My two colleagues were

Mrs. M. Brock and Mrs Clarke. Staff changes were as follows:

15. Sept. 69	Mrs. B. Woollams. Part-time teacher.
19. Dec. 69	Retirement of Mrs. M. Brock after 40 years service at North Lopham School.
5. Jan. 70	Mrs. V. Rout began her duties. Our organisation at this point: Class 1 (9–11) years) myself. Class 2 (7–8 years) Mrs. Rout. Class 3 (Infants) Mrs. D. Clarke.
8. Sept. 70	Mrs. M. Dain appointed as part-time teacher. We had 83 children on roll. Our organisation was now: Class 1 (as before). Class 2 (7–9 years) Mrs. Rout. Class 3 (upper infants—7 years) Mrs. Woollams a.m. and Mrs. Dain p.m. Class 4 (Infants) Mrs. Clark. There was some overlapping of ages between classes. Staffing remains stable until July 1974 when Mrs. Woollams leaves. Between Sept. 1970 and July 1974 our roll varied as follows: Sept '71—94 on roll; Sept. '72—87 on roll; Sept. '73—80 on roll.
3. Sept. 74	Mrs. C. Mills appointed full-time—Mrs. Rout now teaches part time. We have 71 children on roll. Our organisation is as follows: Class 1—myself. Class 2—Mrs. Mills. Class 3—Mrs. Rout (a.m.); Mrs. Dain (p.m.). Class 4 (Infants) Mrs. Clarke.
Sept. 1975	76 on roll.
April 1976	Mrs. Mills leaves.
April 1976	Mrs. S. Saunders begins a full-time but temporary appointment—Class 2.
7 Sept. 76	71 children on roll.
22. Dec. 76	Mrs. Saunders leaves.
10. Jan. 77	Mrs. M. Roberts begins her duties as Deputy Head Teacher—as an interim measure, she teaches Class 2.
1. April 77	Mrs. Clarke leaves.
19 April 77	Mrs. Rout and Mrs. Dain, who were part-time teachers, now both become full-time. Our organisation now is:

	Class 1—myself. Class 2—Mrs. Dain. Class 3—Mrs. Rout. Class 4 (Infants) Mrs. Roberts.
6. Sept. 77	62 children on roll.
26 July 78	Mrs. Rout leaves. There will be no replacement for her—we shall reorganise in Sept. as a 3 class school.
6. Sept 78	49 children on roll. Organisation as follows: Class 1 myself. Class 2—Mrs. Dain. Class 3—Mrs. Roberts.

The school roll has fallen from a peak of about ninety plus children in Sept. 1971 to a low of about 50 children at this present time. This is due in part to the general social immobility of past years, combined with an almost static housing situation in the village. The effect of the nationally falling birthrate has, locally, been minimal. Small groups of housing, both private and local authority are essential in small villages such as North Lopham. We did, up to about three years ago, accept children from Blo' Norton where the village school closed many years ago. Then South Lopham School became the recipient of these children—the effect was to reduce our roll by about ten or so children.

As far as changes in the curriculum are concerned, over the past fifteen to twenty years there has been a greater recognition of the way by which young children learn. In brief, this can be summarised as being the adoption of a more child-centred approach to learning, an approach which seeks actively to involve the children in the learning process instead of merely preaching at or talking to them. Also, this period has seen a breakdown in the traditional syllabus once to be found in many Primary Schools. For example, a visit to a museum would almost certainly be instructive in many disciplines including history, geography, English, mathematics and science, in addition to creating splendid ideas for various forms of art and craft.

Rural life tends not to reflect the more adverse effects of social change which are often so apparent in urban areas. Family groupings can still be found within the village or in reasonably close proximity to it, providing security and warmth for the children.

T.V. is all-pervading. It does offer a tremendous potential for learning as can be seen and heard in the many varied T.V. and radio school broadcasts. Commercial pressures however, dictate that the greatest possible audience must be captured for general viewing, and this often results in trashy and moronic programmes, sometimes extremely violent and totally unsuitable for children. Where a programme is stimulating and its content interesting, then T.V. is exciting and conducive to further thought and reading as increasing book sales show.

SOUTH LOPHAM VOLUNTARY AID PRIMARY SCHOOL MANAGERS

Rev. John Postill, chairman; Mrs. M. Grover, correspondent; Mr. A. Frost; Mr. A. Howard; Mr. I. M. Murdoch; Mr. E. A. Pearce; Mr. K. D. H. Self.

SOUTH LOPHAM VOLUNTARY AID PRIMARY SCHOOL TEACHERS

Head: Mrs. C. R. Twidle; Assistant Teacher: Mrs. M. Hilditch. 38 children on roll.

NOTES ON SOUTH LOPHAM SCHOOL 1946–1971

Staff: from 1946–1971—2 teachers—Miss Battley, Head, 1946–1971; Miss B. A. Coe—Infants Teacher 1929–1972. Until 1955 it was a three-teacher school, the Junior class having several changes of teacher.

The Senior children (11+–15) were transferred to Diss Sec. Modern in April 1955. 13 children went, leaving 40.

Of canteen staff Mrs. M. G. Green served from 1949–1972. School meals were first supplied on October 18th, 1949.

Building: This was greatly improved in 1950s and 60s. Central heating was installed first. Later, a ceiling was added and a new floor laid. This again led to new furniture, and new lighting.

Organisation: This school was originally known as a Parochial School, and belonged to the Church of England. It received Voluntary Aided Status (Jan. 5th 1950) thanks to hard work put in by the "church". The building was formerly in the care of the South Lopham Charities Trustees, but was taken over by the Norfolk Diocesan Board in 1961–1962.

Curriculum: After reorganisation for the "Eleven Plus", children were able to participate in more activities—meeting pupils from other schools for swimming, dancing, singing, sports etc. In school the teaching became more "free and easy"—not quite so "parrot-like". Children were encouraged to "find out for themselves".

NOTES ON SOUTH LOPHAM SCHOOL
BY MRS. C. R. TWIDLE

The movement of people from villages to towns affected this school as it did others. The population of many villages dwindled. Some schools closed, including Blo' Norton, so Blo' Norton children went to South Lopham (and formerly North Lopham) schools. From 90 children at South Lopham at its fullest the numbers dropped to less than 20.

Teachers used to stay in one school for many years. Miss Coe taught in South Lopham for 42 years—Miss Battley was head for 25 years. In recent years attitudes to employment have changed and education, like other professions, has seen more frequent changes in staff. Balance is needed. The stable teacher needs actively to find stimulation. The fleeting teacher needs somehow to provide continuity and dependability for pupils.

South Lopham had several quick changes of staff in the early 70s. At the same time school numbers went down and the school was threatened with closure. A temporary head, Miss S. A. Speed, was appointed for two years. Due to her efforts and those of parents, combined with the increased number of pupils, closure plans were abandoned by the Norfolk Education Committee. A permanent head was appointed in 1976 and the school seems to be thriving. A children's club, the Jubilee Club for ages 5–14, was started in February 1978 and meets every Thursday evening.

Village schools are a vital part of their community. Economic reasons have been given for small school closures, but, if true costings of the advantages of a well-run village school compared to transporting young children out of their village to large schools were possible, it would be interesting to see which actually gives better value. The rapid rate of small school closures in many counties has been very much reduced lately, pointing to a change of policy.

In the 1960s child population was high and there were not enough teachers. Many were trained at this time and a lot of new thinking permeated the practice of teaching. The learning theories of Piaget, the Swiss researcher, were taken into account. Teaching became more child-centred and less subject orientated. It is interesting to note that many schools at that time changed to a system of vertical grouping, i.e. classes of mixed ages, believing that many children worked better and with more initiative in these conditions, gaining socially from the family grouped classes. The idea, of course, came from village schools!

Changes of teaching methods brought changes of inspection procedure. Basic three Rs are still the greatest preoccupation in schools. Social education possibly plays a greater part than in years gone by. South Lopham school, like most schools, hopes to teach the children to appreciate as fully as possible their immediate surroundings of home and village and the wider world of city and nations with the interaction of people. H.M.I.s still visit schools to inspect standards but much of their work is done by County Advisers. They liaise with schools; with headteachers they arrange training sessions for teachers.

Like many schools South Lopham has had its heating problems: in smoking stoves, damp wood etc. Seven or eight years ago a modern oil-fired central heating boiler was installed. Last winter we weathered the deep snow in the knowledge that unlike some, we had plenty of oil. However the boiler motor gave up and proved very difficult to repair.

There have been changes of many kinds. At one time the school house lodged the headmaster and his teaching wife (Mr. and Mrs. Bardwell) and most of their 10 children—what a squash in so small a house! In recent years the school house was empty and deteriorating for many months until the present head moved in and with help from the Diocesan Board of Education drove the spiders out. Formerly the field was used by heads as a kitchen garden and orchard. A recent head arranged for the area to be cleared for the use of the children. It is a small school field but much appreciated.

Playground games have changed. Sometimes "five stones" is played and old skipping rhymes are often heard, but Batman and Robin games and Bank Robbers vie with games of Superman. We never see marbles. Football reigns supreme as a game which never ceases. Hopscotch is popular and the girls like to play dummy.

South Lopham school, with its outside toilets and still lofty ceiling, will never be modern. The soft red Norfolk bricks and pantiles are pleasant. The education provided is a mixture of old methods and new with a variety of equipment chosen with individual children in mind. The children seem to manage well with only two permanent teachers. The teachers manage without office or staffroom. Children and teachers use the school house from time to time. Our dinner ladies and cleaner-in-charge are invaluable members of our school community—the community which most of us enjoy most of the time.

NORTH LOPHAM CHARITIES

Mr. J. D. Alston, J.P., C.B.E., chairman and trustee; Mr. Simon John, Clerk; Trustees: Mrs. M. Brock; Mr. A. A. Crook; Mrs. H. E. Podmore; Mr. W. C. Vernon; Mr. R. D. Griggs; Capt. M. A. N. Mansbridge; Mr. G. L. Nunn; Rev. J. Postill.

SOUTH LOPHAM ESTATES CHARITY: (income principally from land rental) Mrs. R. Bishenden, secretary; Trustees: Mr. J. D. Alston, J.P., C.B.E., Mr. G. J. Beckford; Mr. G. W. Coleman; Mr. H. L. Ford; Mr. A. C. Frost; Mr. A. H. Howard; Mr. D. Huggins; Mr. I. M. Murdoch; Mr. E. A. Pearce; Mr. L. Reeder; Mr. P. N. Reeder; Mr. K. D. H. Self, treasurer; Captain M. A. N. Mansbridge; Rev. J. Postill.

Cash belonging to the Charity is invested and the net yearly income, after various standing payments have been made, is appropriated as directed in the Scheme, that is

One half for Educational purposes which is now paid to and administered by the Norwich Diocesan Board of Finance.

One quarter to the churchwardens to be used for maintenance, repairs and insurance of the church.

One quarter for the benefit of either the Poor of the Parish generally or of such deserving and necessitous persons as the Trustees select. (A small sub-committee of the Trustees is responsible for the distribution.)

The property now owned by the Charity consists of land only which is rented to various people:

The Frith Pastures	26 acres 1 person
Mill Field and Blo' Norton fields	10 acres 1 person
Carrs Allotment, Low Common	2 acres 1 person
27 allotments—approx. ¼ acre each	to various tenants

(15 on High Common—4.154 acres
12 on Gaol House Field 3.483 acres)

SOUTH LOPHAM FUEL ALLOTMENT TRUST

The Charity was formed in 1815 to give "poor persons legally settled and resident in the Parish" the authority to cut peat from the Great and Little Fens, and was duly registered with the Charity Commissioners. The existing Scheme, dated the 15th March, 1965, enabled the Trustees to vary the original and thereby lease the land to the Suffolk Naturalists' Trust for a period of 60 years from July of that year.

That arrangement has ensured that the Fens are well maintained and used to their best advantage; indeed they hold a unique interest among naturalists. In September, 1975, the Charity Commissioners agreed to a proposal by the Suffolk Naturalists' Trust, with the Trustees approval, to sub-let the land to the Nature Conservancy Council for 21 years. This too has proved most beneficial, particularly in regard to the return of the water table to its original level, and the control of fire. In March, 1973, the Fen suffered extensive fire damage.

The Trusts's Income before 1965 amounted to some £8 a year, but by investing the capital payment of £800 in respect of the lease with the Equities Investment Fund for Charities, that has increased to about £80.

Nowadays, the Trustees are able to give immediate financial help in suitable cases, to those who are bereaved, and at Christmas time a small sum to about 10 parishioners as a token of remembrance and friendship. The Trust is administered by seven trustees, at present Mr. A. C. Frost, secretary; Mr. A. H. Howard, vice-chairman; Captain M. A. N. Mansbridge, chairman; Mr. W. R. Havers; Mr. E. A. Pearce; Rev. J. E. Postill; Mr. P. N. Reeder, and Mrs. C. R Twidle.

The Great and Little Fens remain the property of the Parish and it may well be that in the year 2025 the present Scheme will be favourably reconsidered.

LOPHAMS VILLAGE HALL AND PLAYING FIELDS COMMITTEE

The Village playing field was handed over to trustees in 1929 by the Duke of Norfolk and the Hall has been used by nearly all the organizations within the two parishes. Though its popularity has fluctuated from time to time, particularly with the increasing number of entertainments elsewhere, television, and the ease with which many people can now travel; the Hall is still the focal point for local activities and the "home ground" of many groups.

From the early 70s an Annual Fête has been held on the last Saturday in June and as a result of that, and of monthly dances which were well supported until competition and cost became too great a short time ago, the Committee have been able to maintain the Hall satisfactorily and add to its amenities.

The Playing Fields are used mostly by local football clubs and the Schools on occasions. With the kind co-operation of Mr. J. D. Alston the Lophams and District Gun Club set up on the eastern side in 1973 and holds regular monthly shoots, and is a very welcome additional supporter.

It is always hoped that representatives from all the various groups in the parishes will serve on the Committee and indeed without their help and generosity nothing could be done. The members are at present Mr. J. D. Alston, J.P., C.B.E., President; Mr. D. Brock, Mr. A. Crook, Mrs. P. Crowe, Mrs. Y. Culley, Mrs. C. Fuller, Mr. R. D. Griggs, secretary; Mr. M. Grover, Mrs. A. Howard, Mr. A. A. Kerry, Captain M. A. N. Mansbridge, chairman; Mr. I. M. Murdoch; Mrs. A. Rednall, treasurer; Mr. W. Sayer, Mr. J. Sillett, Mrs. C. Solly, Mrs. W. Speer, Mr. D. Spurdens, Mrs. C. R. Twidle.

THE LOPHAMS BRANCH OF THE WOMEN'S INSTITUTE

It was founded in 1926, and the first President was Mrs. Eastwood. Members were very keen: some walked quite a distance to attend; some came from nearby Garboldisham. They brought with them sticks to keep the stove going, also water for the tea making, which was boiled on a primus stove. Flower shows, social and whist drives were held and there was an annual outing. War-time memories are of making large quantities of jam, and doing lots of knitting. On the whole meetings are still conducted in the same way today as they were when the Branch was founded 53 years ago. Mrs. C. Berry, president; Mrs. M. Grover, treasurer; Mrs. E. Gaskin, secretary; Mrs. W. Aldous; Mrs. G. Beckford; Mrs. V. Gilbert; Mrs. A. Howard; Mrs. O. Keer; Mrs. C. Muncila; Mrs. S. Newstead.

THE ROYAL BRITISH LEGION

The Lophams and District Branch of the British Legion was formed in the early 1920s and consisted of ex-servicemen from North and South Lopham and Fersfield. The Armistice Day marches, parades and services were held in rotation at each village with wreaths being placed on the war memorials, with meetings held in Fersfield Crown Inn, South Lopham White Horse, and North Lopham Bull Inn. After the 1939–45 war ex-servicemen from both wars continued the branch functions until the mid 1950s when because of the retirement of the chairman Mr. T. Alexander; the departure from the village of the secretary, Mr. H. Pascoe; and the death of other members; the branch was closed down. In the early 1970s the Kenninghall and District branch took the Lopham area under its "umbrella" and the name was changed to "Kenninghall, the Lophams and District" branch, under the Presidency of Colonel J. B. Chillingworth and the chairmanship of Major C. W. S. Belas, M.B.E.

THE LOPHAMS AND DISTRICT POPPY DAY COLLECTION

This was organised and run by the local branch of the British Legion, incorporating North and South Lopham and Fersfield.

When the branch lapsed in 1954, Mr. and Mrs. Albert Crook became the organisers and have continued up to the present time. The area now covered includes Blo' Norton, with collectors assisting in each village as follows:

North Lopham: Mrs. I. Baker; Mrs. V. Gilbert; Mr. and Mrs. S. Newstead; Mr. and Mrs. Pond; Mrs. E. Potter; Mrs. W. Sayer; Mrs. G. Solly

South Lopham: Mrs. A. Corble; Messrs Desira Garage; Mrs. M. Grover; Mrs. S. Hoskins; Mrs. A. Howard.

Fersfield: Mrs. R. Birch.

Blo' Norton: Mrs. N. Kibble; Mrs. G. Slater. Donations are also received from North and South Lopham church councils.

The total collections now exceed £100, and in 1978 reached £120.

LOPHAMS HAPPY CIRCLE CLUB (over 60s)

Mrs. C. Solly, chairman; Mrs. C. Brock, treasurer; Mrs. C. Solly, secretary; Miss L. Battley; Mrs. P. Crowe; Mrs. V. Gilbert; Mrs. C. Muncila; Mrs. E. Pearce; Mrs. E. Potter; Mrs. L. Reeder; Mrs. G. Solly.

The Club was started on 27th October 1949.

Long serving chairman: Mrs. M. Baker (retired).

Long serving committee members: Mrs. H. Baldwin (retired); Mrs. C. Beevers (retired); Mrs. E. Huggins (retired); Mrs. M. Witton (retired).

NORTH LOPHAM PLAYGROUP

Mrs. C. Fuller, supervisor (qualified teacher); Mrs. L. Eagle, treasurer; Mrs. J. White secretary. Other helpers are: Mrs. J. Holland; Mrs. J. Marriott; Mrs. J. White; Mrs. J. Wood. All work is part time and voluntary. The Playgroup started in November 1975 in the school canteen, two afternoons per week. It is registered with the Pre School Playgroups Association and licensed to take 18 children. The children now have a large amount of play equipment and enjoy outings to local zoos, fire stations etc., and walks during the summer.

LOPHAM UNITED FOOTBALL CLUB

Mr. D. R. Spurdens, chairman; Mr. J. A. Sillett, treasurer; Mr. M. Bradbury, secretary; Mr. Adrian Baker; Mr Anthony Baker.

LOPHAM JUNIOR FOOTBALL CLUB

Mr. S. Newstead, Treasurer; Mr. D. R. Spurdens, secretary; Mr. J. Bailey; Mr. M. Bradbury; Mr. E. S. Burt.

The Club was formed in August 1978 and is entered in the Watton and District League.

LOPHAMS AND DISTRICT GUN CLUB

Patron: Mr. J. D. Alston, J.P., C.B.E. Captain M. A. N. Mansbridge, President; Mr. C. Aves, Chairman; Mrs. M. Kerry, secretary and treasurer; Mr. L. Aves; Mr. and Mrs. M. Bloomfield; Mr. D. Brock; Mr. W. Eke; Mr. T. Emms; Mr. P. Flatman; Mr. R. Gutteridge; Mr. C. Harvey; Mr. A. Kerry; Mr. B. Kindleysides; Mr. C. Rose; Mr. H. Rose; Mr. M. Wade.

THE BELL, NORTH LOPHAM, DARTS CLUB

Mr. W. Speer, Junior, chairman; Mrs. W. Speer, secretary; Mr. C. Levett; Mr. H. Salter; Mr. W. F. E. Speer Senior.

This club has been in existence since 1950 and has once won the Diss Round Table Cup.

SOUTH LOPHAM WHITE HORSE DARTS CLUB

Mr. T. Hoskins, Captain; Mr. G. Hoskins, secretary and treasurer. All players are committee members under the chairmanship of Mr. Hoskins. The club was formed in 1971.

THE LOPHAMS BRANCH OF THE SOUTH NORFOLK CONSERVATIVE ASSOCIATION

Mr. J. Morgan, chairman; Mr. M. J. Grover, treasurer; Mr. A. J. Barnard, secretary; Mr. and Mrs. J. R. Baskerville; Mrs. A. Currie; Mr. M. L. Fuller; Mr. M. G. Podmore; Mr. D. Scott; Mr. L. Shaw; Mr. and Mrs. W. A. Stone; Mr. and Mrs. N. E. Tappenden.

H.M. THE QUEEN'S SILVER JUBILEE

Early in 1977 a committee was formed to arrange a programme to mark Her Majesty's Silver Jubilee. Some twenty people came together for the purpose, and began by raising sufficient money to make their plans possible. A very generous donation of £100 gradually swelled to nearly £500 helped by a Quiz, a Wine and Cheese party, the "Gaiety Group" from Watton, and a Sponsored Walk, the latter bringing in about £270. The ten mile course was extremely well organized, and every entrant, from young children to very mature adults, finished the course!

There was great enthusiasm throughout the months of preparation and all the events were fully supported. The 7th June was cold and wet, yet despite the soaking rain each event was successfully completed to the credit of all concerned. Catering throughout the week was a mammoth task, which the Women's Institute laid on in their usual excellent way, with additional help especially in the way of food of all sorts, much of it cooked by those who so generously provided it.

All children who were not attending school outside the Lophams were presented with Jubilee Mugs by the Parish Councils' to both of which was allocated the balance remaining in the funds raised towards the cost of providing a seat in each village. A subscription was also made to the Queen's Jubilee Fund.

The Committee was supported by many more people, but those initially elected by a well attended public meeting on 16th February, 1977, were:-

Mrs. J. D. Alston. Mr. and Mrs. C. A. Berry. Mrs. R. D. Bishenden (Treasurer). Mr. D. J. Brock. Mrs. G. F. Brown. Mr. A. A. Crook. Mrs. Y. L. Culley. Mrs. C. M. Fuller. Mr. R. D. Griggs (Secretary). Mr. and Mrs. M. J. Grover. Captain M. A. N. Mansbridge (Chairman). Revd. J. E. Postill. Mrs. C. R. Ralph. Mr. A. A. Rednall. Mr. W. A. Sayer. Mrs. S. M. Sillett. Mr. John Sillett. Mrs. A. E. Solly. Mr. W. C. Vernon (Vice Chairman).

From the well attended Church Service on the 5th to the over 60's Party in the Village Hall on the 9th when those who were unable to come were visited in their homes, the Lophams well and truly celebrated the 25 years reign of their Queen with a spirit of communal enthusiasm and joy.

GOD BLESS THE QUEEN, LONG MAY SHE LIVE!

Index of Parts One to Three

"An Index is the *bag and baggage* of a book of more use than honour, even such who seemingly slight it, secretly using it, if not for *need*, for *speed* of that they desire to finde."

Thomas Fuller:
A Pisgah-Sight of Palestine. London, 1650.

Index

Numbers in bold type denote illustrations

A. 1066 road (SEE ALSO Garboldisham Road), 232–233, 262
Adams, John (*fl.* 1680), 23
Adamson, John, S. Lopham (*ob. c.* 1761), 86, 111
air-raid, 256–257
Albemarle, earl of—SEE Keppel
Albert, Prince Consort, 157
Albert Rooms, N. Lopham—SEE Royal Albert National School
Alderson, C., H.M.I., 156
Aldgate, 55
Aldis, Police Constable, 211, 212, 213, 216
Aldred, Christopher, 73
ale—SEE beer
alehouses—SEE taverns
Aleyn, William, chaplain of N. Lopham (?), 53
Aleyn, William, farmer of N. Lopham (*ob. c.* 1500), 45, 52, 53, 59
Aleyn, Margaret, wife of William A., of N. Lopham, farmer, 53
Alfar, The Great—SEE Emms, Alfred
Alfred, King (A.D. 848–900), 16
Allands—SEE Severals, The
Alnwick Castle, 56
Alsi, freeman, 20
America, the United States of, 130, 131
Americans, 257, 260, 261
Anderson, Robert W., N. Lopham, 225
Andrew's Tenement, 80
Anglicans—SEE Church of England
Anglo-Saxons, 11, 13, 20
Anne of Cleves, 104
Apulia, Italy, 27
Arch, Joseph (1826–1919), 197
Arkwright, Sir Richard (1732–1792), 112
arming towels, 85 & n.
Armistice, 1918, 228
Arnold, Matthew (1822–1888), 155, 156
Arundel Castle, Sussex, 32
Arundel, earls of—SEE Fitzalan; Howard
Aslacton, 244
Atkings, Widow, 130
Attleborough, 102, 186, 187, 251
Audley End, Saffron Walden, 89
Augustine, Saint—SEE S. Augustine

Bacon, Nicholas of Redgrave, J.P., (*ob.* 1624) 88
Badger, The Reverend, of Bressingham, 183
Bailey, Alfred, N. Lopham, 225
bailiff of the manor, 36

Baker, Eleanor, Mrs, *née* Ludbrook, of N. Lopham, 201, 202
Baker, Thomas, N. Lopham, 226
Baker, Ted, 216, 217
Baker family of N. Lopham, 211
Baker's Meadow, 214
Baldry, 106
Bale sisters, the—Elizabeth Susannah B., (*ob*. 1912), 192
Georgiana Elizabeth B., SEE Buckenham, Mrs. G. E.
Louisa *Ellen* B., (*ob*. 1925), 146, 192, 194, 198
Balmoral, 202
Bangor, bishop of, 105
Banham, 111, 127, 186
Banham, baker of N. Lopham, 203
Banham, Ducky, N. Lopham, 210
Banham's Meadow, N. Lopham, 189
Baptist Chapel, S. Lopham, 115, 123
Baptists, 90, 91, 114, 115
Bardsley, Samuel, Wesleyan minister, Norwich, 116
Bardwell, Edward, S. Lopham, 227
Bardwell, Marcus George, S. Lopham, 227
Bardwell, Marcus Kerr, S. Lopham schoolmaster, 177, 178, 179, 183, 213
Elizabeth B., his wife, 177
Barham, Mrs Betty, dressmaker of N. Lopham, 201
Bari, S. Nicola's, Italy, 18, 27
Barker, 106
Barker, John of S. Lopham (*ob. c.* 1486), 52
BARKING DICKEY, The—SEE "Ferndale Holding"
barley, 41, 110
Barman, Michael, N. Lopham weaver (1840), 138
Barnes, Doris—SEE Brock, Mrs Doris
Barnes, Edward, (1602), 92
Barningham, Suffolk, 186
Barracks Yard, N. Lopham, 201, **202**
Barrett, Nicholas, S. Lopham (*ob. c.* 1557), 72, 104
Barrow, James, rector 1824–61, 120, 133, 151, 156
Bateman, John Fitzherbert, rector 1861–1895, 151, 152, 154, 156, 160, 161, 177, 179, 187, 205, 208, 220, 240
Bath & Wash Houses, S. Giles's, London, 148
Bawden, Thomas, N. Lopham schoolmaster, 179, 180, **181**, 182
Effie B., his daughter, **181**, 182
Johanna B., his wife, 181, 182
Bayes, William, whitster (1661), 86
Beales family of N. Lopham, 189, 190, 191
Beales, Jeremiah, N. Lopham linen manufacturer (*c.* 1840), 139, 190
Beales, John, Old Buckenham, linen-weaver, (1831), 189
Beales, Lois, *née* Buckenham, wife of William B., 195
Beales, Mary, of Lopham (1831), 189
Beales, Percy Stephen, 160n., 184, 190, 191, 195, 196, 197, 198, 237, 238, 240, 242, 243, 244
Beales, Rita, wife of Percy Stephen Beales, **85**, 195, **196**
Beales, Robert, N. Lopham linen manufacturer, (1875), 149, 210
Beales, Samuel, N. Lopham butcher, (1903), 189, **190**
Beales, Stephen, N. Lopham butcher, (1780), 189
Beales, Stephen, N. Lopham linen manufacturer, (*ob*. 1915), 191, 194, 195, 198
Beales, Walter, N. Lopham, (born *c.* 1836), 190
Beales, William, N. Lopham wheelwright, 195
Beales, Zadia, 240

bearing sheet, 74, 84
Bedfordshire, 148
Beeles, William, Hockham, (1598), 189
beer, 39, 252, 260
Beers, John (1628), 93–94
bees, 21
beet harvest, 1915, 223
Beevor, the Reverend Miles, of Mulbarton House, 109
Belgae, the, 8
BELL, The, N. Lopham, 30, **31**, 41, **91**, 92, 129, 140, 200, 217
Bell Corner, N. Lopham, 262, 263
Bell Meadow, 237n
bells, N. Lopham church, 30, 191
bells, S. Lopham church, 55, **56**, 160, 161
BELLS, The SIX—SEE SIX BELLS
Bergholt, East, Suffolk—SEE East Bergholt
Berners Street, 65, London, 146
Berry Way, N. Lopham—SEE Bury Way
Betts of Wortham family (SEE ALSO Betts, Rev. George, senior and junior), 86
Betts, Arthur Thomas, S. Lopham, 226
Betts, Christopher, senior, N. Lopham town-warden 1826–1879, 121, 153
Betts, George, Rev., senior & junior, squarsons of Wortham, 24
bicycling, 234, 252, 262
Bigod, le, Sir John, (*fl.* 1306), 34
Bigod, Roger, fifth earl of Norfolk (*c.* 1245–1306), 34, 93
Bigod, William, son of Roger Bigot, (*ob.* 1120), 28, 29
Bigot, Roger, (*ob.* 1107), 19, 25, 27
Bird's Lane, S. Lopham, 123
Blackborn Hundred, Suffolk, 23
Black Death, 44, 48
BLACK HORSE, The, N. Lopham, (SEE ALSO "Black Horse Cottage"), 41, 190, **200**
"Black Horse Cottage", N. Lopham, **200**
bleachers, 86, 202
bleaching, 140, 149, 202
Blickling, 148
Blomefield, The Rev. Francis (1705–1752), 3, 17, 23, 37, 38, 44, 69, 86, 96, 102, 103, 132, 133
Blomefield, Mary, *née* Womack, his wife, daughter of Arthur W., rector of Buxton & Oxnead & Caister, 103
Blo' Norton (SEE ALSO Fens), 19, 20, 127, 150, 186, 230
Blo' Norton Road, 7, 123
Blo' Norton, S. Andrew's, 29
Blowland, N. Lopham, 124
Blowland Way, N. Lopham, 124
Boadicea—SEE Boudicca, Queen
bobbin winding, 140, **193**, 198
Bobby, John W., N. Lopham, (1867), 155
Bodney Airfield, 251
Boer War, 225, 226
Bogas, Francis of N. Lopham, gent., (1692), 199
Bolle, 106
Bolle, Robert, of N. Lopham (*ob. c.* 1500), 52
bombs, 257, 258
Bond, George, S. Lopham, 226
Boorde, 106
'bore war, the', 258
Bosse, Richard, 52, 128
Boston, Lincolnshire, 10
Bosworth, battle of, 34
Botesdale, Suffolk, 244
Botesdale Road, 123, 127
Boudicca, Queen, 8, 109
boundary treaty between N. & S. Lopham, 93, 94, 95, 150
"Bourne Cottage", 120
Bowell family of N. Lopham, 90, 106, 149, 150

Bowell/Vowell, Elizabeth, wife of Thomas B./V., 90
Bowell, Ephraim, S. Lopham linen manufacturer, 139
Bowell, Friday, S. Lopham linen manufacturer, 139
Bowell, Saville, N. Lopham, 210
Bowen, John, N. Lopham linen manufacturer (*c.* 1840), 139
Bowhill, S., S. Lopham, 246
Bowles, 106
Bowll, 106
bowls, 244
Boyland Hall, 109
Boys, the Three, of S. Nicholas, 69
breadmaking, 203
breaking hemp, 83
Breckland, 5
Bressingham (SEE ALSO Fens), 55, 71, 111, 150, 186, 202
Brewose, Mary de—SEE (Brotherton?) Mary of, countess of Norfolk, second wife of Thomas of Brotherton
Bridewell, Norwich—SEE Norwich Bridewell Museum
Bridgman, Edward, of Coney Weston, Esq., 156
Bridgman, Mrs Frances, *née* Fox, 48n., 156 & n., 158
Britain, 13
British, 261
British Library, 37
Broadway, the, S. Lopham, 123
Brock, —, of N. Lopham, (1835), 132
Brock, Arthur, N. Lopham, 234
Brock, Mrs Doris, *née* Barnes, district nurse, 230
Brock, Ellen—SEE Stevens, Mrs Ellen
Brock, Thomas, 125
Brockdish, 103
Bronze Age, 7
brooches, 14
Brook House, S. Lopham, 99
(Brotherton?) Mary of, countess of Norfolk, *née* Mary de Brewose, 34
Brotherton, Thomas of, earl of Norfolk, 34
Brown, Charles, farmer of N. Lopham Lodge Farm, **9**, 205 & n., 214, 220
Brown, Frederick, N. Lopham, 226
Brown & Taylor, Surveyors, 36
Bryant, Richard, N. Lopham (*ob. c.* 1592), 101
Brysettway, N. Lopham, 124
bubonic plague—SEE Black Death
Buckenham, New, 51, 111, 186, 251
Buckenham, Old, 51, 111, 186, 251
Buckenham family of Lopham, 150
Buckenham, Mrs Georgiana Elizabeth, *née* Bale, wife of Thomas B. (III), 146, 147, 157, 158, 192, 220
Buckenham, John, S. Lopham linen manufacturer, 139
Buckenham, Lois, wife of William Beales (q.v.)—SEE Beales, Lois
Buckenham, Thomas, (I.), N. Lopham linen manufacturer, partner of William B. of S. Lopham 1800 (q.v.), 142
Buckenham, Thomas (II), (1796–1863) son of William B. of S. Lopham, N. Lopham linen manufacturer, 139, 143, 144, 145, 146
Buckenham, Thomas (III), N. Lopham, 146
Buckenham, Thomas, S. Lopham (1827–1907), farmer and landowner, 146, 192
Buckenham, T. W. & J., Messrs., Linen Manufacturers By Appointment, 86, 184, 189, 191, 194
Buckenham, William, S. Lopham linen manufacturer, partner of Thomas B., (I) of N. Lopham 1800 (q.v.), 142 & n., 144

Buckingham Palace, 147, 202
Buckland, archdeacon, 246
buildings, 33
BULL, The, N. Lopham, 41, **42**, 100, 129, 189, 200, 214, 218, 221, 244, 252, **253**
Buller, Mrs (?), "syster" to John Cowell (q.v.), 76
Bumpstede/Bumstede family, 32 & n.
Bunwell, 88
Burgonys, 106
Burgundy, 106
burial in woollen, 87
Burroughes, Jeremiah, rector of Tivetshall 1636, 115
Bury S. Edmund's, 22, 104
Bury Way, N. Lopham, 124
Bush, miller, of Kenninghall (?), 221
buslusse, 39, 41
Bussey, William, N. Lopham, 211
Busshe, Marion, of N. Lopham (?) (*ob. c.* 1460), 52
Bylnye family of S. Lopham, 150
Bylnye, John, of S. Lopham, 78

Cable, Jonah, 132
Cadogan, George Henry, 6th earl Cadogan, (1840–1933), 148
Caister, 41
Caius (Keys), Dr. John (1570–1573), 76
Caldecott, Alfred, rector 1895–1898, 159, 179, 221
Calvegate, N. Lopham, 124
Calvinism, 90, 114
Calyons/Calyors (?), John, 51, 52
Cambridgeshire, 110
camp meetings, 216
Cantley, S. Margaret's, 70, 71
Cantrell, William of Norwich, gent., 101
capitation grants, 154
Carell, Edward, esq. (1607), 101
carl, 80, 82
Carlton, William, (1628), 93–94
Carman family, 222
Carman, Ky, 217
Carman, Tom, **192**
Carman, Willie and Jim, (1899), **190**
Carrow Nunnery, 71
Cartwright, Edmund (1743–1823), 112
Castell, Charles Finch Delogue, master of N. Lopham school, 196, 228, 230, 231, 242, 244, 250, 251, 258
catapults, 245
Cayley family of Norfolk, 51
Celtic, 8, 10
celts, 5, 7
Chamberlain, Alex, N. Lopham ham (1851), 153
Chamberlain, Hannah, Wesleyan day school teacher, N. Lopham (1851), 153
Chamberlain, Mary, Church day school teacher, N. Lopham (1851), 153
Chamberlain, Neville, 255
Chamberlain, Thomas, farmer & linen manufacturer of N. Lopham (1875), 149
Chambers, John, editor of *General History of Norfolk*, 1829, 17, 131n.
Chancery, Court of, 133
Chapel Fields, N. Lopham, 195
Chapel Hill, N. Lopham, 32
chaplains, 44
Chapman and family, fairmen, 214
Chapple/Chappel Hills, N. Lopham—SEE Chapel Hill
Charitable Trusts Act, 1853, 133
Charity Commission, the, 152
Charles I, King, 93, 95
Charles II, King, 96, 103
Charlton, William (1592), 91, 93–94
Chaucer, Geoffrey (1340?–1400), 11
CHEQUERS, The, S. Lopham, 41, 127, 200, 252

CHERRY TREE, The, N. Lopham, 41, 200, 214
Chestnut Tree Farm, N. Lopham, 96, 98, 100, 147, 216
Chilley, Edmund, 125
Chimbrook, 37
Chimbrook Meadow, 37
Chrightons Show, 214
Christ and the Samaritan Woman, 197
Christianity, 15, 16, 25
church-ales, 46
church-building—SEE buildings
church day school, N. Lopham, 126, 127, 153, 154, 157
Church Farm, N. Lopham, 97, **98**, 262
Churchgate Street, N. Lopham, 124
Churchill, Winston Spencer, 256
Church Meadow, S. Lopham, 245, 252
Church of England, 90, 95, 102, 114, 115, 117, 120, 240
churchwardens' accounts, 46, 152
Churchwardens' Book, N. Lopham, 59, 122, 123, 128, 129, 130, 131, 132, 136
Churchweye, N. Lopham, 124
cinema (SEE ALSO "pictures, the"), 252, 260
citations, 127
Clark, John, N. Lopham, 210
Clarke, Dr Adam (1762?–1832), 117, 118
Clarke, Mrs, dressmaker of N. Lopham, 201
Claydon, Suffolk, 105
Clerk, Edmund (*ob. c.* 1375), 17, 22, 51
clogs—SEE pattens
Cluniac Priory, Thetford—SEE Thetford Priory
Coates family of Lopham, 203
Coates, Jonas & Thomas, N. Lopham linen manufacturers (*c.* 1840), 139
Cobb, Coleby, N. Lopham linen manufacturer, 120, 139, 140, 149, 197
Cobb, Coleby George ("Coby"), 120, 149, 151, 153, 154, 159, 160 & n.
Cockrill, Miss, supplementary teacher at S. Lopham school, 245, 246, 247
Cocksedge, Bert, N. Lopham, 226
Coe, Josiah, shoemaker of N. Lopham, 200
Coffin Pit, 188
coinage, 72, 73n.
Coke, Thomas William, 3rd earl of Leicester, 148
Cole, Aldis, N. Lopham, 210
Coleby, family of, S. Lopham, 139
Coleman, G., S. Lopham, 242
Collings, Laura, 217
Colman, Jeremiah James, of Carrow Hall, Esq., 148
Colman, Russell, Lord Lieutenant, 241, 242
common rights, 37, 38
commonage (SEE ALSO Lopham Commons), 121, 122, 124
Common Market Footway, N. Lopham, 124
commons—SEE ALSO Lopham Commons, 36
Commonwealth Parliament (1653), 96
Coney Lane—SEE Conney Lane
Coney Weston, Suffolk, 156
Congregationalists, 115
Conney Lane, N. Lopham, 124
conscientious objectors, 226
conservation, 33, 38, 135
constables, Lopham, 88, 187
Cooke, Mistress, 71
Cooke, Mr, of Uphall, 183n.
Cooke, Nathaniel, N. Lopham Townwarden 1814–1821, 121
Cooper, John of Suffolk, yeoman (1676), 102n.
Coote, Christopher, 89, 92
Coote family of Blo' Norton, 89

Coote family of Lopham, 89
Anne (Sherwyn) of N. Lopham, 89
Barbara, *née* Harvey, wife of Christopher Coote, 89
Eustas, first-born son of Christopher, 89
Francis, son of Christopher, gentleman usher to Elizabeth I, 89
Coote, Sir Nicholas, knight, 89
copyhold—SEE land tenure
Corbett, J. J., S. Lopham, 257
Corbett, L. J., S. Lopham, 257
Corble, Robert, S. Lopham, 226
Corble, Walter, S. Lopham, 226
coronation festivities, 132, 221, 228
Corpus Christi College, Cambridge, 102
Cotman, John Sell, *frontispiece*, 56
Cotnye, Richard, S. Lopham linen-weaver, (*ob. c.* 1600), 79, 101
daughters: Anne, Mary, Alice, Joane & Frances, 79
"Cottage, The", N. Lopham, 191n.
County Directories of Norfolk, 17, 29
"Court, The", S. Lopham, formerly the SIX BELLS, then "The Limes", 142n.
Coussins, Jonathan, Methodist minister, 118
"Coventry Cycle", the, 47
Cowell, David (*fl.* 1500), 77
Cowell, John, of N. Lopham (*ob.* 1559), 74, 76, 84
Elizabeth, his second wife, 74
Elizabeth, his youngest (?) daughter, 75
Isabell, his married (?) daughter, 75
John, junior, his second (?) son, 75, 76
Margaret "thelder", his daughter, 75
Margaret the younger, his daughter, 75
Mary – , his goddaughter, 75
Robert, his eldest son, 74, 77
Cowell, Elizabeth, wife of Thomas C., 90
Cowell, Thomas, 90
Cowells, 106
Cowl, John, 106
Cowlles, 106
cowmen, 249
cows, 20, 41, 46
Cox, Edward, junior, S. Lopham, 212
Cox, Edward, senior, farmer of S. Lopham, 212
Cox, Miss Mary, dressmaker of N. Lopham, 201
Cox, Thomas, the Reverend (*d.* 1734), 23, 86
Cox & Hall—SEE Cox, the Rev. Thos., and Hall, the Rev. Anthony, authors of *Magna Britannia &c*
Cozens-Hardy, Miss, 246
Crackthorn Bridge, Redgrave, 24
Craneholme Street, S. Lopham, 48n., 123
Cranesholme, S. Lopham—SEE Craneholme
Crécy, battle of (1346), 225
Creightons Show—SEE Chrightons Show
Creke, 105
cricket, 237, 244
Cromer, 180
Crompton, Samuel (1753–1827), 112
Crook, Charles Edward, blacksmith of N. Lopham, 234, **235**
Crook, Mrs Edna Maria, *née* Goddard, 236
Crook, Herbert Augustus, N. Lopham (1886–1970), 234, 244
Crook, Mrs Laura, *née* Ludbrook, N. Lopham, 234
Crossway, Redgrave Common, 24, 185
Cross Ways, the, S. Lopham, 142n.
Crotchet and Dartnell, puppet masters, 214

Crow, Edward H., South Lopham schoolmaster, 177
Crow, Mrs S., S. Lopham schoolmistress, 177
Crowe family, the, of Suffolk and the Lophams, 203
Crowe, Robert, N. Lopham, 204, 226
Crowe, Thomas Peck (*ob.* 1881), 204
Crowe, Thomas, 177, 193, 204, 223, 225, 226, 227
Crowe, William, N. Lopham, 226
Crowe's Book, 191, 203, 204, 206, 211, 223
Crowfield, Suffolk, 204
CROWN, The, S. Lopham, 41, 123, 200, 234, 236
Crown Bridge, S. Lopham, 232
Crowned Mary, The or *L'Incoronata*, 55
Cullum, William, N. Lopham, 226
curates, (SEE ALSO chaplains), 44
Cuttings and Knaveings, 33
cycle business, 233n, 236

Dairy (formerly Noddle) Farm, N. Lopham, 96, 154, 243
Dale, Mr, N. Lopham schoolmaster, 1900, 179
Dale Tree, the Old, 188, 189, 232n.
Dalton, Henry, N. Lopham, (*ob.* 1589), 73
Dalton, Katheryn, daughter of Henry D., 73
damask linen, 86, 145, 146
Danes, 16
Darby, Richard, rector (*ob. c.* 1499), 45, 53
Darracq motor car, 236
Dartnell—SEE Crotchet and Dartnell
darts, 244
Davy, Robert and family, 130
decoy (SEE ALSO fishery), 37
dedications, 15, 16, 17, 32
deer, 35, 59, 92, 93
De Fraine, John, 213
delepol, John, of Lopham (13th c.), 34, 106
de Lopham, family of Norfolk, 32
Cecily de L., formerly wife of Robert de Bumpstede, 31, 32
Dionise de L., notary, son of Symon, 32
Henry de L., the chirurgeon, 32
Ivo de L., tenant of 2nd Bigod earl of Norfolk, 32
Robert de L., bailiff of Norwich 1303–1320, 32n.
Symon de L., clerk, 1334, father of Dionise, 32
de Moor, John—SEE Moor, John of the
Denver, 51, 241
dialects—SEE East Anglian dialects
Dickleburgh, 133
"dirige" and "dirge", 71 & n.
Diss, 96, 105, 111, 113, 115, 186, 194, 242, 250, 260, 264
dissenters—SEE nonconformists
Diss Express & Norfolk & Suffolk Journal, 219
Diss Heywood, 243
Diss Road, 123
Diss, S. Mary's, 118
district nurse, 230
ditches, prescribed, (1815), 123, 125
Dix, John, esquire (1631), 95
Doctor from the Spa, the, 210, 211
doctors, village, 199, 223
Dodd, Charles, 129
Dogger Bank, the, 5
Dolomedes Plantarius, the Great Raft Spider, 11, **12**
Domesday Book, 19, 20, 25, 33, 48
dominoes, 244, 252
donkeys, 132, 143, 185
Dove family of S. Lopham, 149
Dove, Albert, S. Lopham, 226
Dove, John, S. Lopham linen manufacturer, 139
dovecotes, 35
Dovehouse Close, N. Lopham, 32

Dowes Close, S. Lopham, 35
Dowhouse Acre, S. Lopham, 35
Downham Market, 106
Downing, Henry and his sister, 75, 76
Downing, Richard, S. Lopham linen manufacturer, 139
draughts, 244
dressmaking, 182
drinking, 141, 143, 160, 184
Drops, 245 & n.
Duffey, Dr Eric, 11, 12
Duffy's Close—SEE Dovehouse Close
Duke of Norfolk, The, 218, 219
Duke's Palace, The—SEE Norwich House
Dune, river—SEE Ouse, Little, river
Durden, Richard H., S. Lopham, 246
Dyx, William, of Wickmere, esquire, 101

Ealing, 259
Earls Marshal—SEE Marshal, Earl
Earsham, 93
East Anglia, 5, 10, 13, 25
East Anglian dialects, 47
East Bergholt, Suffolk, 30
East Dereham, 101, 148
Eastern Daily Press, 197, 198, 238
Eastgate Street, S. Lopham, 123
Easthall, Kenninghall, 35
East Harling, 21, 47, 213
East Harling, S. Peter & S. Paul's, 46, 47
East London by Matthew Arnold, 155
East Lynne, 214
Eastwood, Charles James, rector 1898–1940, 179, 181, 213, 238, 239, 240, 245, 246, 247, 248
Eastwood, Mrs C. J., 237
Eastwood Hall or Rectory Hall, 240, 258 & n.
Eaton, Mr, vermin killer of N. Lopham 1830–1834, 135, 136
Eden, Sir Anthony, 256
education, 134, 153, 176, 264
Education & Science, Department of, 154
Education, Committee of Council on, 154
Education Committee, Norfolk, 246, 258
Education, H.M. Inspectors of, 155, 156, 175, 176, 178, 179, 180, 181, 196, 228, 247, 248
Education Office, Norfolk County, 248
Edward the Confessor, King, 20
Edward I, King, 34, 93
Edward II, King, 34
Edward III, King, 10, 34, 43, 225
Edward IV, King, 23
Edward VI, King, 90, 104
Egerton, Wilbraham, 1st earl Egerton of Tatton (1832–1909), 186
Egg Hat, 245 & n.
eggs, 40, 41, 43, 47
Egypt, 236
elder-guns, SEE pop-guns
electricity, 250
Elizabeth I, Queen, 57, 70, 72, 73n., 86, 88, 135
Elizabeth II, Queen, 221
Ellacombe's Chiming Apparatus, 160
Ellis, Thomas, "intruder" rector 1654–1663, 96, 115
Elner, Noah, S. Lopham, 212, 213
Ely, 186
emigration, 130, 134
Emms, Alfred (The Great Alfar), 211
Emms, Bertie, N. Lopham, 257
Emms, Frank, N. Lopham, 226
Emms, James, N. Lopham, 226
Emms, Sydney, N. Lopham, 226
Emms, Wilfred, N. Lopham, 226
enclosure—(SEE ALSO Inclosure), 58, 121–6

England, 10
English, the, 261
epidemics (SEE ALSO Black Death), 231
Essex, 23, 80
Eton College (SEE ALSO James, Arthur, esq.), 149
Eure, Oliver, innkeeper of N. Lopham, 1591, 91–92
Europe, Northern, 10, 13
evacuees, 258
"Exodus, Lopham"—SEE emigration

faggot ovens, 203
Fakenham, 106
falgates or fall-gates—SEE folgates
"Falstaff, Sir John", 92
Fandangle, the, 218
farmhouses—SEE buildings
Farsfield—SEE Fersfield
Fenland, the, 8
Fenne, John, linen-weaver of N. Lopham, (*ob. c.* 1586), 78
Fenne, Roger, of N. Lopham, son of John F., 78, 79, 97
Fenn-Common (SEE ALSO Lopham Commons), 33
Fens—Blo' Norton, 5
  Bressingham, 5
  Hinderclay, 5
  Lincolnshire, 8
  Lopham, 5, 9, 11, 87, 93
  Redgrave, 5, 11
  Roydon, 5
  Thelnetham, 5
Fenstrete, S. Lopham, 123
"Ferndale Holding", formerly THE BARKING DICKEY, 185 & n.
ferrets, 182, 213
Fersfield, 44, 71, 96, 111, 230
Fersfield Green, 58
Fersfield Hall Farm, 109
Fersfield Lodge Farm, 109
fertilisers, 110
Filby, All Saints', 71
fimble, 80, 82
Fincham, 106
Finningham, Suffolk, 106
fire festivals, 15
fish emblem, 32n., 69
fishery, 37
fishing, 252
Fit Lane, S. Lopham, 123
Fitzalan, Henry, earl of Arundel 1512–1580, 100
Fitzalan-Howard, (SEE ALSO Howard)
  Bernard Marmaduke F-H, sixteenth duke of Norfolk (1908–1975), 240, 241, 242
  Henry F-H, fifteenth duke of Norfolk (1847–1917), 35, 148, 212
Fivestone Lane, N. & S. Lopham—SEE Fyson's Lane
Five Stones, 15
Flatman, Arthur, S. Lopham, 226
flax cultivation, 79, 80, 195
flaxen yarn, **196**
Flaxlande, 79
Flaxlonde Furlong, 79
Fletcher, John, master of N. Lopham Wesleyan day school, 155, 156, 157
flindermouse or bat, 41
flowers, 252
Flying Fortresses, 257
Foldway, N. Lopham, 124
folgates, 127
Foord/Ford—SEE Lophamford
football (SEE ALSO Lopham United), 244, 252
footpaths, 124, 262, 263
foot-rot, 43
Foresters Club, 214
Forncett, 244
"Fortune's Well", N. Lopham, 195
Founder, the, William—SEE William the Founder
Fox, Thomas, of Coney Weston, esq., 156
Framlingham Castle, 57
France, 43, 225

Francis family of N. & S. Lopham, 86
Francis, Robert, linen-weaver & farmer of N. Lopham, (*ob. c.* 1689), 86
Sarah, his wife, 87
John, his son, 87
Sarah & Mary, his daughters, 87
freebord, 58
freemen (SEE ALSO Alsi, Ofl), 20
freewarren, 35, 58
Frith, the Little and Great, 24 & n.
Frost, Diamond and Sam, N. Lopham, 210
Frost, V. C., N. Lopham, 189n.
Fulham, 49
Fulmerston, Sir Richard, 106
Fulmodestone, 106
Fynchyngham, John, 106
Fyson's Lane (SEE ALSO Five Stones), 15, 195

Gallows Hill, Redgrave, 24
gaol—(SEE ALSO Liberty, the Duke of Norfolk's), 23
"Gaol House", S. Lopham, 24
"Garblesham Game", 46
Garboldisham, 71, 96, 111, 150, 186, 212, 230, 242, 264
Garboldisham Road, 123, 234
Garboldisham, S. John's, 29
GARDEN HOUSE, The—SEE Poplar Tree Farm
gardening (SEE ALSO flowers, vegetables) 178, 228, 252
Garnham, Alan, N. Lopham, 226
Garrod, Henry Edwin, solicitor of Diss, 35, 212, 213
gas masks, 256
Gates, Memorial, at the Lopham Playing Field, 240
Gawdie, Bassingborne, of W. Harling (*ob.* 1590), 88
Gawdie, Sir Bassingborne (1560–1606), 92
Gaze's cattle market, Diss, 264
George V, King (SEE ALSO coronation festivities), 191, 195, 221
Gibson, Andrew, 90–91, 114
gilds, SEE ALSO—S. Andrew's gild, N. Lopham; S. Cross gild, S. Lopham; S. John's gild, N. Lopham; S. Nicholas's gild, S. Lopham; S. Peter's gild, N. Lopham; S. Peter's gild, S. Lopham; Trinity gild, S. Lopham, 45
Gill, Miss Mary, head-teacher of S. Lopham school, 245, 246, 247, 248
Gill, William, N. Lopham churchwarden, 153
Gissing, 244
gleaning, 59, 202
Glover, Emma, N. Lopham, 210
Glover, Jenny, N. Lopham, 210
Glover, Joe, 188, 210
Glover, Thomas Methodist of Leicester, (1770), 115
Glover, W. Joseph Carman, North Lopham, 225
Goddard, Edna Maria–SEE Crook, Mrs Edna Maria
Goddard, Henry, landlord of the CHEQUERS, S. Lopham, 200
Gogosher, the, 218
Goldsmith, Mr, 246
Gonville & Caius College, Cambridge, 74
Gooch, Daniel, 263, 264
Gooch, Thomas, innkeeper and linen manufacturer of N. Lopham, 119, 139
Gooche, John, of London, gent., 92
Gooderham, James, of Thorndon, Suffolk and N. Lopham, 242, 243, 244
Gooderham, Mrs Mary, N. Lopham, 239, 242, 243
Goodman, William, S. Lopham (?), (1628), 93–94
Goryeway, S. Lopham, 123
Grange Farm, N. Lopham, 96, 116, **117**, 120

Graveley, Anne, sister to Graveley, rector John, 71
Graveley, John, rector (*ob. c.* 1545), 70, 71, 73
Great Ellingham, 102
Great or Mill Common (SEE ALSO Lopham Commons), 122
"Great Heathen Army, the", 16
Great Yarmouth—SEE Yarmouth, Great
Grecians, 43
Green, vermin killer of N. Lopham 1847–1852, 135
Green, Elizabeth, N. Lopham linen weaver, (1851), 141
Green, Jesse, **98**, 234, **235**
Greene, John, N. Lopham linen-weaver, 85
Greenhill, William, rector of Oakley, Suffolk (1636), 115
Greens (SEE ALSO Fersfield Green, Lopham Green, Winley Green), 40
Gregory the Great, Pope—SEE S. Gregory
Grey, Lady Jane, 70
Greyfriars Church, London, 35
GREYHOUND, The, Diss, 108
Grove, The, N. Lopham, 78
Guiltcross Hundred, 20, 57, 59
Guiltcross Rural District Council, 230
gunpowder, 126
"Gunwell"—SEE Gonville
Guthrum, King (*ob.* A.D. 890), 15
Gysyer, John, of S. Lopham (*ob. c.* 1558), 72

Hackney, Orchard School & South Hackney Parochial L.C.C. School, 258, 259
Halifax, Bankfield Museum, 112, 198
Hall, Anthony, the Reverend (1679–1723), 23
Halls, Albert, S. Lopham, 226
Halls, Edward, S. Lopham, 226
Hall Way, N. Lopham, 124
Halybbott, John, chaplain of N. Lopham, 52
hām, 10
hand-looms, **112**, 137, 138, 184, 241
hangman, 160, 197
Hangman's Barn, 24
Harbord, Evelyn Louisa, *née* Wilson-Patten, Dowager Lady Suffield, 244
Hare, Sir John of Stow-Bardolph, (*ob.* 1635?), 93
Hargreaves, James (*ob.* 1778), 112
Harling—SEE East Harling, West Harling
Harling Gate, 127
Harling Road, 127
Harrods of Knightsbridge, 191
Harrow School, 149
Harte, Valentine, S. Lopham linen-weaver (1633), 86
harvest festivals, 220
Harvest Holiday, 255
Harvey, Barbara, SEE Coote family of Lopham
Hatch Lane, S. Lopham, 123
haugh, 93
Haughley, Suffolk, 106
Hauville, 106
Hauylye, John, 106
Havers, John, esquire (1631), 95
Havers, Thomas, Mayor of Norwich, 108
Hawes, Charles, landlord of the CROWN, S. Lopham, 200
Hawes, George, S. Lopham, 226
Hawes, Godfrey, S. Lopham, 226
hawkers—SEE pedlars
Hawkeys—SEE Horkeys
Hawks, Mr & Mrs & Leslie, S. Lopham, 246, 247
hay, 41
Heasell, Mary (1628), 93–945
heckling hemp, 84
hedgehogs—SEE sparrows and hedgehogs
helmet, 75

hemp cultivation, 79, 80, 110, 111, 140, 195, 201–202
hempen yarn, 84, 86, 141, 142, 147
hempits, 82, 83
hemplands, 79, 142
Henderson, H. P., H.M.I., 176
Henry I, King, 27
Henry II, King, 29
Henry IV, King, 106
Henry VII, King, 34
Henry VIII, King, 104
Hethersett, 110
Hewtree Furlong & Wattering, 33
High Common (SEE ALSO Lopham Commons), 122
highways, 241, 263
Hilborough, 51
Hill, Henry, gent. (1657), 96
Hinderclay, 5
Hines, Police Constable, 248
Hingham, 244
hire cars, SEE taxi business
Hitler, Adolf, 258
Hobbarde, William, yeoman of S. Lopham, (*ob. c.* 1565), 80, 81, 90
  his wife, Joan, 80, 81
Hockys—SEE Horkeys
Hogg, Arthur, N. Lopham, 226
Hoggison, 106
Holden, Albert, N. Lopham, 226
Holden, Emma, 217
Holden, Jack & his two sisters, N. Lopham, 211
Holland, Sir John, of Quidenham, 1st baronet (1603–1700), 102n.
Holland, John, of Wortwell, Esq., 101, 102 & n.
Holland's Wood, 36
"holy places", 15, 30
Home Guard, 256
hoops, 245
hopscotch, 244
Hopton, Suffolk, 186
Hopton, John, bishop of Norwich (*ob.* 1558), 70, 73
Hopton Road, 24n.
Horkeys, 218, 220
Horne, vermin-killer of N. Lopham 1835–1840, 135
Horne, Dr George, bishop of Norwich (1730–1792), 118
horsemen, 249
horses, 21, 73, 74
Horsham S. Faith's, 104
Horton, Nicholas de, rector 1361–1380, 49
hospitals, 71
Hoskins, Stanley, 233n.
housing, 231
Howard (SEE ALSO Fitzalan-Howard)
  Bernard Edward H., twelfth duke of Norfolk (1765–1842), 240
  Charles H., eleventh duke of Norfolk (1746–1815), 113
  Henry H., earl of Surrey (c. 1517–1547), 106
  Henry H., sixth duke of Norfolk (1628–1684), 108
  Philip H., earl of Arundel & Surrey (S. Philip Howard) (1557–1595), 89, 100, 101
  Thomas H., second duke of Norfolk (1443–1524), 34, 56, 57
  Thomas H., third duke of Norfolk (1473–1554), 56, 57, 104, 105, 106
  Thomas H., fourth duke of Norfolk (1536–1572), 59, 88, 89, 108
  Thomas H., fifth duke of Norfolk (1627–1677), 108
  Thomas H., eighth duke of Norfolk (1683–1732), 108, 109, 151
Howard, "Stumpy", landlord of the BELL, N. Lopham, **91**, 200
Howard Way, N. Lopham, 124
Huggins, Henry, linen manufacturer of S. Lopham, 139
Hugheson, William, clerk, 71
humstrumming, 248, 249
Hundred River, S. Lopham, 232
Hunn's—SEE "Up Hunn's"

Hutson, Frederick, N. Lopham, 226
hyrne, 93

Ice Age, 3
Iceni, the, 8, 9
Imperial Russian Embassy, 148
Inclosure Acts (SEE ALSO Lopham Inclosure Act, 1812), 121, 124, 125
Inclosure Awards, N. & S. Lopham, 1815, 35, 121, 122, 123, 125, 156, 262
Index Villaris, 1690—SEE Adams, John
Industrial Revolution, 137
Inexhaustible Well, the, 3, **4**, 251
intercommonage, 122, 150
interludes, 46, 47
Ipswich, 5, 14
Ipswich Museum, 198
"Ipswich People, the", 14, 15
Irish linen, 147
Iron Age, 7, 8

Jacquard loom, the, 145, 184, 191, 198
James I, King, 92, 93
James, Arthur, esq., of Eton College, 148
jam tarts, 242
Jane, Queen—SEE Grey, Lady Jane
Jeames, Elizabeth, widow, N. Lopham (1598), 189
Jenney, Andrew, rector (*ob. c.* 1507), 70
Jenney, Dame Keteryn, nun, 71
Jente, Thomas, N. Lopham (1479), 52
Jerusalem, 27
Jessopp, Dr Augustus (1823–1914), 231
Johnson, James, N. Lopham linen-weaver (1707), 86
Jolly, Henry, N. Lopham linen manufacturer & butcher (*c.* 1840), 139
"Joppham", *sc.* Loppham, 29
Jubilee, 1887, 220
Jubilee, 1897, 220
Jubilee, 1977 (SEE ALSO Appendix) 221
Jubilee Cedars, South Lopham, 220, 221
Jubilee Cottage, N. Lopham, 220
Jubilee Lane, N. Lopham (SEE ALSO Tann's Lane), 220
Jubilee Meadow, N. Lopham, 220
Jump, Richard James, S. Lopham, schoolmaster, 177
Jutland, 14

"Kailli, John"—SEE Cayley
Kally—SEE Cayley
Keeble, Arthur, N. Lopham shoemaker, 201
Keeble, Jonas, N. Lopham hickler, 1851, 84
Keeble, Walter alias "Pipman", 191 & n.
Kemp, G., 130
"Keningale Game and Players", 46
Kenninghall, 14, 41, 45, 57, 71, 88, 111, 115, 122, 127, 150, 186, 199, 212, 230, 244
Kenninghall Butts, 13, 14
Kenninghall House—SEE Kenninghall Place
Kenninghall Park, 57, 58, 92, 93
Kenninghall Place, 57, 70, 89, 100, 105, 108
Kenninghall Place Farm, 98, 108, 109
Kenninghall Road, 236
Kenninghall, S. Mary's, 32, 53
Kenninghall Union, 209
Kensit, John, 197
Keppel, Arnold Allan Cecil, 8th earl of Albemarle, 186
Keppel, E. G., rector of Quidenham, 158
Keppel, Major, J. P., 212
Kerr, Victoria Alexandrina, *née* Montagu-Douglas-Scott, marchioness of Lothian, 148
Kerridge, Charlotte, 154

Kerry, J., S. Lopham, 246
Keys—SEE Caius
King, landlord of the BLACK HORSE, N. Lopham, 200
KING'S HEAD, the, N. Lopham, **40**, 41, 97, 100, 116, 129, 188, 200, 211, 213, 214, 216, 232
King's Head Green (SEE ALSO Lopham Green, North), 214
King's Head Lane, N. Lopham, 7, 115, 188, 232
King's Lynn, 198, 225
Knaveings—SEE Cuttings & Knaveings

La de dar, the, 210, 213
Lamp Acre, N. Lopham, 46
Lancashire, 191
Land, Christopher, N. Lopham weaver and linen manufacturer, 138, 149
land-mine, 6, 256
land tenure, 48
Langley Abbey, 71
Larance (?Lawrence), 132
largess(e), 218
Last, Joseph, N. Lopham, 225
"Laureate", the N. Lopham, 151
Lawn, The, N. Lopham, 32, 35, 58
Lawrence (?)—SEE Larance
lazar-houses—SEE hospitals
leapfrog, 244, 245n.
"Lechmere", Prestbury, Gloucestershire, 195
Lee, Thomas, Methodist (1770), 115
Leech Mere—SEE Letchmere
Leeder, Robert, N. Lopham linen-weaver, 119
Leeds Spinning Mills, 140
Leet, the, 95 & n.
Leicester, earl of—SEE Coke
Leland, John (1506?–1552), 23
Leper (SEE ALSO lazar-house), 132
Lestrange of Blackmere, 56
L'Estrange, John, 17n.
Letchmere, N. Lopham, 83, 230, 231
Levold, John, of N. Lopham (*ob. c.* 1544), 31, 73
Levould, Thomas, (*ob. c.* 1559) 73, 74
"ley" lines, 15n.
Liberal Party, 197
Liberty, the Duke of Norfolk's, 23, 57, 108, 109, 212
Light Railway Commission, 186
"Limes, The", N. Lopham, **85**, 140, 142, 193, 194, 195, 198
"Limes, The", S. Lopham (SEE ALSO "The Court", S. Lopham), 142 & n., **143**
Lincoln Cathedral, 105
Lincolnshire, 8, 110
L'Incoronata—SEE Crowned Mary, the
"Linden", N. Lopham, 128n.
linen industry, 78–87 *passim*, 111, 137–149 *passim*, 184, 185, 187, 195
linen patterns, 86, 143, 145, 146
"lion sejant", 55, 56
Littlehales, Richard, rector 1801–1822, 150
Little Ouse, river—SEE Ouse, Little
Liverpool, 130, 131
lobbe—SEE loppe
Local Defence Volunteers—SEE Home Guard
Locke, John (1628), 93–94
Lodge Farm,—SEE Lopham Lodge Farm
Lollards, 115
London, 178, 186, 194
Londoners, 258, 259, 260
Longley, Canon R. W., rector of Banham, 240
looms (SEE ALSO Jacquard loom), **81**, **85**, 128, 182, 196, 197, 198
lop, to, 11
lope, to, 11
lope-staves, 11
Lopham, 3, 7, 8, 10, 11, 15, 16, 21, 41, 111, 130, 187, 241, 256
Lopham Charity, 131, 133, 158

Lopham Commons, 109, 122
Fen Common, 122
Great or Mill Common, 122, 127
Low Common, 123
North Common, 122
North Green, 122
Lopham Fen (SEE ALSO Fens & Fenn-Common), 38, 43, 122, 126
Lophamford, 3, 5, 6, 7, 14, 19, 20, 22, 185, 256
Cross, 22
"Foord", village of, 23
land-mine at, 6
"market" at, 22
village of, 23
Lopham Ford Farm—SEE "Gaol House"
Lopham Game, 46
Lopham Gate—SEE Lophamford
Lopham Green, North, 116
Lopham Green, South, 233, 234
Lopham Grove, 36
Lopham Hall, South, 35, 109
Lopham Inclosure Act, 1812 (SEE ALSO Inclosure Awards), 38, 121
Lopham linen, 78–87 *passim*, 137–149 *passim*, 187, 191
Lopham Lodge, 35, 89, 92
Lopham Lodge Farm, N. Lopham, **9**, 13, 109, 220
Lopham Magna,—SEE Lopham, North
Lopham manor, 34, 35, 49, 92
Lopham manorial court Rolls, 37, 48, 51
Lopham market—SEE Lophamford
Lopham Marsh, 34
Lopham Mission Room, South (SEE ALSO "Magdelan House"), 240
Lopham, North, 19, 20, 73, 115, 120, 138, 140, 141, 175, 186, 230, 257
Churchwardens' Book—SEE Churchwardens' Book, N. Lopham
Parish Council, 186, 230, 237, 238, 242, 243, 250, 262
S. Andrew's, **14**, 15, 16, 17, 29, **30**, 31, 45, 49, **50**, 51, 52, 53, 69, 71, 74, 87, 120, 126, 151, 154, 160
School (SEE ALSO Royal Albert National School; Church day school, N. Lopham), 154, 196, 222, 228, **229**, 234, 237, 259
Lopham parish boundaries, 93
Lopham Park, 32, 37, 58, 92, 93
Lopham Playing Field, 240, 241, 244, 255, 262, 263
Lophams, the—SEE Lopham
Lopham Saint Andrew—SEE Lopham, North
Lopham Saint Nicholas—SEE Lopham, South
Lopham, South, 19, 20, 114, 139, 140, 186, 230, 232
Parish Council, 232, 238, 242, 262
S. Nicholas's, *frontispiece*, 15, 16, 17, 22, 25, **26**, 27, **28**, 30, 49, 52, 53, **54**, 55, 69, 70, 71, 72, 74, 120, 132, 133, 134, 160, 220
School, 133, 134, 156, 176, 177, 178, 183, 213, 245–248, 256, 257, 259
Village Hall—SEE Eastwood Hall
Lopham Town Farm, 133
Lopham "treaty" or Indenture of 1628, 93
Lopham United Football Team, 236, 244, 245
Lopham Village (Community) Council, 242, 243
Lopham Village Hall, 237, 238, 240, 241, 242, 243, 244, 255, 262, 263
Lopham Village Hall Committee, 196, 243, 248, 252

Lopham Village Hall & Playing Field Committee, 242, 243
Lopholm, 10
Lopp, the sea of, 11
Loppa, 10
Loppa, the island of, 11
"loppe" and "loppewebbe", 11
Loppington, Shropshire, 10
"Loppon", *sc.* Lopham, 74
lopthorne & lopthorne furlong, 11, 33
lopthreads and lopwebs, 11
lop way, a, 11
lorries, 234
Losinga, Herbert, bishop of Norwich (1054?–1119), 27, 33
Lothian, marchioness of—SEE Kerr
loup, to, 11
Lovack, William, 129
Low Common, S. Lopham (SEE ALSO Lopham Commons), 123
Ludbroke, Elizabeth, N. Lopham, second daughter of Thomas L., 197
Ludbroke, Thomas, N. Lopham, 197
Ludbrook, N. Lopham, 132
Ludbrook, Charles, N. Lopham, 211
Ludbrook, Gordon, blacksmith of N. Lopham, 195, **235**
Ludbrook, Laura, N. Lopham—SEE Crook, Mrs Laura
Ludbrook, "Tip" of N. Lopham, weaver, 191, **192**
"Luppeham", *sc.* Lopham, 11

Magdalene College, Cambridge, 148–149
Magic (SEE ALSO Christianity; relics), 15, 16
"Magdelan House", S. Lopham, formerly Mission Room, 240n.
Magna Britannia &c,—SEE Cox and Hall
mail, shirt of, 75
Mallowes family of N. Lopham, 150
Mann, Sarah Ann, schoolmistress and wife of William Mann, 182
Mann, William, schoolmaster of N. Lopham, 175, 176 & n., 179, 182
manorial courts, 36, 37
marbles, 180, 244
Maria Martin or *Murder in the Red Barn*, 214
Market Weston, Suffolk, 186
Marsh, Francis of S. Lopham (?), 93
Marsh, Thomas, (1628), 93–94
Marshal, Earl, 86
Marshal, Margaret, countess of Norfolk, 34, 35, 36, 78
Marshalcy of England, 34
marshland, 33–34
Martin, Thomas (1697–1771) of Palgrave, 93
Mary, Queen of Heaven, *Maria Regina*, 51, 54
Mary I, Queen, 57, 70, 72, 104, 105
Mary, Queen to King George V, 148, 191, 221
Mary of Teck, H.R.H. Princess, 148, 191
maslin, 80
Mason, William, 125
May Day, 47, 155
"Meadow House", formerly the WEAVERS' ARMS, **185**
mechanisation, 112, 234
Mellitus, bishop of London, later archbishop of Canterbury (*ob.* A.D. 624), 15
Memorial Gates—SEE Gates, Memorial, at the Lopham Playing Field
merman, 41
Mesolithic—SEE Stone Age
Methodism (SEE ALSO Wesley), 115, 116, 150, 151
Mid-Anglian Light Railway, 185
minsters, 25, 27, 29
Mission Room, S. Lopham—SEE Lopham Mission Room

Mitchell, James (1786?–1844), 137, 138, 140, 218
Montgomerie, Cecil F., Esq., 212
Moor, John of the, 78, 106
morion—SEE helmet
Morland, S. Lopham, 78
Mornement, Col. Edward, E. Harling, 240
Mornement, James, N. Lopham churchwarden (1822), 121, 129, 153, 240
morris dancing, 47
Morse, Robert, gent., steward of Lopham manor, (1650), 95
Mothers' Union, 252
motor traffic, 234
Mouncer, Arthur, photographer, 218
Mowbray
  Elizabeth M., *née* Talbot, wife of John M., 4th Mowbray duke of Norfolk, (*ob.* 1506/7), 35, 45, 55
  John M., (1444–1476), 4th and last M. duke, 35, 56
  Thomas M., (1366?–1399) 1st M. duke, 34
Mullenger, James, S. Lopham, 226
Murder in the Red Barn—SEE *Maria Martin*
murrain, 43
Murrell, Richard senior, yeoman of N. Lopham (*ob. c.* 1596), 92
  Katherine M., his daughter-in-law and heiress, 92
Murriell family of N. Lopham, 150
murryon—SEE morion
Murton, Edward, N. Lopham linen manufacturer, (1875), 149
Murton, John, N. Lopham, sometime linen manufacturer, 147, 149
Muskett, Charles of S. Lopham, Esq. (1657), 96
Myra (Dembre) Lycia, Asia Minor, 18
mystery plays, 46, 47
Narrowe Nordale—SEE Nordale
National Union of Teachers, 246
neolithic—SEE Stone Age
netball, 244
Nethergate Street, S. Lopham, 123
newspapers, 40, 226
New Voter's Catechism, The, 197
New York, 131
Nicholas, rector (1225), 151
Nicholas de Horton—SEE Horton, Nicholas de
Nine Acres Field, High Common, 227
Nine Tailors, 241
Noddle (now Dairy) Farm, N. Lopham—SEE Dairy Farm, N. Lopham
nonconformists (SEE ALSO Baptists; Methodism), 114, 220
Nordale, S. Lopham, 123
Norfolk, 5, 14, 16, 23, 25, 29, 43, 48, 79, 80, 93, 110, 111, 219, 241, 260
Norfolk ale, 39
Norfolk and Norwich Archaeological Society, 191
Norfolk, earls & dukes of
  SEE UNDER Bigod, Brotherton, Fitzalan-Howard, Howard, Marshal, Mowbray
Norfolk County Council, 232, 244
"Norfolk Four Course Shift", 110
Norfolk people, 93, 137, 260
Norfolk Show, 252
Norgate, Thomas Starling (1772–1859), 110
Norman architecture, 28, 29
North-Common (SEE ALSO Lopham Commons), 122
North Dale, S. Lopham—SEE Nordale
North Dele, S. Lopham—SEE Nordale
North-Green—SEE Lopham Green, North
  SEE ALSO Lopham commons
North Lopham—SEE Lopham, North

"Northluppeham", *sc.* N. Lopham, 11
Northorpe, Snetterton, 82
North Sea, 5
Northumberland, 56
Norton, Mr, N. Lopham, 210
Nortuna—SEE Blo' Norton
Norway, 11, 195
Norwich, 44, 71, 101, 113, 114, 115, 130, 180, 186
Norwich Bridewell Museum, 143, 197, 198
Norwich Cathedral, 27, 71, 104, 105
Norwich Circuit of Methodist preachers, 115, 117
Norwich City Football Club, 252
Norwich Domesday Book, the, 17, 29
Norwich House, 89, 108
Norwich Rebellion, 1549, 69
Norwich, S. Andrew's, 31
Norwich, S. Peter Mancroft's, 114
Nottidge, S. Lopham farmer, 245
Nottinghamshire, 149
Nuham, Robert, vicar of Kenninghall, 71
Nun, John, 55
Nun, Matthew (1628), 93–94
Nursing Association for N. & S. Lopham, 230

Oakley, William, S. Lopham, 226
Oak Tree Farm, 96
Oddfellows Club, 214
Ofl, freeman, 20
Old Norfolk Sheep—SEE sheep
Ollands, The—SEE Severals, The
"open field system", 36
Orford, 41
"organs, a pair of", 69
Orgill, Miss Mary Catherine, teacher at S. Lopham school, 247
ornaments, 13, 14
Oryell, 106
Ouse, Little, river or Dune, 3, 5, 8, 9, 22, 23, 24n., 29
overseers, 156 & n.
Overwell-Meer, N. Lopham, 124
oxen, 8, 16, 20, 41
Oxfootpiece, the, S. Lopham, 4
Oxfoot Stone, the, 3, 4, 41, 124
Oxfootstone Farm, S. Lopham, 4, 96
Oxford Dictionary of English Place-Names, The, 10
Oysmere, 43

Packway, the, S. Lopham, 123
paganism, 15, 16
Paine, Thomas (1737–1809), 113
"Painters hirne"—SEE Pantshorne Lane
Palestinians, 43
Palgrave, 111
Panter, 93
Panter Hall—SEE Pantshorne Lane
Pantshorne Farm, S. Lopham, 220
Pantshorne Lane, S. Lopham, 93
parish boundaries—SEE Lopham parish boundaries
Parke, Stephen of Forncett, (1657), 96
Parker, Matthew, archbishop (1504–1575), 105
Park Farm, N. Lopham, 214
Park-Hall—SEE Kenninghall Place
Parkin, Charles, (1689–1765)—Continuator of Blomefield's *Norfolk*, 17
parks, 57, 58
Parliamentary Commission (on) the Situation of the Hand-Loom Weavers
SEE Linen Industry
Parochial Church Council, 252
Parson's Idol, The, 151, 160, 197
Partriche, William, N. Lopham linen-weaver (*ob. c.* 1586), 78
Partrydge, John, godson of John Cowell (q.v.), 76
pattens, 205
Payne, Bertie, N. Lopham, 257

Paynters Lane—SEE Pantshorne Lane
Peace Holiday, 1919, 228
Pearce (SEE ALSO Pearse and Peerse)
Pearse, Liney, George & Will, N. Lopham, 211
pea shooters, 245
peat-cutting, 122
pedlars, 142, 148, 194, 264
Peerse family of S. Lopham, 150
Penrose, Thomas, the Reverend, 197
Penterhaugh—SEE Pantshorne Lane
Peterborough, 39
petrol, 234, 236
petrol-rationing, 261
"Pewe, in the", 45
Philip II of Spain, King, 70
pheasants, 35
"pictures, the", at S. Lopham, 240, 252, 260
pigs, 21, 41, 176, 180, 200
Pig's Whistle, 245 & n.
pillow fight, 242
Pitcher, Thomas, S. Lopham linen manufacturer, 139
Pitchers, William, landlord of the WHITE HORSE, S. Lopham, 200
Pitt, R. W., the Rev., curate, 161
playing field—SEE Lopham Playing Field
ploughing, 8
Plumstede, Thomas of London, gent., 92
poaching, 35, 93
politics, 249
Polterabend—SEE humstrumming
Poole, Edward, linen-weaver, 79
poor 'prentices, 129, 130
pop-guns, 245
Poplar Tree Farm, formerly the GARDEN HOUSE, N. Lopham, 96, 99, 100, 185n.
population, 20, 131, 150, 199, 220, 227, 231
Porter, N. Lopham vermin-killer 1842–1847, 135
Porter, Mr, of Snetterton Hall, 119
Porter, John, N. Lopham farmer, 36
Porter, Samuel, senior, N. Lopham farmer, 118
  Mary P., his wife, 118, 119, 120
Porter, Samuel, junior, N. Lopham farmer, 121 & n.
Porter, Samuel, N. Lopham carrier and baker, (1851), 144
Portway, N. and S. Lopham, 95, 124
Post Office, N. Lopham, 230, 250
Post Office, S. Lopham, 250
Poule Chimbrook, 37
poultry, 41, 200
power looms, 112
practical jokes, 248
Prasutagus, King, 8
Pratt, N. Lopham vermin-killer 1813—*c.* 1830, 135
Pratt, George, N. Lopham, 257
preaching house, N. Lopham, 116
Premonstratensian Canons, 104n.
Prentice, Percy, S. Lopham, 226
Preston, emigrant ship, 131
priests, 44
Primitive Methodist Chapel, 120, 160, 216, 230
Primitive Methodists, 120
Primrose, Archibald Philip, 5th earl of Rosebery, 210 & n.
Prince of Wales's Own Norfolk Artillery, 204
prisoners-of-war, 263
pubs, 252
Pulham S. Mary the Virgin, 135
puppets—SEE Crotchet and Dartnell
Purdy of Wortham, 132
Purses, the Three, of S. Nicholas, 69
Pye, Nicholas, of N. Lopham (*ob.* 1559), 73
Pykards Stile—SEE Stelestock Stile

Quakers, 243

"Quaking Bog River", 13
Quidenham, 21, 185
quoits, 244, 252

Race-Ground, The, N. Lopham, 124
radio—SEE wireless
Raft Spider, The Great—SEE *Dolomedes Plantarius*
railway schemes (SEE ALSO Light Railway Commission; Mid-Anglian Light Railway), 185, 186, 187
ranters—SEE Primitive Methodists
Ray, John (1627–1705), 80
Raynor/Raynar, Jack, N. Lopham, 211, 216
Raynor, Towy, N. Lopham, 212
Reade family of S. Lopham, 150
Reade, Edmonde, of S. Lopham, 72
Reade, Francis, of S. Lopham, 72
reading & recreation room, proposed, at N. Lopham, 157, 158
Rectory Hall—SEE Eastwood Hall
Red Bridge, S. Lopham, 123
Redgrave, Suffolk (SEE ALSO Fens), 6, 24, 71, 133, 186
Redgrave Common, 24
Redgrave Road, 6, 24n.
Redgrave, S. Botolph's, 15, 71
Reece, M., supply teacher at N. Lopham school (1919), 228
Reeder, James, N. Lopham, 244
Reeder, James junior, S. Lopham, 247
Reeve, Righteous, senior and junior, N. Lopham thatchers, 210, 211
reeve, the, 36
Reeveland—SEE reeve, the
Reeves Meadow, S. Lopham, 36
Register or Registrar of S. Lopham, 96
Relf, E. W., teacher of S. Hackney Parochial L.C.C. School, 258
relics (SEE ALSO Christianity), 15, 16
Relieving Officer, 222
retting, 82, 83
Reyce, Robert (*ob.* 1638), 22
Rhineland, the, 8
ribskins, 84
Richardson, Michael, Lopham joiner (*ob. c.* 1575), 84, 90
Richardson, Roger, brother of Michael R., 84, 90
Rickinghall Inferior, Suffolk, 186
Rights of Man—SEE Thomas Paine
rights of way, 262
Ringbell, Matthew, S. Lopham, (*ob. c.* 1558), 72
Robin Hood, 47
Rochester Cathedral, 17
Rockland, deanery of, 127
rocks, 84
Romano-British place-names, 10
Romans, 7, 8, 13, 15, 29n.
Roman villa, N. Lopham, 7, 9, 13
rood screen, S. Lopham, 70
Rosebery, earl of—SEE Primrose
rounceys—SEE horses
rounders, 244
Royal Albert Memorial School—SEE Royal Albert National School
Royal Albert National School, N. Lopham (SEE ALSO Lopham North, School), 154, 157, 158, 159, 175, 179, 180, 239, 252
Royal School of Needlework, 149
Royal Warrant—SEE Buckenham, T. W. & J.
Roydon (SEE ALSO Fens), 13, 186
Ruddock family of N. Lopham, 150
Ruddock,—., of N. Lopham, (1835), 132
Ruddock, John, N. Lopham, 59
Ruddock, Peter, N. Lopham tailor, 201
Ruddock, Thomas, N. Lopham, (1814), 122, 123
Rummyng, Elynour, 84
Rural District Council—SEE Guiltcross R.D.C., Thetford R.D.C., Wayland R.D.C.

Rush family of S. Lopham, 150
Rush, Ann, 125
Rush, Robert, S. Lopham (?), 93–94
Rush, William, 216
Russians—SEE Imperial Russian Embassy
Rust, John, brother and heir of Lawrence, 87
Rust, Lawrence N. Lopham linen-weaver (1663), 86, 87

sacrifices, 16
Sadler/Saddler, Miss, uncertificated teacher at S. Lopham school, 246, 247
S. Andrew, 17, 30, 51, 69
S. Andrew's church, N. Lopham—SEE Lopham, N., S. Andrew's
S. Andrew's gild, N. Lopham, 45, 46
S. Andrew's monastery, Rome, 17
S. Augustine, 1st archbishop of Canterbury (*ob. c.* A.D. 613), 17
S. Cross gild, S. Lopham, 45
S. David's—SEE Womocke, Lawrence
S. George and the Dragon, 47
S. Giles—SEE Bath and Wash Houses
S. Gregory the Great (Pope Gregory I, *c.* A.D. 540–604), 15, 16, 17, 46, 219
S. James's Palace, 149
S. John's Acre, N. Lopham, 46
S. John's College, Cambridge, 151
S. John's gild, N. Lopham, 45
S. Mary—(SEE ALSO Mary, Queen of Heaven; Crowned Mary) 32, 51, 54, 55
S. Mary's & S. Andrew's the Great, Thetford—SEE Thetford Priory
S. Nicholas, 18, 27, 69
S. Nicholas's church, S. Lopham—SEE Lopham, S., S. Nicholas's
S. Nicholas's gild, S. Lopham, 45
S. Peter's Acre, N. Lopham, 46
S. Peter's gild, N. Lopham, 45
S. Peter's gild, S. Lopham, 45
S. Philip Howard, SEE UNDER Howard, Philip, earl of Arundel & Surrey
Salisbury, John (1500?–1573), rector of Lopham and suffragan bishop of Thetford, bishop of Sodor and Man, 69, 70, 103, 104, 105; his wife, born-Barrett of Norfolk, 105
Sallowbushweye, N. Lopham, 124
Saltire Cross, 69
Sanders (SEE ALSO Saunder), 86
Sandringham, 191, 195
Saracens, 43
Sare family of S. Lopham, 204
Sare, R. W., S. Lopham, 246
Saunder, Robert, of S. Lopham, (*ob. c.* 1551), 80
  Isabell, his wife, 80
  John, his brother, 80
Saunder, William, of Lopham, (1592), 91
Savage, 106
Saxons (SEE ALSO Anglo-Saxons), 13, 25
Sayers, Dorothy, 241
Scandinavia, 13
"Scheme" for S. Lopham—SEE Lopham Charity
school attendance, 176
scutching, 83
seafaring men, 129
Seakens SEE Seakins
Seakins, Frederick, S. Lopham schoolmaster, 153, 154
Self, Henry, S. Lopham, 212
Selfgrown Stile, the, 3, 124
Semere Hall, Blo' Norton, 89
"Seven Wonders of Lopham", 116
Seven Wonders of the World, the, 1
Seven Years' war, the, (1756–1763), 110
Severals, the, 37
Sewall, Margaret, (1545), 71
sewerage, 230, 231

Shack, the, 59, 203
Shake, the—SEE Shack, the
Shanks, F. W., Ltd., of Hunstanton, 251
Shaw, Arthur, N. Lopham, 210
Shaw, George, N. Lopham, linen manufacturer (1840), 139 & n.
Shaw, George, N. Lopham linen-weaver (1840), 138
Shaw, Honor, N. Lopham, 210
Shaw, Jack, (John), N. Lopham, 194, 210
Shaw, Rodger, N. Lopham, 211
sheep, 8, 20, 41, 43, 53, 59, 109, 200, 223
Sheepmere, 43
Sheep-pen Lane, S. Lopham, 43
Sheet and Blanket Clubs, 239
sheets, Lopham, 74, 76, 79, 84, 85, 146, 202
Shelfanger, 29, 44, 52, 128, 129, 130, 152
shepherds, 223
Sheringe—SEE Sherwyn
Sherwyn/Sheringe, John, of N. Lopham, gent., 89, 90
Robert S., of N. Lopham, (*ob. c.* 1561), 72
Shimpling Thorne, Suffolk, 22
"Ship Money", 95
Shop House, N. Lopham, **125**
Shopehowse yarde, N. Lopham, 124
Shortstubbyng, 33
Shropshire, 10
Singh, Frederick Duleep, Prince, 186, 198
SIX BELLS, the, South Lopham, 142n.
skalbones (? knucklebones), 91
Skelton, John (1460?–1529) rector of Diss, 84
Skowle, William, of Woodrising (*ob. c.* 1481), 53
Slaymaker, 79n.
slays, 79 & n.
Smith, Mrs B. A., head teacher of S. Lopham school, 255, 256
Smith, Frederick E., S. Lopham, 226
Smith, George, landlord of the BULL, N. Lopham (SEE ALSO Smith, Martha, his wife), **42**, 200
Smith, George, of S. Lopham, 257
Smith, John, curate, 118, 150
Smith, Leonard B., N. Lopham schoolmaster, 181
Smith, Martha, of the BULL, N. Lopham, 199
Smith, William, N. Lopham, 226
"smugglers' way", 129
Snetterton (Snitterton, Snytterton), 59, 82
Snetterton airfield, 257
Snytterton—SEE Snetterton
Sodor and Man, Bishop of—SEE Salisbury, John
Sokkiswishwell, S. Lopham, 123
Solly, Miss, supplementary teacher at S. Lopham school, 245, 246
Somerville, Andrew, 110, 111
songs, 252
South African War—SEE Boer War
South Kensington museums, 198
South Lopham—SEE Lopham, South
"South Lopham fifth"—SEE William the Founder
sparrows and hedgehogs, 135, 136
Speer, W. F. E. of the N. Lopham BELL, 244
Spelman, Sir Henry (1564?–1641), 3
Spicer's Hill, S. Lopham, 142n.
"Spider village", 12
Spiders, the Great Raft—SEE *Dolomedes Plantarius*
"Spider Web" linen pattern, 194
Spincke, Margaret of Garboldisham, widow (1657), 96
Spinke, John of S. Lopham, Register, (1654), 96
spinning wheels, 84, **85**, 195, 202
Spitalfields, 155

Sporle, Henry, of Bunwell, 88
squatters, 125
Staghorns, 245
standing stones, 15
Stangate, N. Lopham, 124
Stanton, Suffolk, 186
"steeple", 53, 54
Stelestock Stile or Pykards Stile, N. Lopham, 124
Stevens, Ambrose, 203, 213, 234
Stevens, Mrs Ellen, *née* Brock, assistant at N. Lopham school, 180, **181**
Stevens, Timothy, N. Lopham, 239, 242
steward, the lord of the manor's, 36
stoats, 182
stocks, North Lopham, 126
Stone, Mrs F., Quidenham, 242
Stone Age, Middle and Late, 5
stool-ball, 244
Stourbridge or Sturbitch Fair, 148
Strachan, David, linen-weaver of Scotland, 145, 184
"Strachan, James", 145
Strachan, Sarah, N. Lopham, wife of David S., 145
Stradbroke, Suffolk, 131
Strangeways Murder, 197
stubbinges, 33
Sturbitch Fair—SEE Stourbridge Fair
Styles, H. P., S. Lopham, 243
Sudbury, 22
Suetonius Tranquillus, Gaius (*ob. c.* A.D. 250), 8
Suffield, Evelyn Louisa Harbord, *née* Wilson-Patten, Dowager Lady—SEE Harbord
Suffolk, 5, 14, 16, 23, 24, 43, 79, 80
Surrey, 23
Surrey, Earls of—SEE Howard
Sussex, 23
Sweden, 13
swingles, 83
Syrians, 43
Syzling, Lionel, N. Lopham, 257
tallage, 34
Tann's Lane, N. Lopham, 116, 195, 214, 230, 232
Tann's Meadow (SEE ALSO Jubilee Meadow), 231
Tann's Mill, N. Lopham, 214
taverns, 39, 45
taxes, 21, 43
taxi business, 236
Taylor, John, S. Lopham schoolmaster, 177
Teck—SEE Mary of Teck
telephone service, 230, 250
television, 40, 226, 255
temperance, 160
Thelnetham (SEE ALSO Fens), 24
Thetford, 27, 29, 71, 93
Thetford, Great S. Mary's—SEE Thetford Priory
Thetford House, 85
Thetford Museum, 151, 197
Thetford Priory, 27, 29, 30, 49
Thetford Rural District Council, 236
Thetford, S. Nicholas's, 27
Thetford, suffragan bishop of—SEE Salisbury, John
Thomas, A. A., solicitor for N.U.T., 246
Thorndon, Suffolk, 243
thrashing machine, steam, 203, 213, 233
Three Boys, the—SEE Boys
Three Purses, the—SEE Purses
Three Wonders of Lopham, the—SEE Wonders of Lopham
Thurlow, Albert, N. Lopham, 211
Thurlow, "Bleacher", of Bressingham, 202
Tiberius II, Emperor of the East (A.D. 578–582), 18
tied cottages, 222, 249
Tit-Bits, 178
Titchfield, abbey of, 104
Tivetshall, 115
Toftwood, Christopher, Mr & Mrs, 91
Top Drag Way, N. Lopham, 185n.

"Top shop", N. Lopham, 201
tops, spinning, 245
Tower of London, 57
"town", 33
Town Barn, N. Lopham, 123 & n.
Townhouse, N. Lopham (SEE ALSO Workhouse Row and Weavers' Cottages), 126, 127, **128**, 147
Townsend, Sir Roger, 105
trackways, 5
Travellers' Club Loom—SEE Jacquard loom
"treaty" or Indenture of 1628—SEE Lopham "treaty"
Trennel House, N. Lopham, 98
Trinity Gild, S. Lopham, 45, 46
Trinity, the Holy, 51, 54
Trudgill, Roger & Billy, N. Lopham, 211
Turks, 43
turnips, 109, 110
Turnour, Katherina, of N. Lopham (*ob. c.* 1498), 53, 128
Tusser, Thomas (*c.* 1524–1580), 79, 81, 82, 105
Twiddy, Lionel, master of N. Lopham school, 228, 237 & n. 238
Tyler, Albert, 192, **193**, 194, 195
Tyler, Dubbs, 193
Tyler, Harry, 193, 204
Tyler, James, 193

UFOs—SEE Unidentified Flying Objects
Underwood, John (xv c.), 106
Unidentified Flying Objects, 41
United States Army Air Force (USAAF), 257, 261
United States Cavalry, 260
Uphall, Garboldisham, 183 & n.
"Up Hunn's", 252

vans, 143, **144**, 147
vegetables, 252
Vice de Lou, manor of, Shelfanger, 128
Victoria, Queen, 132, 157
Vigerous, William, rector (1332–1341), 49
Village Community Council—SEE Lopham Village Council
Village Hall and Playing Field Committee—SEE Lopham Village Hall and Playing Field Committee
Village Hall Committee—SEE Lopham Village Hall Committee
Village Pump, The, 253, 254
Vincent, A. S., S. Lopham, 239
visitations, 45, 126, 127
Vynor, Edward, S. Lopham linen-weaver (1703), 86
Vyse, Richard, Colonel (1746–1826), 113

Wacton, 244
Wade, Bartholomew of S. Lopham, yeoman (*ob. c.* 1567), 90
Wade, Robert, S. Lopham (?) (1628), 86, 93
wages, agricultural (SEE ALSO Appendix), 221, 227, 249
wagons, 147, 216
Wallis, Robert Ellis, S. Lopham, 226
Wallis, Sidney, S. Lopham, 226
Wallis, Spencer G., S. Lopham, 226
Walnut Tree Farm, S. Lopham, 99
Walsham-le-Willows, Suffolk, 186
Wamuke, James, rector of Yaxham, 101
war casualties 1914–1918, 226–227
war casualties 1939–1945, 257
Warne, Richard, N. Lopham, (1502), 53
wars, 43, 225, 226, 255, 264
"*Watercress song, The*", 216
Water Gate, S. Lopham, 123
water supply (SEE ALSO wells), 251
Watry Lane, S. Lopham, 123
Wattisfield, Suffolk, 186

Waveney, river, 3, 5, 9, 13, 22, 23
Wayland Rural District Council, 251, 263
weapons, 5, 7, 245
weather, 40, 43, 181
WEAVERS' ARMS, the—SEE "Meadow House"
Weavers' Cottages, N. Lopham (SEE ALSO Townhouse), 127
webster, 78
wells, 227, 251
Wesley, John (1703–1791), 115, 117, 118
Wesleyan Chapel, 118, **119**, 160, 216
Wesleyan day school, 153, 154, 155, 157, 159, 175
Wesleyan Methodists, 117, 118, 119
Wesleyan Sunday school, 182, 183
West, L. J., N. Lopham, 237n., 239
West Harling, 8
Wetheringsett, Suffolk, 203
wharrows, 84
Wharton, George, innkeeper, weaver & farmer of N. Lopham, 116, 118
Wharton, George, junior (II), 118, 119, 120
Wharton, George, III, 120
wheat, 8, 41, 202
Whinbergh, 101
Whist Drive & Dance, 252
Whitebread Farm, N. Lopham, 147
WHITE HORSE, the, Kenninghall, 100
WHITE HORSE, the, South Lopham, 41, 100, 129, 214, 219, **233**, 257, 258
White House, Boyland, 109
Whiting, Sidney, blacksmith of Garboldisham, 236
Whitinge, John (1657), 96
whitsters— SEE bleachers
Whitsuntide, 47, 214
Wickgate, N. Lopham, 124
Wickmere, 101
Wild, Mr G., of London, 178, 213
Willbush, N. Lopham, 52
Willesden, 259
William of Lopham (1347), 225
William I, King, the Conqueror, 19
William II, King, "Rufus", 27
William the Founder, of Aldgate, 55
Williamson, Anne of N. Lopham (1657), 96
Williamson, Mistress (i.e. Miss) Mary, of Garboldisham, 129, 152
Williamson, T., of Lopham, 244
"Willow Tree Cottage", N. Lopham, 96, 99
Wilney Green—SEE Winley Green
"Wimsey, Lord Peter", 241
Windsor Castle, 146, 194
Winfarthing, 29, 111
Winfarthing Park, 92, 93
Wingfield, Borlase, rector 1760–1768, 150
Winley Green, 58
wireless, 40, 226, 255
Witting, John, S. Lopham linen manufacturer, 139
Witton, L., S. Lopham, 239
Wolsey, Cardinal, 104
Womack, Womock, Womocke family (SEE ALSO Wamuke), 101, 116, 150
  Arthur (Womock), rector 1578–1607, 77, 95, 96, 100, 101, 102
  Avice, his wife, 102
  Arthur (Womocke), rector of Fersfield & Guidenham, 96, 97, 102
  Baker (Womack) of Tann's Mill, **94**
  Elizabeth (Womack), 132
  Henry (Womack), rector of Fersfield & Gt. Ellingham, 102
  J. (Womack), N. Lopham, miller & banker (1837–1846), 132
  James (Womocke), rector of Whinbergh, 101
  John (Womack), S. Lopham (*ob.* 1698), 103

John (Womack), Chestnut Tree Farm, N. Lopham, 197, 207 (?)
John (Womack), junior, linen-manufacturer & farmer, N. Lopham, (1875), 149
Laurence (Womock/Womack), bishop of St. David's &c., (1612–1686), 102, 103
Anne, his daughter, 103
Laurence (Womocke), rector 1607–1656, 93–94, 95, 96, 101, 102, 114, 115
Laurence (Womack), of Mautby, gent., 103
Mary (Womack)—SEE Blomefield, Mary
Oswald (Womack) of N. Lopham, 197
Percy (Womack) of ditto, 236
Robert (Womack) of ditto, (m. 1668), 103
Robert (Womack), miller of S. Lopham (1882), 234
Thomas (Womack), Park Farm, N. Lopham, 214
Thomas (Womack), S. Lopham, 102, 103
William (Womack), do., linen manufacturer, 132, 139
William (Womack), do., farmer & linen-weaver, (1771), 111
William (Womack), of Tann's Mill, N. Lopham, 214, 221
William Wharton (Womack), N. Lopham, 240, 244
William, (Womack), of the King's Head, N. Lopham, **94**, **192**, 210, 211
his wife & daughter, 211
Women's Institute, the Lopham, 237, 243, 252, 255
Women's Land Army, 227, 263
Womock(e)—SEE Womack
Wonders of Lopham, the Three (SEE ALSO Seven Wonders), 31
woodland, 3, 5, 8, 11, 19, 21, 33, 36, 38, 58, 78–9
Woods, Bilham, N. Lopham, 239
Woods, Mrs Bilham, N. Lopham, 243
Woods, Charles, brewer of Thetford and N. Lopham, 116
wool—SEE ALSO burial in woollen, 43
Worby, Charles, N. Lopham, 257
Workhouse Row, N. Lopham (SEE ALSO Townhouse), 127
Wortham, Suffolk, 132, 133, 186
Wortham Hall, 24
Wortwell, 101, 102n.
Wramplingham, 244
Wretham, 240
Wrongeyeld, le, 34
Wryght, 106
Wuffings, the (SEE ALSO "Ipswich People, the"), 15
Wyatt, Thomas Henry (1807–1880), 56, 70
Wylton, Katherine, 90
Wymondham, 113

Yarmouth, Great, 44, 113, 131, 180
Yaxham, 101
Yorkshire, 5, 110, 149
Young, Arthur (1741–1820), 80, 109, 110, 111, 138
Yongs, Marion, of S. Lopham (*ob. c.* 1511), 46

zeppelins, 227

NORTH LOPHAM
NORTH DALE CLOSE
DEAL
School
Top Drag Way
Lower Drag Way
MILL OR HIGH COMMON
Oak
Hangman's Barn
Noddle Farm
Red Barn
Malting Farm
S O U T
BARN MEADOW
BIRD'S LANE
NEW CROSS
Lodge Farm
BIRD'S PIECE
TRIANGLE
SITE OF FALGATE
LOWER SAND FIELD
Whitehouse Farm
The Grange
Chequers (P.H.)
Poplar Tree Farm
Self's Lane
T O N
Fernleigh
SITE OF FOLGATE
LADIES' CLOSES
HOPTON ROAD
Gaol
LITTLE FRITH
GREAT FRITH
The Banks
Lopham Ford
Crown & Anchor (P.H.)
Hinderclay Fen
Bridge Farm
R E D
Fen Street
Grove Farm
Fen Farm
Crackthorn
Pound Farm